The New Politics of Crime and Punishment

The New Politics of Crime and Punishment

edited by

Roger Matthews
Jock Young

WILLAN
PUBLISHING

Willan Publishing
Culmcott House
Mill Street, Uffculme
Cullompton, Devon
EX15 3AT, UK
Tel: +44(0)1884 840337
Fax: +44(0)1884 840251
e-mail: info@willanpublishing.co.uk
Website: @www.willanpublishing.co.uk

Published simultaneously in the USA and Canada by

Willan Publishing
c/o ISBS, 5824 N.E. Hassalo St,
Portland, Oregon 97213-3644, USA
Tel: +001(0)503 287 3093
Fax: +001(0)503 280 8832
Website: www.isbs.com

First published 2003

ISBN 1-903240-92-1 (hardback)
ISBN 1-903240-91-3 (paperback)

British Library Cataloguing-in-Publication Data
A catalogue record for this book is available from the British Library

Typeset by TW Typesetting, Plymouth, Devon
Printed and bound by T J International Ltd, Trecerus Industrial Estate, Padstow, Cornwall

Contents

Editors' Preface

The political climate in the United Kingdom has changed dramatically over the past decade, and the expectation has been that this would result in a significant shift in government policy on crime and punishment. This expectation has in part been met, although the nature of the changes which have taken place are not always those that were expected.

When New Labour swept to power in 1997 it was widely anticipated that this would lead to a less punitive, more informal and community-based approach, which would place greater emphasis on crime prevention and addressing the causes of crime, particularly since there was growing evidence of a decrease in most forms of crime. The popular slogan 'tough on crime, tough on the causes of crime', which was coined by Tony Blair, signalled his desire to make New Labour the party of 'law and order' and his commitment to take crime seriously, because he believed that this issue was a priority for the electorate.

During the first period of administration there was a predictable emphasis on young people, who increasingly came to be seen as responsible for a disproportionate amount of crime. There was also a growing focus on the protection of victims as well as the development of inter-agency partnerships and 'evidence-based' policy. There was a clear commitment to increasing police numbers and to addressing growing concerns about police effectiveness, particularly following the publication of the Macpherson Inquiry and claims about institutional racism. At the same time, the continuing increase in the number of people imprisoned led many critics to claim that New Labour had in fact adopted a largely Conservative agenda, and that in their attempt 'to get tough on crime' they had moved increasingly to the right.

In the first few years of the new century, however, the assessment of government policy has become more diverse and more positive. The passing of the Crime and Disorder Act (1998) has increasingly been identified as a watershed in policy, by its linking of crime with disorder and its placing them both within a broader framework of community safety. This, in turn, has broadened the focus from crime control to issues of social and distributive justice. It has also involved a realignment of the major regulatory agencies, with responsibility for crime control and community safety shifting increasingly to local authorities. Within this changing context, crime and disorder are increasingly linked to issues of urban decline and regeneration. This broadening of the focus of intervention has resulted in a growing interest in the dynamics of social inclusion and exclusion.

The main objective of this book is to examine these developments and to assess their significance. In doing so the authors are faced with the perennial task of distinguishing rhetoric from reality and appearances from underlying processes. A cursory examination of recent policy, however, indicates that the Labour government is no longer offering 'more of the same' and simply trying to outdo its Conservative predecessors. In fact, there is a growing realization that New Labour is now moving in a different direction, involving different priorities, methods and objectives. A more complex and differentiated strategy is emerging, which no longer simply mimics 'get tough' policies, but which is in the process of developing a more diverse approach, which will undoubtedly have profound consequences not only on 'law and order' but also on social life in this country in general.

All of the contributors to this volume have a close association with Middlesex University. The criminology group at Middlesex have regularly contributed over the past two decades to the ongoing debates on the politics of crime and punishment, and have attempted to contribute to the development of policy. It is also 30 years since the Masters Programme in Criminology was introduced at Middlesex, and a number of those who have studied on this pioneering course are now involved in developing and implementing the policies discussed in this volume.

About the contributors

Anthony Goodman is a Principal Lecturer at Middlesex University. He has extensive experience of probation practice and teaching, and a special interest in the changing nature of probation practice, which was the subject of his doctorate. He is currently researching the effect of parenting programmes on young offenders.

Lynn Hancock is Lecturer in Criminology and Criminal Justice at the Open University. She was Senior Lecturer in Criminology at Middlesex University 1997–2002, and Lecturer in Criminology at Keele University, 1993–96. She held a Leverhulme Special Research Fellowship between 1996 and 1998 at Keele University and Middlesex Universities respectively. The research entitled 'Neighbourhood Change, Crime and Urban Policy' was published in her book *Community, Crime and Disorder: Safety and Regeneration in Urban Neighbourhoods* (Palgrave, 2001). Her current research interests focus on urban/neighbourhood change and crime, community responses to crime and disorder, and public attitudes towards criminal justice.

John Lea is Professor of Criminology at Middlesex University. He is author (with Jock Young) of *What Is to Be Done about Law and Order* (Pluto Press, 1993). He has published on issues such as postmodernism in criminology ands racism in criminal justice agencies. His most recent book is *Crime and Modernity* (Sage, 2002).

Denise Martin is a doctoral student at Middlesex University researching Best Value in the Police Service. She previously worked as a research analyst for Bedfordshire Police and has conducted research for The Children's Society on Youth Justice

Roger Matthews is Professor of Sociology at Middlesex University. His research interests include prisons and penal policy, prostitution and community safety. His publications include *Doing Time: An Introduction to the Sociology of Imprisonment* (Palgrave/Macmillan, 1999), *Crime, Disorder and Community Safety*, edited with John Pitts (Routledge, 2001), and *Prostitution*, edited with Maggie O'Neill (Ashgate, 2003).

Jayne Mooney is Principal Lecturer in Criminology at Middlesex University. She is author of *Gender, Violence and the Social Order* (Palgrave, 2000) and was the research coordinator of the North London Domestic Violence Survey. Her current research is on comparative patterns of interpersonal violence.

John Pitts is Vauxhall Professor in Socio-Legal Studies at the University of Luton. He has worked as youth worker, youth justice development officer, group worker in a Young Offender Institution, and consultant to justice system professionals in the UK, mainland Europe, the Russian Federation, and China. His publications include *The Politics of Juvenile Crime* (Sage, 1988), *Crime Disorder and Community Safety*, edited with Roger Matthews (Routledge, 2001) and *The New Politics of Youth Crime: Discipline or Solidarity* (Macmillan, 2001).

Patrick Slaughter is a Senior Lecturer in Criminology at Middlesex University. His current research is on the effectiveness of sporting interventions on high crime estates in East London.

Betsy Thom is a Principal Lecturer in drug and alcohol studies at Middlesex University, responsible for the MSc programme 'Drugs in Society: Policy and Intervention'. Her research interests and writings deal with alcohol/drugs and gender, alcohol and drug policy, and community responses to alcohol and drugs. She is the editor of the peer-reviewed journal *Drugs: Education, Prevention and Policy* and has worked as a consultant for UNDCP. She is currently a member of the Alcohol Education and Research Council and a consultant to the Health Development Agency.

Catriona Woolner was awarded an MA degree in Criminology during 2000 and is currently working towards a Doctorate, at Middlesex University, on homicide in the United States, England and Wales. Her research interests include firearms, interpersonal violence and illegal drugs. Publications include 'Guns, Crack Cocaine and Ethnic Minorities', *Safer Society* (NACRO, 2002).

Jock Young is Professor of Sociology at Middlesex University and Distinguished Professor at John Jay College of Criminal Justice and the Graduate Centre, City University of New York. His most recent book is *The Exclusive Society* (Sage, 1999) and he is nearing completion of its sequel, *Crossing the Borderline*. He is also working on a book on criminological theory, entitled *Merton's Dream and Quetelet's Warning*.

Chapter 1

New Labour, crime control and social exclusion

Jock Young and Roger Matthews

As has been well documented, the countries of the First World, from the late 1960s onwards, experienced a yearly increase in crime, which lasted for over 30 years. There were a few exceptions, and there were some countries in which the rise started comparatively later; but the impact on criminology and on the criminal justice system was widespread. That is to say that there was a prevalent feeling that 'nothing worked' – the phrase of Robert Martinson (1974) – which became a widespread belief, whatever Martinson's actual position or intentions. At times the whole modernist project of crime control through tackling the causes of crime and rehabilitating the offender seemed forced back on its heels and all that could be proffered was the advice of more locks and bolts, greater care and caution, with the admonition to be circumspect about guarding your home and travelling around the city. Indeed David Garland, as recently as 1996 in his survey of the field, sketched out what he saw as 'the limits of the sovereign state' (Garland, 1996), where governments could no longer claim the ability to control crime rates and provide security for their citizens, where the public itself acquiesced, however fearfully, to high crime rates, and where crime itself became normalized.

In the more recent period a seachange would seem to have occurred. Crime rates in very many industrial countries have begun to level out or decline (Barclay *et al.*, 2001). Crime, like stocks and shares, can fall as well as rise. The most iconic example of this is 'the New York miracle', where the homicide rate of this city fell by just under 50 per cent between 1993 and 1996. It is important here not to embrace the urban myth of the exceptional provenance of New York politicians and police officers, but to note that the crime rate also fell in a large number of American cities (see Blumstein and Wallman, 2000) and indeed in many urban areas of the First World. Yet the widely publicized success in a city of such importance, one that had an extreme notoriety for violence and danger, had important reverberations around the world. Further, the actual appearance of such statistics, whether local or national, whether about burglary or taking and driving away, imbues a new feeling of confidence. It reveals that crime statistics do not always go up, they can fluctuate, and indeed fall. The mindset of 'nothing works' begins to change to 'maybe things do work' – what is needed is to catalogue good practice in various parts of the world and above all to monitor and evaluate each initiative.

Multi-agency crime-intervention partnerships evolved in the period of rising crime in order to mobilize resources, in an attempt to stem the increasing problem of crime (Lea et al., 1989). In part, these represented the correct understanding of the situation: that criminal justice initiatives alone are insufficient to tackle the crime problem, whether on the level of prevention or of ameliorating the impact of victimization (see Young, 1992, pp. 45–9). They were not the abnegation of responsibility for security by the state, but rather a realistic adjustment to the problem where state agencies maintained central coordination and control. Such a transformation occurred amid the much larger movement in the relationship between public service agencies and the state, that is, education, health, social services and the criminal justice system all became subject to what has been called the 'New Public Management' (see Clarke et al., 2000; Flynn, 1997). This attempt to control the cost and effectiveness of public-service budgets involves the by now familiar imposition of performance indicators, publication of league tables illustrating comparative performance, the costing and market testing of all activities (see McLaughlin et al., 2001).

The more benign assessment of the possibilities of a successful intervention against crime in the present period melds well into this general trend of stress on effectiveness and good value. In Britain in particular, under the auspices of the Crime and Disorder Act 1998, a regime of finely assessed targets and intricately constructed indicators are set for the multi-agency partnerships of police and council agencies set up to combat crime (see Hough and Tilley, 1998). What is important to stress here is that such a matrix of targets and evaluation would scarcely have been possible in the context of the previous scenario of seemingly inexorably rising crime rates.

Such a situation of sporadic, if patchy, decline in crime rates allows those agencies involved to claim success. The research data with regard to changes in crime rates suggest that outside of the influence of changes in public reporting levels and tolerance of crime, a high proportion of variation can be explained by changes in economic and social conditions, rather than by the impact of the various criminal-justice and other agencies, which, so to speak, *administer* crime (see Field, 1990). For example, the exhaustive analysis of the dip in the American crime rate conducted by Al Blumstein and his associates for the National Consortium on Violence Research (Blumstein and Wallman, 2000) pointed to demographic and economic factors being the most powerful influences on crime change (see Young, this volume). This, of course, does not rule out the impact of police, prisons, and crime prevention techniques, but points to the fact that interventions have to be massive and continuing to have influence (e.g. mass incarceration has had an impact in the United States, although even there not as much as is often made out) and that marginal increases in, say, the number of police officers have only minor impact on the crime rate. Whatever the reality of influences, the existence of declining rates allows single agencies – particularly the police – to make claims to be the sole causes of such change. It also generates a competition for the ownership of the crime problem. In the period of rapidly increasing crime rates there was a tendency for disavowal. A particularly pertinent example of this was the Metropolitan Police Report of 1986, which pretty accurately described the dramatic rise in crime as a result of a Treasury-led monetarist policy, which gave rise to mass unemployment with all the social dislocation that this entailed: 'The Government pursues an economic policy which includes Treasury driven social policy that has one goal – the reduction of inflation. Any adverse social by-products are accepted as necessary casualties in the pursuit of the overall objective.'

The police, quite correctly, deplored the fact that they were being blamed for a crime wave that was not within their behest to control. But in times of declining crime rates a totally different scenario unfolds, where the ownership of the crime problem is acutely contested. The most public example of this was the spat between Mayor Rudy Giuliani and Commissioner William J. Bratton as to who had instigated the zero-tolerance policies, which had supposedly been so successful in reducing the crime rate in New York City.

Daniel Moynihan, in a famous article written in 1993 entitled 'Defining Deviancy Down', suggested that a major response to the rising tide of crime and disorder that occurred up until the recent period was simply to become more tolerant of crime, disorder, disturbance, and mental illness. Indeed, he argues, this is precisely what occurred, and a careful reading of events, from the 'permissive

3

1960s' through to the decriminalization of juvenile delinquency and the decarceration of the mentally ill, gives some support for this. But more recently, from the late 1980s onwards, the very reverse of this process would seem to have been set in motion, namely the 'defining of deviancy up'. Such a process has come from different directions, both liberal and conservative. For conservatives, control of incivilities became a central plank of the zero-tolerance campaigns against crime; for the liberals, the pursuit of anti-racist and sexist harassment policies, as well as the campaign of zero-tolerance against domestic violence, also contributed to a lowering of tolerance of crime and incivilities (see Hancock and Matthews, 2001; Young, 1999).

The postwar period up to the 1960s was characterized by a tendency to view crime as vestigial, and increased prosperity would eventually reduce it to a minimum. Crime was a propensity of isolated dysfunctional families or inadequate individuals. The rise in crime of subsequent years was closely associated with a very different picture: the notion of a sizeable underclass, cut off from the main body of society, spatially located in the sink estates of the inner city and the outer suburbs, lacking the norms and values of the wider society. The association between crime and a relatively small proportion of citizens – especially boys and young men in these areas – became a motif that would recur throughout the world (see Patrick Slaughter, this volume). The crime problem, therefore, becomes localized, and offenders have a distinct social membership – often racialized. Furthermore, such a group is perceived as a threatening 'Other' – something beyond the limits of normal society. The concern with race is fraught with a deep ambiguity, seeing ethnic minorities as disproportionately the perpetuators and victims of crime. The racist murder of Stephen Lawrence and the subsequent Macpherson Report served, as John Lea argues in this volume, to redefine the meaning of racism, while drawing attention to the ways in which the criminal justice system fails victims.

Despite the perceived danger associated with the growth of the underclass, there is a greater tendency for optimism in terms of intervention. There is a demand for the monitoring and evaluation of programmes closely related to the emergence of the New Public Managerialism, a greater competition for the ownership of programmes, and deviancy is defined up. At the same time there is a widespread decrease in tolerance with regard to crime and incivilities that impact on the quality of life, and, lastly, it is recognized that crimes and incivilities are widespread throughout the structure, although unevenly distributed spatially and socially. As Garland (2001) has quite correctly indicated, all such motifs in crime control are subject to interpretation within specific political, historical, and social contexts. Indeed, if the present authors have any difference with his book, *The Culture of Control*, it is that he does not take this interpretative position far enough. Thus, to our mind, he makes too much of the similarities between the United States and the United Kingdom, as well as, incidentally, discerning quite different general motifs from our own. What is of interest is convergence and differences between the various advanced industrial countries in their perceptions of the crime problem and their techniques of crime control (see Matthews 2002; Young 2003).

In the next section, we wish to examine the politics of New Labour, where general patterns emerge amid very specific interpretations, reflecting both the Third Way philosophy of the party and the particular political and social context of contemporary Britain.

Hard on crime, hard on the causes of crime

Tony Blair's article 'Crime is a Socialist Issue', published in the *New Statesman* in 1993, which contains the catchphrase 'tough on crime, tough on the causes of crime', is a very much cited but little-read piece. Yet the article, written while Blair was shadow Home Secretary, contains all the seeds of the subsequent crime policy of New Labour, both in terms of analysis and policy implications. It is an article remarkable for its clarity, and what is of particular interest is the consistency of these ideas over time, as New Labour entered government for its first and second terms, and the continuity of the tensions in policy.

First of all, Blair recognizes in his article the normality of crime, that crime is part and parcel of everyday life and a serious problem in the inner cities and in the suburbs. He points to 'our core voters [who] look to Labour to reflect their anxiety and anger, not to respond with patronizing sympathy or indifference' (Blair, 1993, p. 27). The impact of crime is not localized: it affects both Labour's traditional voters in the inner cities and those in the suburbs and rural areas. The article is intensely critical of Conservative ineptitude in this area – it calls for the Labour Party to make crime a genuine 'people's issue' and the subject of a campaign 'for better and safer communities' (ibid.). Secondly, it clearly demarcates the 'third way': 'we are moving the debate beyond the choice between personal and social responsibility – those who want to punish the criminal and those who point to the poor social conditions in which crime breeds' (ibid.). And he adds: 'the obvious common sense of the matter – which would be recognised instantly by any member of the public – is that the choice is false and misleading' (ibid.).

As far as 'tough on crime' is concerned, he points out that people have a right, and society a duty, to punish those offenders who have violated the rights of other citizens in a way that 'properly reflects the seriousness of the crime. To act otherwise would be to betray the interests of those we serve' (ibid.). However, equally, punishment and deterrence should be combined with rehabilitation – these are not alternatives – and for this reason we must reform 'our monstrous prison regime' (ibid.).

Yet we must also be tough on the causes of crime: 'Above all, any sensible society acting in its own interests . . . will recognise that poor education and housing, inadequate or cruel family backgrounds, low employment prospects and drug abuse will affect the likelihood of young people turning to crime' (ibid.). And here he introduces the motif of social exclusion, which is to dominate New Labour's thinking with regard to the causes of crime: 'if these young people are placed outside mainstream culture, offered no hope or opportunity, shown no respect for themselves, there is a greater chance of their going wrong' (ibid.). This can only be challenged by active community intervention: 'to see this requires not a Ph.D in sociology but a small experience of life' (ibid.). Undergirding Blair's argument is the distinctly New Labour credo of rights and responsibilities. People have the right to security, job opportunities, a stable community; against this they have the responsibilities to act honestly, not violate the rights of other citizens, and actively participate in the workforce.

Crime, then, centres on the relationship between the individual and the community; crime occurs where communities disintegrate; and crime contributes to the disintegration of communities: the individual who contributes to this disruption must be held responsible, while the state, on the other hand, must create the conditions for the establishment of effective and safe communities. We will turn now to examine how these ideas were developed when New Labour entered office, focusing first of all on the notion of social inclusion.

Crime and social inclusion

Tony Blair's first speech after coming to power in a landslide victory in 1997 was in the Aylesbury Estate in South London (Southwark, 2 June), selected for its poverty and exclusion from the mainstream of British society. His speech was to incorporate the *Leitmotif* of New

Labour – a core theme, which resonated throughout both its first and second term of office. He talked of the decline of old industries, the shift in the economy, which left some behind and created a new class, 'a workless class': these were the people who were either forgotten by society or, as with the previous (Conservative) government, became the object of blame. There would, he insisted, be 'no forgotten people' under New Labour, and he declared that the greatest challenge for government was 'to bring this new workless class back into society and into useful work'. On 8 December 1997 the Social Exclusion Unit (SEU) was set up by Peter Mandelson with a strategic relationship to all government departments. It was located in the Cabinet Office, 'putting it at the heart of government'. Since that time it has characteristically focused on a wide range of issues; on, for example, deprived neighbourhoods, unemployment, drug use, teenage pregnancy, truancy, school exclusion, and most recently on reintegration of ex-offenders into society.

It is important to stress the underlying dimensions of this concept of social exclusion. First it is seen as a global problem of social and economic change, which has impacted considerably on Britain. As Blair more recently put it:

> We came into office determined to tackle a deep social crisis. We had a poor record in this country in adapting to social and economic change. The result was sharp income inequality, a third of children growing up in poverty, a host of social problems such as homelessness and drug abuse, and divisions in society typified by deprived neighbourhoods that had become no go areas for some and no exit zones for others. All of us bore the cost of social breakdown – directly, or through the costs to society and public finances. And we were never going to have a successful economy while we continued to waste the talents of so many.
>
> (Blair, 2001, p. 1)

This text illustrates both the centrality of social exclusion to his thinking and that its amelioration is seen as the radical project of New Labour: for exclusion is the way in which poverty and inequality are seen to configure in these new times. Note also that the problem is seen as one that impacts on not only the excluded, but also on the included in terms of taxes, economic inefficiency and incivilities.

Second, social exclusion is seen as a series of linked problems. It is a 'shorthand term for what can happen when people or areas suffer from a combination of linked problems such as unemployment, poor skills, low incomes, poor housing, high crime, bad health and family breakdown' (Social Exclusion Unit, 2001, p. 1.1). Further, 'only when these links are properly understood will policies really be effective' (ibid., p. 3).

Third, corresponding to the across-the-board, linked nature of the problem is the necessity of a response that is 'joined up'. The Social Exclusion Unit works across departments, it demands multi-agency intervention, it is overseen by the Deputy Prime Minister, John Prescott, whose role is coordinating cross-departmental issues. Further, as he put it recently in an address to the Fabian Society; 'Departments cannot ignore social exclusion any more – it is part of their everyday work. It is the day to day business of every Secretary of State.' (Prescott, 2002).

Finally, social exclusion is seen in the context of rights and responsibilities. This 'makes Government help available but requires a contribution from the individual and the community' (Social Exclusion Unit, 2001, p. 3). Benefits can be withdrawn if job opportunities are not taken up, educational maintenance depends on regular attendance, neighbourhood funding depends on community involvement. How does this position inform policy on crime and, more specifically, how does it relate to Blair's famous couplet on crime, the promise to be 'tough on crime and tough on the causes of crime'?

Let us approach this question systematically, noting that the SEU quite clearly posits that 'social exclusion is a key driver' (2001, p. 2.3) in the genesis of crime, and indeed that crime and fear of crime are part of the complex of problems that indicate social exclusion. Because of this insistence on the interlinked nature of these problems, the explanation of crime, and the policy recommendations, become, obviously, subsumed under the general problem of how to tackle social exclusion.

Causes of social exclusion

To explain the United Kingdom's high level of social exclusion the SEU points to two sets of factors: economic and social changes, and weaknesses in government policies. On the economic level the emphasis is on globalization – on the rapid change in industry, higher competition, the decline of manufacturing and the rise of knowledge-based industries: in short, the demands for a flexible labour force and the inequality that results from some being left behind. At the same time, on a social level, there have been changes in the wider society which have weakened or removed the support systems that helped people to cope in the past. These involve the breakdown of the family and the community.

Finally, it is acknowledged that government policies – by this the SEU presumably refers particularly to previous Conservative administrations – have not coped well in helping people come to terms with these changes. They list a series of managerial problems (insufficient emphasis on partnership, on sustained change rather than short-term programmes, top-down initiatives, etc.) but also a 'passive welfare state that sometimes trapped people on benefits rather than enabling them to help themselves' (Social Exclusion Unit, 2001, p. 3.7).

What problems constitute social exclusion?

Social exclusion is seen as a series of problems that are 'linked and mutually reinforcing [which] can combine to create a complex and fast-moving vicious circle' (Social Exclusion Unit, 2001, p. 1.4). The list of problems is extensive and almost eclectic: drug use, educational under-achievement, truancy, child poverty, rough sleepers, ill health, inadequate housing, alcohol dependency, unemployment, poor access to services and to information sources, having a criminal record, sink estates, teenage pregnancy and, of course, crime and fear of crime. Crime, within this mutually reinforcing network, is seen as both a product of social exclusion and a cause of social exclusion. All these interlinking factors are seen to lead to crime just as crime creates disorder and fear, thus promoting social exclusion in its own right.

How large is the socially excluded population, and how does this relate to the number of people who commit crime?

Preventing Social Exclusion, the most recent SEU analysis of this phenomenon, points to the fact that 'there is no agreed way of measuring overall social exclusion' (2001, p. 1.5), but gives a range of figures, of 'a fraction of one per cent' who suffer the most extreme forms of multiple deprivation to 'as many as a third or more [who] are in some way at risk' (ibid.). The authors are, however, much more precise as to the numbers with regards to crime, noting that 'about ten percent of all active criminals may be responsible for half of all crime: about 100,000 individuals. Of this 10 percent, half are under 21 and nearly two-thirds are hard drug users.' (2001, p. 5.71).

Mechanisms that produce crime

Although all the interlinked problems are seen to relate to crime, they take two forms: those problems concerned with the lack of control and socialization of young people (the maladministration of youth) –

primarily poor childrearing (e.g. single mothers presumed to be associated with teenage pregnancy) and inadequate schooling, particularly relating to truancy or school exclusion (see Mooney, this volume) – and those activities such as drug or alcohol abuse, which necessitate high incomes in order to satisfy addictions. The central mechanism here would seem to be, in the first instance, an implicit control theory; namely that lack of adequate socialization or supervision leads, quite simply, to crime, or in the case of illicit drug use, a second-stage-removed process, whereby lack of community, school and family controls fail to contain drug use, which then leads on to crime (see Woolner and Thom, this volume).

Tackling social exclusion

The New Labour government delineates a three-pronged strategy to counter social exclusion: the *prevention* of social exclusion, the *reintegration* of the excluded, the delivery of *basic minimum standards*. The strategy extends across a wide variety of policy areas, and within each area the outputs under the three headings – prevention, reintegration and basic minimum standards – are ticked off. We have chosen the most fundamental areas – 'children, families and schools', 'skills, job and income', 'homes, neighbourhoods and communities' and 'crime' – to illustrate this (see Tables 1–4). Once again, some of these measures would seem to sit rather eclectically with each other – at the very least some items are of a totally different level – basic bank accounts, the New Deal and the Minimum Wage, for example in Table 2. But what

Table 1   Children, families and schools

Strategies	Prevention	Reintegration	Minimum Basic Standards
Sure Start	✓		
Support for Parents	✓		✓
Children's Fund	✓	✓	
Literacy and Numeracy Strategies	✓		✓
Excellence in Cities	✓	✓	✓
Truancy and School Exclusion	✓	✓	✓
Connexions Service	✓	✓	✓
Education Maintenance Allowance	✓	✓	✓
Teenage Pregnancy Strategy	✓	✓	✓
Access to Childcare			✓
Children in Care	✓		✓
Sport and Culture	✓	✓	✓

Table 2   Skills, jobs and income

Strategies	Prevention	Reintegration	Minimum Basic Standards
Adult Skills	✓	✓	✓
Individual Learning Accounts	✓	✓	
Access to New Technology	✓		✓
New Deal	✓	✓	✓
Working Families Credit	✓		✓
Minimum Wage	✓		✓
Phoenix Fund		✓	
Supporting Enterprise	✓	✓	✓
Basic Bank Accounts	✓	✓	✓

Table 3   Homes, neighbourhood and communities

Strategies	Prevention	Reintegration	Minimum Basic Standards
Neighbourhood Renewal		✓	✓
Role for Communities in Renewal	✓	✓	
Volunteering		✓	
Transport for Communities		✓	✓
Mixed Communities	✓		
Decent Homes	✓	✓	✓
Affordable Rents	✓		✓
Tackling Fuel Poverty	✓	✓	✓
Rough Sleeping	✓	✓	✓

Table 4   Crime

Strategies	Prevention	Reintegration	Minimum Basic Standards
Crime and Disorder Reduction Partnership	✓		✓
Youth Justice Board	✓		
Youth Offending Teams	✓	✓	
Intensive Supervision and Surveillance Programme		✓	✓
Drug Testing and Treatment Orders		✓	✓
National Treatment Agency	✓	✓	✓
Arrest Referral Schemes		✓	
Neighbourhood Wardens	✓		✓

is important to stress is the systematic integration of policy which attempts to manage social exclusion by attempting to prevent and reintegrate the excluded within the context of much more basic interventions.

Inclusionary and exclusionary strategies

It is obvious also that the New Labour government has adopted both intensive inclusionary and exclusionary strategies towards crime. The two seemingly contradictory processes – the source of the frisson in the 'tough on crime, tough on the causes of crime' couplet – make sense in terms of the position of crime in the discourse. Crime is a product of exclusion; it must, therefore, be tackled at a fundamental level by policies of inclusion, which will, in time, bring down crime rates. But crime *in the here and now* disintegrates communities, it undermines the forces of inclusion; it must therefore be combated strongly where it arises. Let us summarize at this point the posited relationship between social exclusion and crime:

1. Although crime is widespread, a small number of offenders commit a large proportion of these offences.
2. These offenders are clustered within a socially excluded underclass.
3. The social disorganization and drug use endemic in these areas permit and sustain crime.
4. The cause of social exclusion lies in lack of motivation and capability, itself a product of dependency culture.
5. Such disorganized communities produce and perpetuate inadequate families, particularly those with a high proportion of single mothers, often in their teenage years.
6. Such inadequate families are criminogenic, reproducing disorganization over generations and perpetuating delinquency.
7. The policy solution is inclusionary; back-to-work programmes to tackle the 'causes', backed up with a forceful criminal justice system to deal with the problems of the present.

Social inclusion, for and against

The whole notion of social exclusion, and consequently of a socially excluded underclass who are a focus of multiple social problems including crime, has come under a considerable barrage of criticism. Before turning to this let us first point to some of its more favourable features:

Globalization, insecurity and crime

Let us first note that the SEU clearly recognizes the global background to the economic and social problems. The cause of crime is not located in the individual *per se*, however much individuals may be harmed by the wider social factors. It is thus distinctly different from the notion of crime being a product of isolated dysfunctional individuals (as with 'Old' Labour positivistic notions of crime and delinquency) or of opportunistic, voluntaristic individuals (as with the neo-liberalism of Margaret, Thatcher with its classicist ideas of criminal motivation). The approach thus distances itself from the analytical individualism of the past. Further, it locates these global processes in the production of social and economic inequality. Thus, if we are looking for the causes of crime (in the Blairite couplet), we can find it in the inequalities engendered by globalization. The concept of social exclusion is, in this sense, an advance. Further, it sets the local in the context of the global; just as it does not presume criminal behaviour stems from the characteristics of an individual, it does not locate the criminogenic within the delineated limits of a geographical area. Its emphasis on the role of flexible labour markets, global competition and the decline of manufacturing industry begins, at least, to embrace the notion of the transition to late modernity as the key to understanding the transformation and problems of contemporary society. Indeed, the Scottish Social Exclusion Network, in its report *Three Nations: Social Exclusion in Scotland* (1998), adopted the categories 'Excluded Scotland', 'Insecure Scotland' and 'Settled Scotland', which echo the well-known '30:30:40' divisions of the liberal commentator Will Hutton (1995) and which are incisively demonstrated by the Marxist writer on social exclusion, David Byrne (1999).

The linked nature of crime as a problem and the response to it

Crime is not seen as a separate problem, but as part of a matrix of problems and possessing interrelated causes. There is not a separate criminology nor a hermetic aetiology but the various manifestations of social exclusion are linked together – and their causes reside at the level of the family, the community, and the economy. Further, interventions must occur on all these levels and be part of a linked and co-ordinated response; indeed this is the *raison d'être* for the Social Exclusion Unit itself. If one looks across the array of interventions which the SEU suggests, it would not look out of place in the repertoire of interventions suggested by radical criminology – particularly of a realist variety. Indeed, there is very little here which one would not find resonance in, say, Elliott Currie's *Crime and Punishment in America* (1998).

The emphasis on prevention and reintegration

The real test for the SEU is its attitude to ex-offenders, and this is amply exemplified in the recent report, *Reducing Re-Offending by Ex-Prisoners* (2002). Here the emphasis is on the offender as a product of social exclusion, the ex-offender as a target of exclusionary attitudes and on the need to provide measures to reintegrate him or her into society. It is a programme of re-entry, not of stigmatization or retribution. We will return to this later, but suffice it to say such a rehabilitative programme is a welcome change from that of previous administrations and, indeed, pursues the notion of rehabilitation in a much more elaborate and thought-out fashion than the more usual limited and gestural acknowledgement of its worth (see Matthews in this volume).

This being said, the overall thrust of SEU policy emphasizes *prevention* rather than *cure*. Thus, it sees the role of intervention as to deal with the root causes of social exclusion, *not* to merely attempt to ameliorate the plight of the excluded, hence the emphasis on work rather than benefits. This is brought out well in *Three Nations*:

> Low pay is not only a cause of poverty but in part a symptom of low skills. In the long term tax and benefit changes will not assist enough of the low-paid to move up and stay up the earnings ladder. The growth of low-paid jobs (even those underpinned by a national minimum wage) becomes a vicious trap when workers never have a chance to leave them for something better. Low-paid work leads to long-term poverty because access to in-work training is so biased towards those who already have higher skill levels. Without a stronger commitment to skills development, a national minimum wage can only tackle the symptoms of low pay rather than its root causes.
>
> (Scottish Council Foundation, 1998, p. 24)

Note here the emphasis on skilled work rather than low-paid jobs. Here again such an argument has resonance within radical criminology. Witness Currie's stress on the relationship between stable, well-paid work and crime re-education and his charge that unstable, low-paid work would worsen the situation:

If the reduction of extreme poverty is our goal, what most needs reforming is the labor market itself and particularly the spread of low-wage unstable work. We will not sever the links between poverty and crime by increasing the number of poorly paid stressful jobs and forcing low-income parents to take them. If anything, the research tells us that diminishing the time available to parents to nurture and supervise children could make the crime problem worse, not better. A far more rational approach is to boost the rewards and the stability of work, in order to strengthen families and stabilize local communities.

(Currie, 1998, p. 149)

Many's the slip 'twixt cup and lip: New Labour's obsessional neurosis

All of this so far would seem promising. As noted by John Pitts, New Labour might well claim 'that its deliberations on crime and justice have paid due attention to "background" socio-structural factors and that it is precisely these factors that its social exclusion strategy is designed to address. Indeed, in *Bringing Britain Together* (SEU, 1999a) ... there is a clear acknowledgement of the structural origins and the interrelatedness of crime, poverty and inequality.' (Pitts, 2001, p. 146). Yet in the end, Pitts notes, the discussion of structure ends up being seen as a problem of lack of joined-up administration: 'Suddenly the problem is reduced from one of social structure to one of social administration. Like the victim of an obsessional neurosis, incapacitated in the face of real problems s/he reverts to an obsessive preoccupation with the detail of that which s/he cannot control.' (Pitts, 2001, p. 147).

The structural causes of crime are clearly delineated, but that is as far as it goes; rather than these being located in the deep structures of society, and its inevitable divisions of class, the concept of social exclusion carries with it the notion that the problem is that of inadequate management of society. The solution becomes managerial rather than transformative. Thus, a constant theme is that Britain performs less well than its European equivalents. Thus, 'In the mid-1990's, this country was distinguished from its EU competitors by high levels of social exclusion' (Social Exclusion Unit, 2001, p. 1). To demonstrate this, a series of tables are presented by the SEU showing that the United Kingdom has the worst record in terms of percentage of children living under the poverty line, children living in households without an adult in employment, and levels of adult illiteracy, teenage births, drug use, crime, etc. By this simple presentational tactic the SEU suggests that good practice exists already out there, in Europe, and all we have to do is replicate it.

Let us look diagrammatically at this account of social exclusion:

Figure 1   Social Exclusion and New Labour

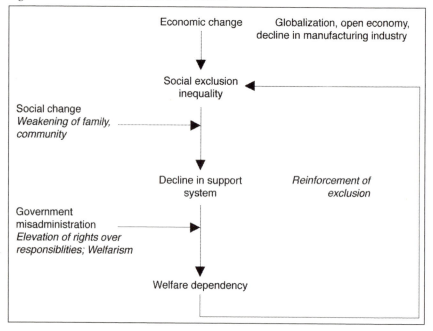

What is interesting is that this discourse on social exclusion takes the stronger structural version of radicals such as William Julius Wilson (1987) and bolts on to it the right-wing notions of exclusion of writers such as Charles Murray (1984) and Laurence Mead (1992) (see Pitts, 2003). That is, as we shall see, it moves from blaming the structure to blaming the social actors.

Let us turn now to the basic criticisms of social exclusion:

Criticisms of social exclusion

Dualism

The discourse of social exclusion has encapsulated a notion of a dualism of the included and the excluded. The chief flaws of this conception are:

1. *Homogeneity.* It suggests a homogenous group of people in the category of excluded, whereas in fact the social excluded incorporate the young, the old, the temporarily poor, etc. (see Gans, 1995).

2. *Social Immobility.* The presumption of a fairly static underclass is misleading. There is in fact a great deal of social mobility across categories (see Hills *et al.*, 2002).

3. *Fixed Locality and Separate Morality.* The concept harbours the notion of a group of people outcast, spatially cut off from the rest of society, with perhaps different values and motivations. In fact, no such spatial segregation occurs (physical mobility in and out of the ghetto, for example, is frequent) and values are shared with the wider society (see Young, 2002a; Nightingale, 1993);

4. *Focus on Poverty and Deprivation.* The notion of a socially excluded underclass gives the false notion that the majority of social problems are located in these areas. In fact, problems exist across the city, the majority outside of the poorest areas (see Mooney and Danson, 1997).

Losing class

Thus the opposition of, say, 20 per cent, the 'excluded', to a wider society of 'included' massively underestimates the economic and social problems of those in the wider society. It suggests that the included do not suffer the problems of class – indeed, that if they make the transition from the zones of exclusion to the inclusive world of mainstream society, the rest of their problems would vanish. Most importantly, this notion of social exclusion carries with it the implication that the problem is a Durkheimian one of a failure of integration, rather than a socialist one, which would emphasize problems of class. That is, globalization is seen as having resulted in problems of social cohesion – those left behind by change – rather than as an exacerbation of existing class divisions (Levitas, 1996). Indeed, John Andersen argues that this notion of social exclusion involves a major conceptual transformation:

> Theoretically, the notion of social exclusion points to a shift in the conceptualization of poverty from extreme class inequality and lack of resources in the Townsend tradition ... to a broader insider–outsider *problematique* – that is, a change of focus in the poverty and inequality discourse from a vertical to a horizontal perspective. The shift of focus can to some extent also be described as a shift from Marxist and Weberian tradition of class and status analysis to a Durkheimian 'anomie–integration' discourse.
>
> (Andersen, 1999, p. 129)

17

From RED to SID

Ruth Levitas (1996) notes how the concept of social exclusion became popular after the publication of Peter Townsend's book *Poverty in the United Kingdom* (1979). At that time it was used in tandem with the notion of relative poverty where people's *relative* (rather than absolute) impoverishment does not allow them to take part in the normal social and political activities associated with citizenship. Here is, of course, a loud resonance with the work of T.H. Marshall and the argument that without greater economic equality, full citizenship cannot be achieved. But the present discourse is, according to Levitas, distinctly different:

> The original popularity of this term does therefore derive, like the 'outcast poverty' version of the 'underclass', from a concern with inequality, even if it always contained a tendency to present an overly homogeneous view of the situation of those included in society. But the way it is currently being used actually obscures the questions of material inequality it was originally intended to illuminate: it has been co-opted into a different discourse, with different purposes and different effects. It is a discourse unable to address the question of unpaid work in society (work done principally by women), or of low-paid work, and completely erases from view the inequality between those owning the bulk of productive property and the working population, as well as obscuring the inequalities among workers. It presents 'society' as experiencing a rising standard of living by defining those who have not done so, who have become poorer, as 'excluded from' society, as 'outside' it.
>
> (Levitas, 1996, p. 7)

Levitas (1997) famously describes this transition as from a 'Redistributive, Egalitarian Discourse' (RED) to a 'Social Integrationist Discourse' (SID).

From structure to agency: the weak thesis

John Veit-Wilson (1998) makes the important distinction between 'strong' and 'weak' versions of social exclusion. The strong versions of this discourse emphasize the role of those excluding, whereas the weak versions involve focusing on the qualities of the excluded, where 'the solutions lie in altering those excluded people's handicapping characteristics and enhancing their integration into dominant society' (Veit-

Wilson, 1998, p. 45). David Byrne, in his key book *Social Exclusion* (1999), notes how it is his intention to focus on the strong version, emphasizing, as he does, 'that exclusion is not a property of individuals or even social spaces. Rather it is an inherent characteristic of an unequal post-industrial capitalism founded around a flexible labour market and with a systematic constraining of the organizational powers of workers as collective actors.' (Byrne, 1999, p. 128). Here the underclass are a reserve army of labour, who shift in and out of work, and who interface in terms of upward and downward mobility with a more traditional working class that has a higher standard of living but also a new degree of insecurity characteristic of late modernity.

Note that Byrne's formulation involves a more robust discourse around social exclusion. It emphasizes the strong thesis with its focus on exclusion, it tackles the criticism of the dualistic notion of the discontented underclass and the contented majority by pointing to the widespread insecurity occurring throughout society, and places this within the context of a reserve army of labour, the surplus population which the market cannot incorporate. He points to the political process of social exclusion, where there has been a systematic undermining of the power of trade unions and the elevation of neo-liberal notions of the individualistic contract between employee and employer. Lastly, he places this process in the transition from modernity to late modernity, contrasting it with the Fordist deal between worker and employer in the 'golden years' of Keynesianism, where work was relatively secure and well paid. Here the postwar consensus on wages, the compromise negotiated between capital and labour, although not involving genuine economic equality at least granted the notion of a fair day's wage for a fair day's work, security of employment and some shift towards the decommodification of labour. This inclusiveness of the wage deal was lost in the process of globalization and economic liberalization.

As to New Labour's version of social exclusion, Byrne has no doubt that it is the weak version, and, echoing many other writers, he dismisses the discourse 'as a method of closure in relation to challenges to inequality as a general social issue' (Byrne, 1995, p. 5). Indeed, Helen Colley and Phil Hodkinson (2001) point to the reversal of structure and agency in the discourse of the Social Exclusion Unit, focusing particularly on its analysis of youth in *Bridging the Gap* (1999c). Thus:

> ... the young people we meet in this report are at best passive victims of inevitable processes ... sponging off society as a whole in their costly benefit dependency. At worst they are deviant perpetrators of criminal behaviour and drug abuse who pose a

sinister threat to the rest of society. Somewhere in the middle are the pregnant teenagers reproducing future non-participants at alarming rates, ready to pass on their misconceived negativity about education, training and employment to perpetuate the cycle of social exclusion.

(Colley and Hodkinson, 2001, p. 341)

Salvation through labour: equality of opportunity, not outcome

Work is the key theme in New Labour discourse; the entry into work is seen as a major route out of social exclusion. Here again the focus is on manipulating agency (the supply side of labour) rather than on structure (the demand for work). Here the danger is that any work is seen as better than no work (Young, 2002a), that unpaid work such as child care is seen as not real work (Levitas, 1996) and that, in any case, the policies will work only geographically where there exists a high demand for labour (Peck, 1999).

The focus becomes preparing the excluded for work by coaxing them with the threat of benefit cuts, coupled with energetic programmes of retraining. Behind this, the critics argue, is a position that considerably rewrites Labour's traditional emphasis on justice and substitutes for this inclusion. As Normal Fairclough, in his thoroughgoing analysis of the language of New Labour, puts it: 'The meaning of "social justice" has also shifted through the omission of "equality" in the sense of equality of outcomes (entailing redistribution of wealth) and its substitution by "fairness" and "inclusion" ' (Fairclough, 2000, p. 46).

Ignoring stigmatization and criminalization
Byrne's critique of the 'weak thesis' tackles the problems of the loss of class (it sees globalization as having an impact across the class structure) and the rigid dualism of underclass and mainstream society. A parallel argument concerning the fluid nature of the underclass and the post-Fordist nature of exclusion was made in Young's *The Exclusive Society* (1999), written in the same year. However, in this latter text, written from a more sociological point of view, it became clear that the discussion of social exclusion even in the 'strong version' did not go far enough. That is, there is a tendency for writers on the impact of globalization (such as Byrne himself, but see also William Julius Wilson, 1987) to view the process of exclusion as occurring solely on an economic level and involving simply a hydraulic withdrawal of labour markets. Work disappears elsewhere, or becomes more com-

plex, particularly with regard to information technology, so that the excluded are, so to speak, *non-intentionally* stranded. This view ignores the processes of social exclusion that occur on the level of civil society and the criminal justice system. That is, parallel to the process of economic exclusion, there occurs the *active* social exclusion by stigmatization and the 'othering' of the poor as inadequate, criminogenic and troublesome. Frequently this involves the blaming of single mothers, and the invocation of the sins of welfare dependency are often racialized, particularly in terms of immigrants. Such a social process of moral panic and stigmatization is captured well in Herbert Gans's *The War Against the Poor* (1995), and by Zygmunt Bauman in *Work, Consumerism and the New Poor* (1998). Such a phenomenon of scapegoating and blame is a major component of social exclusion, yet is scarcely touched upon in the discourse. Indeed, it may well be argued, as Colley and Hodkinson (2001) imply, that the discourse of the Social Exclusion Unit, with its obsession with dependency, teenage pregnancy (see SEU, 1999b) and anti-social behaviour, contributes volubly to this process of 'othering' (see Young, 2002a).

Similarly, a staple of criminological discussion is the manner in which the criminal justice system discriminates against the poor, both in a heavy-handedness of suspicion as offenders and in inadequate provision when victims of crime. Such a palpable force for social exclusion is ignored in this discourse (see Mooney and Young, 2000). Indeed, what is remarkable when one compares the crime audits set up by New Labour on a borough by borough basis under the remit of the 1998 Crime and Disorder Act with the radical crime and policing surveys conducted by Labour boroughs in the 1980s (see Jones *et al.*, 1986; Painter *et al.*, 1989) is the absence of any public assessment of police illegalities and lack of accountability. Thus, the 'strong' thesis can be strengthened even further by adding to the non-intentional exclusion by market forces the intentional exclusion produced within civil society or by the criminal justice system (see Young, 2002a).

Beyond the 'weak' thesis

We have seen how the 'weak' thesis on social exclusion overplays agency over structure, wrongly stresses the binary nature of inclusion/ exclusion and ignores social stigmatization and prejudice within the criminal justice system. It starts off from the global and structural and ends up with the local and personal. Further, it is widely argued, most powerfully by Ruth Levitas, that New Labour's concept of social exclusion represents a retreat from redistribution to a concern with integration that it is unable to address, and which indeed conceals the fundamental problems of inequality.

Yet at the same time it must be noted that some of the criticisms are overdrawn. In compensation, there are, for example:

1. An awareness of the widespread impact of globalization: witness the title of the Scottish policy paper, *Three Nations*. Indeed this essay makes a point of denying the simple dualism. Structure, here, takes priority over agency.

2. A place for redistribution and greater equality of outcomes: witness the inclusion in *Preventing Social Exclusion* (Social Exclusion Unit, 2001) of levels of *income inequality*, and propositions of *children living in poverty* as key indicators of levels of social exclusion.

3. An emphasis on minimum basic standards (including, importantly, working family credit, the minimum wage), which involves a redistributive move (see Table 2, above);

4. The stress on enabling the individual to learn the skills to obtain a job and to be capable of taking up jobs (e.g. through better child-care facilities) (see Tables 1 and 2, above), which are undoubtedly beneficial. To focus on agency in terms of empowering the individual actor need not necessitate blaming the excluded.

5. An awareness in some of the Social Exclusion literature that Welfare to Work programmes can shift people from unemployment to badly paid employment, with insecure conditions, merely replicating social exclusion. Witness the passage in *The Three Nations* (cited above) on the need for well-paid secure jobs. Such criticism is well made.

There is in much of this social exclusion discourse, like in so much of New Labour policies, a social-democratic impulse heavily patinated with caution, hesitation and conservatism. This exists somewhere in the contradiction between the instincts of the Party membership and the government's pursuit of the central ground of voters, and it resonates in deep-seated conflicts within the Party leadership. All in all, however, the major theme of the discourse remains agency; it is interested in disciplining the underclass rather than genuine empowerment for them. Nowhere is this more evident than in the area of political exclusion.

Social and political exclusion

'It is interesting to reflect', Janie Percy-Smith notes, 'that, while there is an increasing literature on social and economic exclusion, there is relatively little on political exclusion'. And she adds that the first annual government report on poverty and social exclusion, *Opportunity for All: Tackling Poverty and Social Exclusion* (Department of Social Security, 1999), 'despite being extremely wide-ranging, reporting progress on all the myriad initiatives which are being developed to address social exclusion, makes no mention of political exclusion (Percy-Smith, 2000, pp. 148–9). And the same situation exists today. Let us examine the subjects illustrated by tables in the SEU Report of 2001, *Preventing Social Exclusion*, intended to measure trends in levels of social exclusion: Long Term Unemployment; Workless Households; Income Inequality; Exclusion from School; Drug Addicts; Crime; Children Living in Low Income Households; Adult Literacy; 18-Year Olds in Learning; Teenage Births. (see Social Exclusion Unit, 2001, pp. 1.6–1.12)

Once again note the eclectic mix of measures, and once again note that few people would, from a social democratic perspective, object to measures that reduced these key indices. Indeed, the only immediately problematic category is 'teenage births', which is closely associated with the discourse of single mothers and welfare dependancy, although, of course, as has been argued, the interpretation of many of these items (particularly the central concerns of unemployment and income inequality) are cast in a way that puts the emphasis on inadequacies of agency rather than structure. However, what is of interest here is what is omitted. For there is no mention of any measures of political inclusion, for example: voting levels; membership of political parties; community participation; social capital; tenants' organizations; trade union membership; participation in local community decision-making; candidature in local political forums; participation in pressure groups.

Now, of course, all studies of the lower part of the class structure have indicated that political involvement is extremely low (see Burchardt *et al.*, 2002). Such a situation creates an extremely unequal relationship between powerful interests and a local community. This is clearly revealed in the massive inequalities in urban regeneration schemes between the interests of capital and those of local working-class communities. As Byrne points out:

This is not simply because the interests of development capital have been given absolute priority. That has been possible only because in 'partnership' there has been no real countervailing power from the 'community' precisely because the 'community' is so fragmented and disorganized. Given the fragmented nature of 'community' and the logic of personal mobility in space, the proposals contained in the Cabinet Office Social Exclusion Unit 1998 White Paper *Bringing Britain Together: A National Strategy for Neighbourhood Renewal* (Cm 4045) can be described only as vacuous. The authors of this piece seem simply not to know how people actually conduct their lives in the divided city. It is plain that organization is the key to any kind of re-empowerment of the dispossessed. That is the issue to which we now turn in the conclusion of this book. It is process which matters most when we are dealing with issues of power.

(Byrne, 1999, p. 123)

And, however much the Third Way politicians talk about a new contract between the citizen and the state, based on rights and duties, and modernizers argue for a *reciprocity* between the state and citizens (Corrigan *et al.*, 1988), the old welfare state, which bestows problems and grants rights to its citizens, remains very much to the fore (see Young, 1999, pp. 197–199). As such it becomes more understandable how progressive discourses about social exclusion are undermined by those that stress the faults of actors. Indeed, as Mooney (in this volume) indicates, the social democratic emphasis on the dysfunctional family in relation to crime present in 'Old' Labour is replicated by New Labour, but this time read in the context of welfare dependency. There can be little doubt that the individuals themselves, if they had some political input into the debate, would not describe themselves as inadequate, nor would they stress lack of ability over lack of opportunities.

Let us turn now to what is the likely effect of political exclusion on levels of crime and disorder. The most prominent of all symptoms of social exclusion are riots (see Percy-Smith, 2000). The background to large-scale civil disturbances in the last 30 years has involved a situation where a population which is both economically *and* politically marginalized; where people have felt left out of the economic success of the wider society, have had no obvious means of political change in the near future. The spark for such rioting has most frequently been some gross example of police malpractice, preceded by a history of corrupt, violent and non-effective policing. Indeed, police malpractices represent very palpably the lack of political power of marginal groups – the inability of localized politics to deliver basic legal and civil rights and keep policing within the rule of law (see Lea and Young, 1993;

Power and Turnstall, 1997). Urban riots, such as those in England in 1981, 1984 and 1991, the French riots of 1981, and the most recent English riots in the northern cities of Burnley, Bradford and Oldham, represent dramatic expressions of failure of inclusion. Indeed, one commentator, John Pitts (2003), has suggested that the northern riots of 2002 represent a major setback for the social inclusionary policies of the New Labour government which we have detailed in this article.

The origins of civil disorders and of crime are similar in many ways. A major source of endemic criminality is economic marginalization coupled with a feeling of political and social marginalization. And, as with rioting, this latter marginalization is made evident to a group or locality by them being the disproportionate focus of police attention and malpractice (see Mooney and Young, 2000). Riots differ in that they are more collective and, to some extent, more targeted; but the background of economic despair and hostility to the police is common.

Pitts, in *The New Politics of Youth Crime* (2001), makes an illuminating comparision between the responses of the British and the French to the riots that occurred in 1981 in both their countries. The response of the former gave rise to the *Scarman Report* (1982); the latter produced the report of Henri Bonnemaison (1983), the result of an inquiry set up by the new socialist administration of François Mitterand following nationwide riots in the multiracial *Banlieues*. Pitts's conclusion is that while both reports recognized the problem of economic marginaliz-ation as a core part of the problem, the Bonnemaison report went further in pointing to the key problem of political alienation.

Thus, if Scarman emphasized economic exclusion, Bonnemaison affirmed this, but placed it in the context of a problem of citizenship, of political exclusion. And here, of course, we return ironically to earlier commentaries on the concept of social exclusion, which distin-guish a 'Durkheimian' concept of inclusion, that is concerned with horizontal integration, and that which is more social democratic and class-based in its emphasis, focusing on vertical integration. (This, as is described above, is the basis of the argument of critics such as Levitas, who castigates New Labour's formulation of social exclusion as being too integrationist (SID) and not sufficiently redistributionist (RED).)

The truth, however, is that *both* an integrationist and a redistribution-ist element of policy is necessary if a more egalitarian, social-inclusionary policy is to be achieved. A 'strong' thesis must not only strengthen its economic policies with a greater emphasis on structure than agency, but it must pay attention to the empowerment of the excluded. That is, it must have *policies* of political inclusion and *politics* which are inclusionary.

Crime and social inclusion

In the light of such criticisms, as described above, what likely effect could such policies have on the problem of crime? Let us look briefly at two aspects: tackling the conditions that give rise to crime, and tackling the problems of controlling crime:

The conditions which give rise to crime

Social inclusion – the realization of full citizenship economically, socially and politically, and the identification of a common interest within a community – mitigates against crime. Conversely, social exclusion – feeling economically deprived, socially alienated and politically and legally marginalized – creates a high level of discontent, which frequently gives rise to crime. In particular, feeling denied the normal rewards of society, being relatively poor, while being treated as second-class citizens on the street (especially with regards to maltreatment and unfairness by the police) classically create the conditions to sever allegiance from society and encourage criminal behaviour.

The inclusionary policies advocated by the SEU, with its emphasis on the 'weak' thesis and dragooning people into work at whatever level, does not solve the problem of social exclusion. To be at the bottom of the heap in the worst paid jobs does not ameliorate feelings of exclusion; indeed, by making easier comparision with other workers more comfortably off, such a policy might actually exacerbate relative deprivation. Rather, what is necessary is a strengthening of the progressive features of present policy – for example, educational provision for better jobs and social mobility, state intervention to ensure jobs are available in depressed areas, *and* a widening of the terms of social inclusion to include the political in order to achieve a 'strong' thesis that would directly cut out the roots of crime.

Tackling problems of controlling crime

The notion of a reciprocal relationship between the citizen and the state – one which neither follows a neo-liberal notion of the citizen catering for him or herself (and despises the 'nanny state') nor simply accepts the traditional social democratic notion of delivering rights and services to the citizen – is based not only on a normative imperative, which stresses both the responsibilities of the citizen and those in authority, but also on the empirical facts of successful service delivery: such as that schools cannot simply provide knowledge – homes and families are obviously also key elements in a child's education; doctors and clinics do not grant good health – individuals' habits of eating, exercise and hygiene are vital parts of the process. Such social goods are produced within civil society, outside of the institutions of the state, and, moreover, the contribution of state agencies is facilitated and augmented by the level of cooperation of the citizen. No more so is this true than in the area of security from crime and incivilities. First of all, it is the strength of community and family that is paramount in law-abiding behaviour. Second, the police and the courts are heavily dependent on public cooperation for the provision of knowledge.

On the first point, as Elliot Currie (1998) has clearly documented, inclusionary policies that insist on the importance of work, with long and inflexible hours, serve to undermine the family and the community. They lessen social control and the supervision of adolescents rather than strengthen it. As to the second point, the police rely heavily on the public, from knowledge of offenders (*reporting*) to suggesting the likely offender (*identifying*), to giving evidence in court (*witnessing*). The information-flow theory of policing points to the key part public cooperation plays in police effectiveness and the wide variation among areas and sections of the community willing to cooperate with the police (see Kinsey *et al.*, 1986). There is little doubt that such cooperation is lowest among the socially excluded. Thus, we have the paradox that those who live in high-crime areas, who are the most vulnerable victims of crime and have the highest knowledge of crime, are also those least likely to cooperate with the police. The reason for this is undoubtedly that the socially excluded are very much the focus of police attention, experience higher levels of police malpractice, and are thus those most alienated from the police (see Mooney and Young, 2000).

A vivid illustration of this is that, at the time of writing (January 2003), there is a public furore about gun crime. Two Black teenage girls, aged 17 and 18, were shot dead at a party in Birmingham, caught in the crossfire of a feud between members of rival Black gangs. The police admitted they could not get far in their investigation, because of the unwillingness of members of the Black community to testify. Similarly, in March 2002, Gladstone Johnson was shot dead in front of hundreds of revellers at the West Indian Federation Club in Winston Green, and, despite the shooting being witnessed by many people, no witnesses came forward. Part of the reason for this is, of course, fear of reprisals; but a significant element is a culture of unwillingness to aid the police because of experiences of police stigmatization and malpractice.

It is extraordinary that the discourse built up around the Macpherson Report into the murder of the Black teenager Stephen Lawrence, which openly admitted to 'institutionalized racism' within the police service (see John Lea, this volume), does not seem to have any resonance in the wider discourse of social exclusion, the central motif in New Labour's social policy.

Conclusion: decline in crime in society, increase in crime in the margins

Let us conclude this section by noting that despite the general decline in crime throughout England and Wales, there has been an increase in the more blighted, socially excluded areas. To this extent the continued high public concern about crime has some rational kernel, and the worries, for example about gun crime, have some basis in reality, however distorted by their presentation in the mass media. Part of this development is no doubt the greater level of crime prevention in more well-off areas, which displaces, or contains, crime in the sink estates and poorer areas; but also the level of economic inequality has increased, further compounded by the inequalities in criminal victimization (Hope, 1997, Trickett *et al.*, 1995). Such economic inequalities, localized in certain areas, are, of course, part and parcel of the process of globalization, which the policies of social inclusion are intended to tackle. It may well be that a generally propitious economic climate and relatively good employment prospects have resulted in a fall in crime in all but these blighted areas. Here one should note Peck's ironic comment (1999) that the prospects for social inclusion are greater in those areas with high labour demands and fewer in those geographical areas that most need them. Once again this calls for structural intervention in these areas to generate employment; the situation is not a symptom of supposed deficiencies among the actors involved. Such a genuine equalization of opportunities must be combined with a more egalitarian approach to security. In this context it is refreshing to see Paul Wiles, Head of Research Development and Statistics at the Home Office, quite categorically arguing for progressive crime-reduction targets, tackling the uneven distribution of public safety. Thus, he argues:

> ... the challenge for the next few years ... is how do you equalize the distribution of crime ... What we really need to start thinking about are what are referred to as floor targets – say, no community or city in the country ought to have a burglary rate that is twice as high as the best area in the country. We need to get crime down

in those high crime areas – that has to be the next big objective, because crime is so unequally distributed . . .

(Wiles, 2002, p. 23)

References

Andersen, J. (1999) 'Social and System Integration and the Underclass', in I. Gough and G. Olofsson (eds) *Capitalism and Social Cohesion*, New York: Palgrave Macmillan.

Barclay, G., Tavares, C. and Siddique, A. (2001), *International Comparisons of Criminal Justice Statistics 1999*, London: Home Office.

Bauman, Z. (1998) *Work, Consumerism and the New Poor*, Buckingham: Open University Press.

Blair, T. (1993) 'Why Crime is a Socialist Issue', *New Statesman*, 29(12), 27–8.

Blair, T. (2001) Foreword to *Preventing Social Exclusion*, London: Stationery Office.

Blumstein, A. and Wallman, J. (eds) (2000), *The Crime Drop in America*, Cambridge: Cambridge University Press.

Bonnemaison, H. (1983) *Face á la delinquance: prévention, répression, solidarité*, Paris: La Documentation Française.

Bottoms, A. (1995) 'The Philosophy and Politics of Punishment and Sentencing', in C. Clarkson and R. Morgan (eds) *The Politics of Sentencing Reform*, Oxford: Oxford University Press.

Burchardt, T., LeGrand, J. and Pichaud, D. (2002) 'Degrees of Exclusion', in J. Hills, J. LeGrand and D. Pichaud (eds) *Understanding Social Exclusion*, Oxford: Oxford University Press.

Byrne, D. (1999) *Social Exclusion*, Buckingham: Open University Press.

Cabinet Office (2002), *United Kingdom National Action Plan on Social Inclusion – 2001–2003*.

Clarke, J., Gerwitz, S. and McLaughlin, E. (eds) (2000), *New Managerialism, New Welfare*, London: Sage.

Colley, M. and Hodkinson, P. (2001) 'Problems with Bridging the Gap: The Reversal of Structure and Agency in Addressing School Exclusion', *Critical Social Policy*, 21(3), 335–59.

Corrigan, P., Jones, T., Lloyd, J. and Young, J. (1988) *Socialism, Merit and Efficiency*, London: Fabian Society.

Crawford, A. (2001) 'Joined Up But Fragmented: Contradiction, Ambiguity and Ambivalence in the Heart of New Labour's Third Way', in R. Matthews and J. Pitts (eds) *Crime, Disorder and Community Safety*, London: Routledge.

Currie, E. (1998) *Crime and Punishment in America*, New York: Metropolitan Books.

Daly, K. (2002) 'Restorative Justice: The Real Story', *Punishment and Society*, 4(1), 55–79.

Department of Social Security (1999) *Opportunity for All: Tackling Poverty and Social Exclusion*, Cm 4445, London: Stationery Office.

Fairclough, N. (2000) *New Labour, New Language?*, London: Routledge.

Field, S. (1990) *Trends in Crime and Their Interpretation*, London: HMSO.

Flynn, N. (1997), *Public Sector Management*, Hemel Hempstead: Harvester Wheatsheaf.

Gans, H. (1995) *The War against the Poor*, New York: Basic Books.

Garland, D. (1996) 'The Limits of the Sovereign State', *British Journal of Criminology*, 36(4), 445–71.

Garland, D. (2001) *The Culture of Control*, Oxford: Oxford University Press.

Hancock, L. and Matthews, R. (2001) 'Crime Community Safety and Toleration', in R Matthews and J. Pitts (eds) *Crime Disorder and Community Safety*, London: Routledge.

Hills, J., LeGrand, J. and Pichaud, D. (eds) (2002) *Understanding Social Exclusion*, Oxford: Oxford University Press.

Hirst, P. and Thompson, G. (1992) 'The Problem of Globalization: International Economic Relations, National Economic Management and the Formation of Trading Blocs', *Economy and Society*, 21(4), 357–96.

Home Office (2001) *Through the Prison Gate: A Joint Thematic Review by HM Inspectorates of Prison and Probation*, London: HMSO.

Hope, T. (1997) 'Inequality and the Future of Community Crime Prevention', in S. Lab (ed.) *Crime Prevention at a Crossroads*, Cincinnati, Ohio: Anderson Publishing.

Hope, T. (2002) 'What's What: And What Does "What Works" Mean?', paper presented at the British Criminology Conference, Keele University, July.

Hough, M. and Tilley, N. (1998) *Auditing Crime and Disorder: Guidance for Local Partnerships*, Police Research Group, paper 91, London: Stationery Office.

Hutton, W. (1995) *The State We're In*, London: Jonathan Cape.

Jones, T., MacLean B. and Young, J. (1986) *The Islington Crime Survey*, Aldershot: Gower.

Kinsey, R., Lea, J. and Young, J. (1986) *Losing the Fight against Crime*, Oxford: Blackwell.

Lea, J. (2002) *Crime and Modernity*, London: Sage.

Lea, J., Matthews, R. and Young, J. (1989) *The State, Multi-Agency Approaches and Crime Control*, Middlesex University: Centre for Criminology.

Lea, J. and Young, J. (1982) 'The Riots in Britain 1981', in D. Cowell, T. Jones and J. Young (eds) *Policing the Riots*, London: Junction Books.

Lea, J. and Young, J. (1993) *What is to Be Done about Law and Order?*, 2nd edition, London: Pluto.

Levitas, R. (1996) 'The Concept of Social Exclusion and the New Durkheimian Hegemony', *Critical Social Policy*, 16(1) 5–20.

Levitas, R. (1997) 'Discourses of Social Inclusion and Integration: From the European Union to New Labour', paper presented at the European Sociological Association Conference, University of Essex, August.

Lister, R. (1998) 'From Equality to Social Inclusion', *Critical Social Policy*, 18(2) 215–25.

McLaughlin, E., Muncie, J. and Hughes, G. (1991) 'The Permanent Revolution: New Labour, New Public Management and the Modernization of Criminal Justice', *Criminal Justice*, 1(3), 301–18.

Marshall, T.H. (1996 [1950]) *Citizenship and Social Class*, London: Pluto.

Martinson, R (1974) 'What Works? – Questions and Answers about Prison Reform', *The Public Interest*, 34, 22–54.

Matthews, R. (2002) 'Crime Control in Late Modernity: A Review Essay', *Theoretical Criminology*, 6(2), 217–27.

Matthews R. and Pitts J. (2001) 'Beyond Criminology?', in R. Matthews and J. Pitts (eds) *Crime, Disorder and Community Safety*, London: Routledge.

Mead, L. (1992) *The New Politics of Poverty*, New York: Basic Books.

Metropolitan Police (1986) *Metropolitan Police Strategy Department*, London: Metropolitan Police.

Mooney, G. and Danson, M. (1997) 'Beyond Culture City: Glasgow as a Dual City', in N. Jewson and S. MacGregor (eds) *Transforming Cities*, London: Routledge.

Mooney, J. and Young, J. (2000) 'Policing Ethnic Minorities', in B. Loveday and A. Marlow (eds) *Policing after the Stephen Lawrence Inquiry*, Lyme Regis: Russell House.

Moynihan, D. (1993) 'Defining Deviancy Down', *American Scholar*, 62, Winter, 17–30.

Murray, C. (1984) *Losing Ground*, New York: Basic Books.

Nightingale, C. (1993) *On The Edge*, New York: Basic Books.

Painter, K., Lea, J., Woodhouse, T. and Young, J. (1989) *The Hammersmith Crime and Policing Survey*, Middlesex University: Centre for Criminology.

Pawson, R. and Tilley, N. (1997) *Realistic Evaluation*, London: Sage.

Peck, J. (1999) 'New Labourers? Making a New Deal for the "Workless Class"', *Environment and Planning C Governmental Policy*, 17, 345–72.

Percy-Smith, J. (2000) 'Political Exclusion', in J. Percy-Smith (ed.) *Policy Responses to Social Exclusion*, Buckingham: Open University Press.

Pitts, J. (2001) *The New Politics of Youth Crime*, London: Palgrave.

Pitts, J. (2003) 'New Labour and the Racialisation of Youth Crime', in J. Hagedorn (ed.) *Gangs in the Global City: The Limitations of Criminology*, Champaign, Illinois: University of Illinois Press.

Power, A. and Tunstall, R. (1997) *Dangerous Disorder: Riots and Violent Disturbances in Thirteen Areas of Britain 1991–1992*, York: York Publishing Services.

Prescott, J. (2002) 'Social Exclusion in the Twenty-First Century', Speech to Fabian Society, London.

Scarman, L. (1982) *The Scarman Report*, London: Penguin.

Simon, J. (2001) 'Entitlement to Cruelty: The End of Welfare and the Punitive Mentality in the United States', in K. Stenson and R. Sullivan (eds) *Crime, Risk and Justice*, Cullompton, Devon: Willan.

Scottish Council Foundation (1998) *Three Nations: Social Exclusion in Scotland*, Edinburgh: SCF.

Social Exclusion Unit (1999a) *Bringing Britain Together*, London: Stationery Office.

Social Exclusion Unit (1999b) *Teenage Pregnancy*, London: Stationery Office.

Social Exclusion Unit (1999c) *Bridging the Gap: New Opportunities for 16–18 Year Olds*, London: Stationery Office.

Social Exclusion Unit (2001) *Preventing Social Exclusion*, London: Stationery Office.

Social Exclusion Unit (2002) *Reducing Re-Offending by Ex-Prisoners*, London: Stationary Office.

Taylor, I. (1999) 'Limits of Market Society. European Perspectives', in H. Steinert (ed.) *Politics Against Social Exclusion*, Vienna: Institut für Rechts- und Kriminalsoziologie.

Townsend, P. (1979) *Poverty in the United Kingdom*, London: Penguin.

Trickett, A., Ellingworth, D., Hope, T. and Pease, K. (1995) 'Crime Victimisation in the Eighties', *British Journal of Criminology*, 35, 343–59.

Veit-Wilson, J. (1998) *Setting Adequate Standards*, Bristol: Policy Press.

Wiles, P. (2002) 'Crime's Vital Statistics', *Safer Society*, 11, 22–4.

Wilson, W.J. (1987) *The Truly Disadvantaged*, Chicago: Chicago University Press.

Young, J. (1992) 'Ten Points of Realism', in J. Young and R. Matthews (eds) *Rethinking Criminology*, London: Sage.

Young, J. (1999) *The Exclusive Society*, London: Sage.

Young, J. (2002a) 'Crime and Social Exclusion', in M. Maguire, R. Morgan and R. Reiner (eds) *The Oxford Handbook of Criminology*, 3rd edition, Oxford: Oxford University Press.

Young, J. (2002b) 'Critical Criminology in the Twenty First Century: Critique, Irony and the Always Unfinished', in K. Carrington and R. Hogg (eds) *Critical Criminology: Issues, Debates, Challenges*, Cullompton, Devon: Willan.

Young, J. (2003) 'Searching for a New Criminology of Everyday Life', review of D. Garland, *The Culture of Control*, *British Journal of Criminology*, 42, 445–61.

Chapter 2

Winning the fight against crime? New Labour, populism and lost opportunities

Jock Young

Between 1995 and 1999 there was a 23 per cent fall in the crime rate, according to the authoritative British Crime Survey (Kershaw *et al.*, 2000). The less reliable figures of those crimes known to the police mirrors this, albeit imperfectly, with a decline in the region of 20 per cent in the period 1991–1999: it is difficult to be precise because of the change in counting rules (see Matheson and Summerfield, 2001). The long rise in crime from the 1960s, which has dominated the thinking of criminologists, politicians, and law-and-order officers, has finally turned. The steady annual increase in pressure on the criminal justice system, *at least at source*, has halted. Furthermore, such a decline has not been restricted to property crimes as might be expected; the British Crime Survey indicates a 20 per cent decline in violent crime over the same period (1995–99), with falls occurring in all offence categories (that is assault, wounding, theft from person). The only exception to this decline is robbery, which has been buoyed up by the inclusion of school bullying – particularly with regards to mobile phones (see below). This decline in violent crime is more recent than that of property crime, but is more than welcome, set against the backcloth of a similar long increase since the 1960s. Homicide has been increasing on average by one per cent a year since the mid-1960s, but much of the recent increase relates to the crimes surrounding the cocaine trade and to the discovery of some particularly productive serial killers. The United Kingdom's homicide rate, it must be emphasized, is low from an international perspective; for example, it is one quarter of the rate in the United States. In 1999 London had a homicide rate 19 times smaller than Washington D.C., almost one third of New York's and, within Europe, smaller than, for example, Edinburgh, Brussels, Prague, Berlin, Dublin, Madrid and Stockholm (Barclay *et al.*, 2000). UK rural areas too, it should be noted, have low crime rates: risks of violence are much lower than in the towns, and are also decreasing, indeed slightly more rapidly so. (Both burglary and violence are almost twice the rate in urban than rural areas.) (see Kershaw *et al.*, 2000, p. 75).

The current Labour Government, then, has been fortunate in the law-and-order stakes. No administration, whether Conservative or Labour, since Churchill's 1951–55 government has been so lucky. With Labour's huge majority and an often commanding lead in the polls one would have imagined radical innovations to occur in this area, or at the very least a celebration of government policy. Joined up thinking might have linked successes in economic policy to the decline in property crime, or to the government crime-reduction strategies, or, in particular, could have highlighted the extensive social inclusionary projects of Neighbourhood Renewal and Welfare to Work (see Matthews and Young, this volume). At least that is what I would have been tempted to do if I had my hands on the spinometer at Labour Party HQ. But none of this has occurred; rather, the emphasis from the government has been on violent crime, social disorder, and the need for increased numbers of police officers and prison expansion.

The international dimension

Lest one think that this decrease in crime is something idiosyncratic or a blip in the statistical record let me put it in an international context.

On November 16 2000, in San Francisco, a packed meeting of the American Society of Criminology gathered together to discuss a most extraordinary happening in the world of crime. For from 1991 onwards, violent crime in the United States, which had led the advanced world by far in rates of murder and robbery, had begun to fall. Homicide dropped by 35.7 per cent from 1991 to 1998 (from 9.8 to 6.3 per 100,000) (Blumstein and Wallman, 2000). Al Blumstein, of the National Consortium on Violence Research had brought together a dazzling array of experts: demographers, economists, sociologists and criminologists, all contributing their views on the change with graphic charts and probing statistical analysis. I listened with fascination to how they factored each of the developments over the period to explain the phenomenon, from changes in the distribution of handguns, the extraordinary prison expansion, zero-tolerance policing, down to changes in crack-culture and technology. At the end of the session they asked for comments from the audience, no doubt expecting some detailed remark about policing levels or the influence of handgun availability, or such like; but the first question, from a Canadian woman, was something of a revelation. She pointed out, ironically, how Canadians were supposed to be condemned to culturally lag behind their American cousins, but that they too had had a drop in violence, despite the fact that they had not experienced such a period of rapid prison expansion, that zero-tolerance policing was not *de rigueur* and that Canada had only a small problem of crack-cocaine. She was followed by a Spanish woman, who said something very similar about her country. And, in fact, there was a crime drop in 13 out of 21 industrial countries during 1997–98 (Barclay *et al.*, 2001).

So what is happening? Methods of policing or extra police numbers would seem to have little effect on crime rates. There has been a decline in crime in countries that have increased, decreased *or* left unchanged their prison population[1]. Even in the United States, where imprisonment of so many of its population has obviously had some impact on crime, by virtue of taking out so many of its young, working-class citizens – 2 million in all – just as it has affected unemployment levels and voting patterns, the effect is less than one might think. Indeed, the National Consortium on Violence Research suggests that the enormous amount spent on prison in the United States (more than on a higher education for each person) has not made as great a contribution as an expanding economy and changes in the age proportions in the population (Blumstein and Wallman, 2000). Indeed, if we were looking for explanations we might pinpoint the economy, demographic factors, and in addition the intensive crime-reduction and target-hardening strategies that have occurred in the majority of the advanced industrial countries. Demography apart, the British government could well have claimed to have managed the economy efficiently, and it has spent enormous sums on crime reduction. The fact that the crime drop has occurred internationally would not rule out of court New Labour's claims to have facilitated the process. But none of this occurred; instead the Labour government has competed with the Conservatives in playing up the image of a disorderly Britain, while its policies have been in the very opposite direction of what the research evidence suggests. That is, Labour has attempted to increase the size of the police force while embarking on a massive prison-expansion programme.

It would be difficult to find one academic criminologist in this country who supports prison expansion, and there are few who believe that an increase in police manpower can have anything more than a marginal effect on crime rates. Government policies fly directly in the face of research evidence, and would seem almost wilfully to ignore expert opinion. All of this might be expected from the Conservatives, whose 'common sense revolution' would turn to the saloon bar rather than the research centre for its inspiration; but it is surprising from a Labour administration, one which lays such stress on the need for evidence-led policies.

How did such a situation come about? I want to point first of all to a mass media which has consistently taken the most pessimistic view of the crime problem, and thus reinforced the pessimism of politicians of the two major parties. Second, there has been a widespread and mistaken view, actively fuelled by the police lobbies, that we have a crisis in police numbers. Third, the ideas which New Labour has assimilated with regards to crime control are, paradoxically, those of the American Right. Lastly, there is a simple populism at work – a notion of giving the public what they want.

Violent Britain

In February 2001 the result of the annual International Crime and Victim Survey conducted by the University of Leiden in the Netherlands was published, to headlines in *The Daily Telegraph* (23 february 2001) that 'England Tops Crime League and We Are the Crime Capital of the World'. This was linked inevitably, and with seeming justification, with Tony Blair's plans for an ambitious £700 million prison programme as part of the Government's 'National Crime Plan', including plans to boost police recruitment. 'Vicious Brits' topped the *Economist*'s chart of violent nations: with England and Wales second only to Australia in the Crime Survey findings, while down at the bottom of the chart were the United States and Spain. What is strange about these results is they are almost exactly the opposite of reality. The most reliable index of violence is the homicide statistics. Here the United States is easily at the top out of all the First World countries, however improved of late, while Spain is at the top of the league within the European Union. England and Wales are, in fact, bottom of the homicide stakes in the countries listed, while Australia is a relative haven of tranquillity internationally.

Let us say that the figures of the International Crime and Victim Survey – which are used widely in the media and in official reports – are greeted annually with dismay and a general gnashing of teeth by the worldwide criminological community. These maverick results, however welcome to the British press, are a result of surveys conducted by telephone, naively expecting strangers to tell them about violence over the phone. And, more significantly, the paradox is that countries with genuinely high rates of incivilities are less sensitive to violence, and do not register relatively minor acts of violence, whereas those where violence is more distasteful record the slightest violent act as serious.

Such gross exaggeration and alarmism about crime is regularly exercised in both the tabloid and the broadsheet press. Thus, on 3 June, the *Observer* had the headline 'UK Matches Africa in Crime Surge' (2001) in which it was claimed that violent crime in Britain was rising at a faster rate than in the United States or Russia, and was 'escalating at the same rate as the crime-ridden South Africa'. This report was based on the figures given in the recent Home Office report on *International Comparisons on Criminal Justice Statistics* (Barclay *et al.*, 2001). The warning, in the report, to be very cautious about making direct comparisons was completely ignored. To start with, with the exception of homicide only a small proportion of violent crime is reported to the police, and furthermore this varies widely among countries, so that comparison of these rates is of little utility. The more robust homicide rate would show that the rate in South Africa is 40 times that of England and Wales, while the Russian rate is 14 times greater and the American rate is four times higher. The base level of violence is thus much lower in England and Wales than these other countries. Furthermore, the British homicide rate at the time of writing – the best indicator of violence – has risen only by 3 per cent from a very low figure in the last five years.

This attempt to portray Britain as a violent society is therefore grossly inaccurate: to equate the dire situation in South Africa with the relative safety here trivializes the problems of the new South Africa, just as it sensationalizes the problem in Britain.

What I have shown above are examples, which could be replicated on almost a daily basis, of what Bill Chambliss, in his recent book *Power, Politics and Crime*, talks of as the 'systematic attempt to make the problem of crime as bad as the data will allow'. In these instances it involves serious journalists taking absurd figures at face value, forgetting all they have ever been told about the nature of statistics. More frequently in the recent period it involves ignoring the generally benign drift in the crime statistics and focusing on the one blemish, street robbery. So we are informed, breathlessly, that robbery is up by 20.8 per cent without discussing what we mean by robbery or without pointing out that robbery is a small part (12.6 per cent) of all violent crime, and indeed only 1.7 per cent of the total crime figures.[2]

The crisis in policing

On May 17 2001, in the *Guardian*'s Truth Watch column, one might have been slightly alarmed to see a graph that recorded the precipitous decline in the number of police officers in this country. In fact, the artist had imaginatively adjusted the axes of the graph so that an actual decline between 1991 and 1999 of 3 per cent looked like a steep slope. Indeed, if one had allowed for the considerable civilian backing, the actual number of police-service personnel over the period had increased by 2 per cent. But more significantly let us look at the police case-load over the period, as represented by the number of crimes reported. This, as we have seen, fell by about 20 per cent. The case-load thus had a considerable decline even if we allow for the slight decrease in police numbers, we have a decrease in case-load per police officer of 19 per cent. There is hardly any argument here for increasing the amount of police resources, or, indeed, the number of police officers. But let us take this investigation a little further by looking at the number of crimes cleared up. These have fallen since 1991 by 10 per cent. Furthermore, the most useful indicator of police efficiency is crimes cleared up per police officer per year. This is now in the region of ten – that is, only ten crimes cleared up per officer per year – a figure that surprises many, although it is even lower in the Metropolitan area. Further, there has been a decline in this figure, from almost 12 in 1991. There has, therefore, been a considerable drop in police efficiency during this period. One should also ask oneself how many police officers at the rate of 10 clear ups a year would be needed to solve the 4 million crimes not detected every year?

Where is the crime drop dividend?

Such a decline in crime represents a reduction in pressures on the police and prisons, and ought to result in some sort of a public dividend, with significantly less money spent on police and prisons. But just as after the Cold War the peace dividend from military expenditure never seemed to materialize, so any reductions in the law-and-order budget seem remote. Indeed, the very opposite is the case, so that we are repeatedly warned of the crisis in police numbers and the need for prison expansion. It is paramount that a future government should face up to the need to reduce the prison population and, in particular, to tackle the problem of police inefficiency, even though to do so will incur considerable ire from police lobbies and sections of the media. In particular, we should note the shifting of money from welfare to criminal-justice budgets – as is evident in the United States, with its increased spending on prisons and decreased expenditure on higher education (see Chambliss, 1999, Chapter 6, 'Trading Textbooks for Prison Cells').

The influence of the new right

In 1993, in an article in the *New Statesman* entitled 'Why Crime is a Socialist Issue', Tony Blair first presented his, at the time, encouraging couplet 'tough on crime, tough on the causes of crime', which at least suggested some commitment to dealing with structural causes. Unfortunately, like the word 'socialism', which soon disappeared from Blair's vocabulary, structural causes became transmuted, as Jayne Mooney shows in this volume, into the typically Conservative concern with the 'inadequate' family as the main cause of crime; while 'tough on crime' has become immediately transposed into a fascination with zero-tolerance policing and greater numbers of prisons in an emulation of the American model. The three theoretical influences constituting the 'big idea', if that is what you could call it, all came from the United States: Charles Murray, the maverick anti-state libertarian more at home with the militias than liberal democracy; John DiIulio (1995), the right-wing advocate of American prison expansion; and James Q. Wilson, an advisor to presidents Nixon, Reagan and the elder Bush. Thus, the vocabulary of underclass and social exclusion came to dominate New Labour discourse. Crime was the provenance of a small minority of excluded, the realm of dependency: single mothers, teenage pregnancy, dysfunctional families, the work-shy and the substance abusers. The solution was to drum them into work, regiment benefits, etc. From Charles Murray was taken the view of the underclass as those unwilling to work rather than as, in the social democratic version of William Julius Wilson, those cut off from work. From DiIulio Labour absorbed the notion that a small number of young people – sited in the underclass – committed a large proportion of street crime, and the task of government was to target them. So it was claimed that 6 per cent of young males committed 50 per cent of all delinquencies.

John Birt, the ex-governor of the BBC – bizarrely drafted into the Home Office in 1998 as a 'crime czar' – focused his attention on these 'super-predators' as a technical fix to the delinquency problem.[3] Such claims have become a key part of New Labour's policy. Thus Tony Blair in a speech delivered on 30 May 2001, set out the Government's crime-reduction plans in the second term:

We will take further action to focus on the 100,000 most persistent offenders. They are responsible for half of all crime. They are the core of the crime problem in this country. Half are under 21, nearly two-thirds are hard drug users, three quarters are out of work and more than a third were in care as children. Half have no qualifications at all and 45 per cent are excluded from school. . . . Spending on the police will be an extra £1.6 billion per year by 2003–2004. And we are pledged to recruit another 6,000 police officers . . . that investment must be matched by radical reform. We plan the most comprehensive reform of the criminal justice system since the war – to catch, convict, punish and rehabilitate more of the 100,000 persistent offenders.

(Blair, 2001 speech)

Let us note that these figures are totally hypothetical, yet very politically convenient. They ignore the fact that a large proportion of young people commit crime, and that only a few are caught; that generalization about their background from these few is grossly unreliable; that the number of crimes committed is based on police interviews with apprehended young offenders, who are encouraged to exaggerate to boost the clear-up figures; that even given this, only one quarter of offences are cleared up, so that for 4 million uncleared offences we haven't the faintest idea of the identity of the offenders. Furthermore, for youthful offences such as burglary and robbery the clear-up rate is even lower, 18 per cent and 13 per cent respectively, and the culprits even more difficult to categorize (*Criminal Statistics, England and Wales*, 1999). And even in those instances where a small number of youths are involved in crime, it is not the same youths every week. Four muggers may commit most of the street robberies in one locality in a month but with such an amateurish crime, the culprits are often different people from one month to the next.

Via DiIulio and James Q. Wilson Labour adopted the metaphor of the war against crime and against drugs, and incarceration as the key weapon in this war. From Wilson, it took the concept of zero-tolerance, the idea that we best tackle crime through dealing with incivilities. Indeed, at times Blair's pronouncements on crime look like liberal transcriptions from James Q. Wilson's *Thinking about Crime*. Thus, on December 5 2000, Blair suggested curfews and a zero-tolerance campaign to stamp down hard on petty criminals, drunken yobs and juvenile delinquents. In an exclusive interview with the *Daily Express*, the Prime Minister said:

If you are tolerant of small crimes, and I mean vandalism and the graffiti at the end of the street, you create an environment in which pretty soon the drug dealers move in, and then after that the violent people with their knives and their guns and all the rest of it, and the community is wrecked.

I am not suggesting, of course, that either Tony Blair or the Home Secretary at the time, Jack Straw, have any direct acquaintance with these commentators. Merely that it is the ideas of such thinkers filtered through the lenses of policy advisors and speech-writers that have greatly influenced New Labour's policy on law and order. What is important to note, here, is that the ideas imported from the United States were not those of liberal criminology, not the ideas of Elliott Currie, William Julius Wilson, or Frank Cullen, but of the highly contested American Right.

Defending populism

In the last resort spokespeople for New Labour will turn to their focus groups and to opinion polls and argue that they merely do what the people want. But is it really surprising, given the direction of political leadership and the prevalent mass media coverage of crime, that public opinion is pushed in a pessimistic and vindictive direction? Indeed the evidence is particularly worrying. Widespread public pessimism about levels of crime was discovered in the 2000 *British Crime Survey*. Two thirds of the respondents believed that crime at the national level had increased over the previous two years, but that is contrary to the actual rates (Kershaw *et al.*, 2000, p. 59). Indeed, only 6 per cent of the population realized that there had been a decrease. Furthermore, more people believed that the crime rate was increasing than in the 1998 *Survey* (1998, 59 per cent; 2000, 67 per cent) (ibid., Table A7.1, p. 95). Thus, as the situation was getting better, public perception (or should we say misperception?) was getting worse.

Of course, politicians and a media banging the law-and-order drum are not the sole reason for such views existing. The level of economic and ontological insecurity in late modernity guarantees that public anxieties are constantly generated, and that delinquents, drug users, immigrants, and a host of other folk-devils are ready targets (see Young, 2003). But it is in precisely such a context that the government should provide objective assessments of the crime situation.

Let me close with a discussion, from not long ago, but seemingly from another world. While writing this article I reached up for a book, and a pamphlet, long forgotten, fell out of the bookcase. It was entitled *Politics and Prison* and is the edited Prison Reform Trust Lectures. One of them, given on 11 December 1985, was by Clive Solely MP, then Labour front-bench spokesman on prison issues. Clive Solely argued trenchantly for an improvement in prison conditions, and a reduction in sentencing and the prison population:

There will be opposition to penal reform – I have already mentioned that – and the popular press is an important part of it. But I think there is evidence that people will accept shorter sentences if we do more to help prevent crime and to help victims of crime. I am not saying it will be easy. At the end of the day what we need and what no one can guarantee you, from any political party, is a Home Secretary who has the courage to come in and carry out the sort of things I am laying out to you today.

What I want to do is put all these matters on the record for the Labour Party, to say that is what we intend to do, this is what we are setting out to do. I have discussed all these issues with Gerald Kaufman, who is our Home Affairs Spokesman, and I can say on behalf of the Labour Party that the British criminal justice system has become inhumane, inefficient and is generally now a bad system, right the way through. What we need to do is to take a root-and-branch look at it, to change things round. There is no reason, no reason at all, why this country should have fallen to such an abysmally low level compared to many of the countries in Western Europe and the Western world generally.

(Solely, 1986, p. 28)

Then there were 47,000 people in prison, a fact which Solely deplored. At the time of writing (July 2002) there are 71,000.[4] Britain has the second-highest rate of imprisonment in the European Union, and is predicted to take a leadership position in the very near future. In 1985 we had Labour out of power confronting a remorselessly increasing crime rate, bravely proposing to reduce imprisonment; today we have Labour in government, facing a decreasing crime rate, proposing exactly the opposite policy. The turnaround could not have been more complete.

Postscript: the promise of the second term

The Labour government successfully gained its second term in 2001 with still a commanding lead over the Opposition, both in parliament and in the polls. Surely this was a chance to pursue a more radical and rational policy on law and order? Indeed the new Home Secretary, David Blunkett, entered office with a programme that would seem to take on board all these criticisms and to well nigh reverse the policies of his predecessor, Jack Straw. First of all, in December 2001, he attempted to grasp the nettle of police reform, pinpointing police inefficiency, particularly the low clear-up rate of 24 per cent, the extraordinarily high level of sick leave (38 per cent higher than the average worker), and the scale of ill-health retirement. Second, in a speech to the Prison Service Annual Conference in February 2002, he was intensely critical of recidivism rates for those sent to prison, highlighting the expense and inefficiency of prisons, and arguing that their role should be rehabilitation rather than incapacitation. He also argued for a reduction in prison numbers, and for the increased use of intermediate measures such as open prisons and hostels. Prison reformers could not believe their ears – the very use of the term 'rehabilitation', a word that had seemingly disappeared from the discourse of Home Secretaries, and the pledge to reduction, to buck the trend of remorseless prison expansion, were warmly, if cautiously, welcomed. Third, the Home Secretary seemed very well aware of the overall drop in crime, and was quite willing to link this to the improved economic climate and the fall in unemployment. He was, therefore, seemingly poised to concede that it was structural problems that caused crime – rather than problems of the family or the school – and, indeed, to connect this up to the government's favourable economic performance.

But the new dawn was not to last long. Remember Clive Solely's admonition as to the need for a strong Home Secretary and the opposition of the popular press. Let us take this a little bit further: the opposition to a rational penal policy occurs from two sources:

1. Mass media: As has been frequently noted, the media have an institutionalized focus on negative news – the crime rate going up sells newspapers, and settles audiences in front of their television sets watching programmes such as Crime Watch. The crime rate going down is, or so it is believed, less of a draw. Couple this with a majority of news sources being hostile to the government, and the focus on negative news is reinforced.

2. Vested interests: law enforcement agencies are threatened by crime rates dropping. It bodes badly for continuing or increased resources.

The problem of street robbery has been periodically bubbling up as an issue for the last 20 years; it has been used, mistakenly, in the mass media as the archetypal image of crime and as representing a rising crime rate in our society. What was different about the recent period is that street robbery, one of the few crimes that was on the increase, was widely taken to represent all crime, despite the overall crime rate reduction. Furthermore, this was tied to strident demands for an increase in police numbers. Thus, street robbery, at only 1.7 per cent of all crime as observed above, was focused upon. While the huge graph of total crimes slumps by over 1 million, the tiny graph of street robbery with a rise of 40,000, becomes the centre of attention. With no attempt to define what is meant by 'robbery', or the fact that somewhere between a third and a half of the increase is of mobile phones – more a consequence of ease of access than anything else hardly represents a deterioration in the nation's moral fibre. This is not to suggest that street robbery is not a problem but to put it in perspective. It is scarcely comparable, for example, to domestic violence, with over one third of all homicides occurring in the family. (Only 11 per cent of homicides in England and Wales are motivated by theft, and only a tiny proportion of these are as a result of street robbery – see Mooney, 2002). And, of course, in a rational world the large scale decline ought to imply a moratorium on police numbers, not an increase. The mass media, of course, played its role: 'Scared to Walk Our Streets' was the front-page headline in the *Daily Express* (18 March 2002), in riposte to a speech by Blunkett, while the *Sun* echoed with 'Muggers Rule our Streets'. The hysteria was kept in motion by a steady stream of Police Federation press releases highlighting the problem ('Rising Street Crime Links to Cops Shortage', 'More Cops Mean Less Crime'), and other, perhaps stranger, interest groups began to argue for an increase in police numbers. Thus, Ken Livingstone took the opportunity of New York Mayor Giuliani's visit to London in February to argue that London's police force should be expanded to reach New York levels, demanding an increase of 12,000 police officers. Apart from the naive belief in the urban myth that it was zero-tolerance policing that achieved the decrease in crime in New York (the crime rate went down generally in many American cities), this argument ignores the fact that New York City is a much more dangerous place than most Western cities, with a homicide rate of over three times that of London. Indeed, if there was any justice, New York politicians and police commissioners should be visiting London to find out how so large a city can be so relatively tranquil, rather than the other way around.

The upshot of all this, on 1 May 2002, was £62 million of extra funding for the Metropolitan Police service in order to help meet its twin 'priorities' of combating terrorism and street robbery. The Home Secretary, seemingly intent on tackling police inefficiency and reducing prison numbers, was, therefore, immediately confronted with a vociferous policy lobby putting the worst possible spin on the crime figures, a mass media fanning public concern, and senior police officers announcing that there was a crisis in the criminal justice system, in the juries, in the conviction rate, in the courts, in the legal profession – anywhere else but in the police service.

To bring the matter more up to date, on 12 July 2002 the annual criminal statistics were published in the form of a joint publication of the *British Crime Survey* and the figures of Crimes Known to the Police. The former is, of course, by far the more authoritative publication, and even more given its substantially increased sample size (33,000 interviews); the police figures are, of course, dependent on levels of public reporting and police recording, and are considerably distorted by changes in counting rules. The *Survey* showed a 2 per cent drop in crime; the police recorded statistics showed a rise of 7 per cent, at least 5 per cent of this being due to changes in recording practices. If one looks at the newspaper headlines one gets some idea of how this was reported in our national press:

Daily Express	Street Crimes Rocket by 28 per cent
Sun	Robbery up 28 per cent
Daily Mirror	Tough on Crime? They'd Laugh if It Didn't Hurt So Much (accompanied by pictures of badly beaten up people)
Daily Telegraph	Robberies Fuel Rise in Crime Figures
Independent	Alarm over Huge Rise in Street Crimes and Theft
Times	Robbery Sends Crime Soaring
Daily Star	Blunkett Calm on Street Crime
Guardian	Abrupt End to Six-Year Fall in Crime.

The focus in these headlines was once more street robbery, with the only exception being the *Guardian* – although it is difficult to see how a 2 per cent actual decrease, however statistically insignificant, can be portrayed as an 'abrupt end'. The articles all led with the less reliable police figures, and nearly all ignored the *Survey* finding that there was 'a notable increase in the proportion [of the population] believing that crime had risen "a lot" in the first quarter of 2002, rising to 35 per cent from 27 per cent in the final three months of 2001'. This period witnessed a heightened degree of press coverage on crime, which particularly focused on the claimed rise in crime (Simmons, 2002, p. 4). This was, of course, despite the actual fall and the belief was greater among tabloid readers (42 per cent) than broadsheet readers (27 per cent). The only oasis of reason was an article by Polly Toynbee in the *Guardian*, which pointed out the fact that crime rates are largely a result of economic conditions and are not affected by marginal changes in police numbers (Toynbee, 2002). All of this seemed over the head of the Home Secretary, who noted that 'an important factor in sustaining the fight against crime is the investment we are making in the police service', and who welcomed the fact that England and Wales had now a record-high number of police officers (130,000). Finally, the Home Secretary, faced with seeking an extra 10,800 prison places over the next years, was forced to go cap in hand to the Chancellor, Gordon Brown, for reputedly an extra £1 billion. The level of unreason displayed by such actions beggars belief, the benign trend in the level of crime is constantly under pressure from being interpreted in the most negative light, and each progressive moment is submerged amid a welter of populism.[5]

Notes

1 See the interesting analysis in the conclusion of *The 2000 British Crime Survey* (Kershaw *et al.*, 56–8).

2 Robbery, as is well known in the literature, is an extremely flexible category, particularly at its borderline with 'theft'. Thus the authors of *The 2000 British Crime Survey* note: 'Closer examination of robbery incidents for 1999 . . . revealed that there were a few instances where school age respondents had reported multiple incidents of robbery. Although the incidents met the criteria for robbery, they might be viewed as nearer to bullying incidents. These and other incidents involving school age respondents had a marked impact on estimated changes in violence victimisation rates. Excluding 16 year-olds from the analysis reduced the 14 per cent increase between 1997 and 1999 in robbery to a 2 per cent increase. For mugging the percentage increase of 4 per cent becomes a decrease of 7 per cent'. (Kershaw *et al.*, p. 35). Police statistics on robbery are even more susceptible to 'cross-criming'. (For the classic analysis, see Blom-Cooper and Drabble, 1982.)

3 In an amusing letter to the *Guardian*, Joe Sim, Professor of Criminology at Liverpool John Moore's University, congratulated John Birt on his new appointment, and offered his services as a criminologist to help out with the restructuring of the BBC.

4 The government's ten-year plan *Criminal Justice: The Way Ahead*, published in February 2001, made a commitment to 2,600 extra prison places.

5 The overt populism of New Labour's law-and-order politics can be gauged from Tony Blair's fairly accurate and optimistic assessment of the crime situation. Thus, in a *Sunday Times* interview just before the 2001 General Election he was taxed with the question of the crime problem, and violent crime in particular. He replied: 'We've only just made a start. . . . When we came in, we were told that crime was going to rise for demographic reasons by 20 per cent; instead it has fallen by 10 per cent.' Further, the 'rise' in violence 'is to do with things like domestic violence, which is reported more, low-level street violence, mobile phones . . .' (White, 2001, p. 48).

References

Barclay, G., Tavares, C. and Siddique, A. (2001) *International Comparisons of Criminal Justice Statistics 1999*, London: Home Office.

Blair, T. (1993) 'Why Crime is a Socialist Issue', *New Statesman*, 29(12), 27–8.

Blom-Cooper, L. and Drabble, R. (1982) 'Police Perceptions of Crime', *British Journal of Criminology*, 184–7.

Blumstein, A. and Wallman, J. (eds) (2000) *The Crime Drop in America*, Cambridge: Cambridge University Press.

Chambliss, W. (1999) *Power, Politics and Crime*, Boulder, Colorado: Westview.

DiIulio, J. (1995) 'Crime in America: It's Going to Get Worse', *Reader's Digest*, August, 57.

Home Office (2001) *Criminal Justice: The Way Ahead*, Cm 5074, London: The Stationery Office.

Kershaw, C., Budd, T., Kinshott, G., Mattinson, J., Mayhew, P. and Myhill, A. (2000) *The 2000 British Crime Survey*, London: Home Office.

Matheson, J. and Summerfield, C. (eds) (2001) *Social Trends*, 31, London: Stationery Office.

Mooney, J. (2002) 'Get a Grip on Reality: Let's Put Street Crime in Perspective', *Safer Society* (NACRO), Summer, 6–7.

Simmons, J. (2002) *Crime in England and Wales 2001/2002*, London: Stationery Office.

Solely, C. (1986) [1985] 'Labour's Prison Policy', in *Politics and Prisons* (no editor), London: Prison Reform Trust.

Toynbee, P. (2002) 'What Really Causes Crime', *Guardian* (12 July), 17.

White, L. (2001) 'The Hot Ticket', *Sunday Times*, 3 June, 42–51.

Wilson, J.Q. (1975) *Thinking about Crime*, New York: Basic Books.

Young, J. (1999) *The Exclusive Society*, London: Sage.

Young, J. (2003) 'Merton with Energy, Katz with Structure: The Sociology of Vindictiveness and The Criminology of Transgression', *Theoretical Criminology* 7(3), 389–414.

Chapter 3

Institutional racism in policing: the Macpherson report and its consequences

John Lea

The Macpherson report (Macpherson, 1999) began as a specific inquiry into the failure of the (London) Metropolitan Police to successfully apprehend the killers of Stephen Lawrence, a young black man murdered by a gang of white racists in South London in 1993. The report concluded that the police investigation was sabotaged by 'a combination of professional incompetence, institutional racism, and a failure of leadership by senior officers' (46.1).[1] In order to gain a fuller understanding of the dynamics of police racism, Macpherson, in the second part of his inquiry, held a series of general meetings with representatives of Black and other minority communities in several cities in the United Kingdom on the general problems of police–community relations. One of Macpherson's central aims was to show how the conduct of the police, both in the flawed Lawrence murder investigation and more generally, was influenced by what has come to be called 'institutional racism', that is, racial prejudice and discrimination generated by the way institutions function, intentionally or otherwise, rather than by the individual personalities of their members (Lea, 1986). Macpherson attempts to deploy the concept in a more sophisticated way than did the Scarman report of 1981, the result of an earlier major inquiry into the state of relations between the police and ethnic minority communities. The argument of this article will be that Macpherson's discussion of institutional racism fails to locate with sufficient precision its roots within the structure of operational policing and in the relationship between police and minority communities. The result is that a major opportunity to spell out a policy agenda adequate to the task of eliminating racist policing has been missed.

Beyond Scarman

As regards the understanding of racism, Scarman left an ambiguous legacy. He drew attention to the problem of police racism, but in doing so he defined institutional racism as only overtly racist policy *consciously* pursued by an institution. He thereby rendered it of marginal relevance to an understanding of the British situation. He confirmed the focus of policy, in the police as in other public bodies, as that of the elimination of the racism of prejudiced individuals. Yet, as Macpherson notes (6.7), Scarman's view of the types of racism was not exhausted by the prejudiced individual on the one hand and the overt policy of institutions on the other. Lord Scarman responded to the suggestion that 'Britain is an institutionally racist society' in this way:

> If, by [institutionally racist] it is meant that it [Britain] is a society which knowingly, as a matter of policy, discriminates against black people, I reject the allegation. If, however, the suggestion being made is that practices may be adopted by public bodies as well as private individuals which are unwittingly discriminatory against black people, then this is an allegation which deserves serious consideration, and, where proved, swift remedy.
>
> (Scarman, 1981, 2.22)

It was this latter category, of practices that are unwittingly discriminatory, which remained untheorized and lacking emphasis in Scarman. Macpherson continues (6.15):

> ... if the phrase 'institutional racism' had been used to describe not only explicit manifestations of racism at direction and policy level, but also unwitting discrimination at the organizational level, then the reality of indirect racism in its more subtle, hidden and potentially more pervasive nature would have been addressed.

So there are now, for Macpherson, three categories of racism of equal importance. First, the racism of overtly prejudiced individuals; second, racism as a conscious and deliberate policy of public institutions, which is not to be found in Britain; and third, racism as unintentional or unwitting discriminatory practice in the operations of organizations which are formally non-discriminatory. This type of institutional racism, rather than that for which Scarman reserved the term, is widespread in British public institutions. A new definition of institutional racism is thereby elaborated (6.34) as:

> The collective failure of an organization to provide an appropriate
> and professional service to people because of their colour, culture,
> or ethnic origin. It can be seen or detected in processes, attitudes
> and behaviour which amount to discrimination through unwitting
> prejudice, ignorance, thoughtlessness and racist stereotyping
> which disadvantage minority ethnic people.

It was this re-elaboration of the concept of institutional racism that
made it possible for Sir Paul Condon, Metropolitan Police Commissioner, to agree that it existed in his force. He had previously
challenged any characterization of the police as institutionally racist,
but from the standpoint of Scarman's original definition.[2]

An approach to institutional racism that goes beyond the level of
overt policy of the kind that characterized policing in South Africa
under the apartheid regime, for example, is to be welcomed. The
unintended consequences of the working of institutions is the appropriate framework for analysis in a liberal democracy formally committed to the principles of equal citizenship. Nevertheless, it will be
argued, Macpherson's discussion of institutional racism suffers from
crucial ambiguity concerning the precise location of the processes that
sustain racial discrimination, in both distinguishing individually generated from institutionally generated behaviour and in specifying
which institutional dynamics are conducive to racism.

The first problem concerns the fact that the working of institutions
is, of course, encountered as the actions of the individuals within them,
and it is not possible to immediately infer from the characteristics of
the latter the nature and dynamics of their institutions. Unwitting and
unthinking prejudice *can* be simply milder forms of the individual
racism of 'bad apples'. What has to be shown is precisely how such
attitudes and actions derive from the working of the institution itself.
Macpherson is not always able to demonstrate that the racism he
identifies is institutional as opposed to individual.

This problem is illustrated in the discussion of the Lawrence murder
investigation. An inquiry into the conduct of a single murder investigation by its very nature involves a focus on the actions of individual
police officers – how they treated suspects, witnesses, relatives of the
victim, etc. In such a context, even if it can be concluded that 'there
was a "collective failure" of a group of officers to provide an
appropriate and professional service' (44.11), they remain a particular
group engaging in actions not shared by all officers. It is difficult in
such a context, particularly where other factors such as professional
incompetence and failure of leadership are also seen to be important

ingredients (46.1), to distinguish institutionalized from individual racism, or racism from incompetence. For example, one of the indications of institutional racism used by Macpherson was the failure to characterize the Lawrence murder as a racist crime. Yet 50 per cent of officers involved (19.35) including the Senior Investigating Officers (19.38) characterized the incident precisely in such terms. At the level of the actions of some individuals rather than others, the institutional dimension is necessarily backgrounded. To establish institutional racism it would be necessary to survey a series of such inquiries and look for patterns of behaviour, which could then be located in the patterns of institutional operation. Macpherson was obviously not in a position to conduct this type of research. However, as will hopefully emerge in the discussion which follows, the most important problem is that even where Macpherson focuses more clearly on the police institution rather than the actions of individual officers he locates the source of racism in the social and cultural life of police officers rather than in the dyamics of operational policing itself.

Occupational culture

There is indeed a sustained attempt to see unwitting prejudice, thoughtlessness and deployment of racist stereotypes as located in the norms and values through which police officers define their roles and the legitimacy of their activities. Macpherson quotes approvingly (6.32) the following passage from the submission of sociologist Robin Oakley:

> The term institutional racism should be understood to refer to the way institutions may systematically treat or tend to treat people differently in respect of race. The addition of the word 'institutional' therefore identifies the source of the differential treatment; this lies in some sense within the organization rather than simply with the individuals who represent it. The production of differential treatment is 'institutionalized' in the way the organization operates.

Prejudice is something into which individuals are socialized rather than something they bring to the organization from outside. The issue, then, is to identify precisely what it is about the day-to-day work of the police institution that generates and sustains an occupational culture supportive of racism. The key factor identified by Macpherson is the particular forms of contact between police and various sections of the public. This theme was stressed in testimony by an officer speaking on behalf of the Black Police Association (quoted at 6.28):

> Given the fact that ... predominantly white officers only meet members of the black community in confrontational situations, they tend to stereotype black people in general. This can lead to all sorts of negative views and assumptions about black people, so we should not underestimate the occupational culture within the police service as being a primary source of institutional racism in the way that we differentially treat black people.

The officer continued:

> Interestingly I say we because there is no marked difference between black and white in the force essentially. We are all consumed by this occupational culture. Some of us may think we rise above it on some occasions, but, generally speaking, we tend to conform to the norms of this occupational culture, which we say is all powerful in shaping our views and perceptions of a particular community.

There is a clear understanding here that it is not the character of the contact between predominantly White police and Black people in law enforcement situations as such that is the root of the problem, but rather the lack of other contact *outside* that relationship. The reason that the White police officer knows that not all Whites are suspects is that he or she meets a diversity of non-criminal Whites both within and outside the police organization and, above all, outside the policing relationship. The problem for the Black community at large, in this analysis, is that officers impose upon it attitudes derived from their restricted interactions with ethnic minorities. By deflecting attention away from the policing relationship as such, Macpherson arrives at a policy agenda that is largely a reiteration of strategies that have been in existence for over a decade, and which have manifestly failed. It is an agenda whose focus lies on issues of cultural communication and understanding rather than structural locations and inequalities of power and resources. From this standpoint there are two main strategies, both of which are articulated by Macpherson. First, attempts can be made to change the occupational culture of policing through a widening of ethnic recruitment combined with measures to increase police officers' contacts with, and awareness of, the cultural diversity of contemporary Britain. Second, there can be attempts to minimize the impact of officers' cultural assumptions on the application of legal and procedural rules in law-enforcement encounters with citizens.

Cultural change versus power and community

Attempts to change police culture, if they start from the assumption that lack of contact between police and ethnic minorities outside law-enforcement situations is the key problem, generally involve measures aimed at an increased recruitment of ethnic-minority officers, race awareness training for White officers, and various 'meet the community' initiatives. Macpherson calls for a significant reorganiz-ation and expansion of race-awareness training in the police service (recommendations 48–54) as well as measures to increase the recruit-ment and retention of officers drawn from ethnic-minority communi-ties (recommendations 64–66).

But such strategies have a considerable history. Scarman called for an increased recruitment of ethnic-minority officers having noted that in 1981 Black officers constituted 0.5 per cent of the Metropolitan Police (Scarman, 1981, para 5.6). The proportion of minority officers is currently 3.3 per cent, a figure still dwarfed in comparison to the 20 per cent of London residents who are members of ethnic-minority commu-nities. Similarly, various forms of race-awareness training have been on the agenda of police forces throughout the United Kingdom for many years. Scarman called for training aimed at 'an understanding of the cultural background of ethnic minority groups' and indeed was 'satisfied that improvements in police training are in hand' (Scarman, 1981, 5.16 and 5.17). Macpherson found, however, 18 years later (6.45) that: 'not a single officer questioned before us in 1998 had received any training of significance in racism awareness and race relations through-out the course of his or her career'. He noted the 'identified failure of police training', yet provided little in the way of analysis as to why it had failed, providing simply an exhortation for more such training, more vigorously implemented (see Recommendations 48–54). Similar-ly, if the issue was simply that of increasing the contact between police and ethnic minorities outside a law-enforcement situation, then devel-opments during the period should have been considerable. The fact that they were not suggests, perhaps, that some important factors were overlooked, not only by Scarman in 1981 but also by Macpherson in 1998.

Power and community relations

The thesis that racism, institutionalized and reproduced in police occupational culture, can be signficantly reduced by increased contact between (White) police and ethnic minorities in non law-enforcement situations tends to be couched in terms of very generalized concepts of 'Black' and 'White', and to see these groups as monolithic. In fact, the majority of White police officers interact with a very restricted segment of the White population – overwhelmingly other police officers. They also tend to live in outlying White upper-working-class or middle-class suburbs. There is no obvious reason why they should see all other Whites as akin to themselves. The fact that White police officers meet other Whites in a non law-enforcement situation does not stop them stereotyping those sections of the White population from whom they are separated by geography, socio-economic status, gender and age. The key issue is power rather than ethnicity *per se*. In traditional police culture the surrounding population is 'differentiated according to the power of particular groups to cause problems for the police ... [thus the] ... power structure of a community, and the views of its elites, are important sources of variation in policing styles' (Reiner, 1992, p. 137; see also Holdaway, 1983). In other words, the crucial aspect of the relation between police and White communities is less the existence of contacts outside the law-enforcement relation than police perception of significant power groups in the White population, both nationally and locally. Middle-class Black people are not seen as significantly power-ful enough to cause trouble for the police or to be seen as worthwhile allies to further police goals. The recruitment of more Black police officers, while desirable in itself, would not necessarily change this relationship. The half-hearted pursuit of race-awareness training is perhaps explicable – though not condonable – if police do not perceive a necessity to accommodate to the demands of minority communities. Police–community liaison schemes have suffered a similar fate. The strategy of liaison with 'respectable' members of minority communities stretches back to the Community Relations Councils of the 1960s. The aim of these was rather to depoliticize race relations by linking immigrant communities to the state 'through buffer institutions, replicating key features of traditional colonial relationships' (Katznel-son, 1973, p. 178). In the wake of Scarman a new effort was made to establish police–community liaison committees more specifically oriented to discussion of local policing needs, and to get the police to see the advantages of discussing crime control with community groups. Liaison was made statutory under the 1984 Police and

Criminal Evidence Act. While there were some successes, most such groups were largely 'talking shops' with little impact on relations between police and minority communities (Kinsey *et al.*, 1986; Morgan, 1987) What had been ignored was the issue of power. Police were willing to listen to those who agreed with them and would act as their supporters. But otherwise there was little incentive to listen to the demands or grievances of those not perceived to be politically powerful at either a local or national level.

However, there is currently an increasing prominence of locally based crime-prevention initiatives and community-safety partnerships, in which police and local authorities work together to reduce crime. These arrangements have been given a statutory basis under the Crime and Disorder Act 1998. Some commentators have detected a seismic shift in relations between police and community, in which police monopoly of expertise is no longer taken for granted but rather 'the community and its leaders are to be involved in determining what are the policing needs of the locale, and what styles of police work are seen to be effective in these terms, and forms of intervention are regarded as desirable or undesirable' (O'Malley and Palmer, 1996, p. 145). Such an enhanced role for the local community might be seen as the occasion not simply for increased interaction between police and ethnic minorities but also for a police reorientation to the latter as valuable sources of expertise about crime and policing needs. Home Office testimony to Macpherson underlined commitment to the implementation of the recent HM Inspectorate of Constabulary *Thematic Inspection Report on Police Community and Race Relations*, which noted:

> ... a greater awareness that the police cannot win the battle against crime without the support of the communities they serve. As communities become more plural, gaining their trust will require both improvements in the quality of service they receive and the adoption – as a core element of all policing activity – of a community focused strategy which recognizes diversity. ... In effect this means that all the various components ... of the police organization should reflect a community and race relations element in their individual plans and strategies. (Her Majesty's Inspectorate of Constabulary, 1998, paragraph 4.)

The question is which communities? Are the most deprived communities likely to be partners in this process? Macpherson saw the willingness of the police to respond effectively to racial violence against ethnic minorities as the key to winning the latter's confidence in such partnerhsips. He was optimistic (45.19) that the 1998 Crime and Disorder Act, which strengthens the ability of police and local authorities to deploy civil powers to exclude disorderly individuals from neighbourhoods, would be used to tackle racist violence. If police and local authorities, acting through partnership structures, are seen to be acting in this area, then minority communities can be expected to show greater confidence in these bodies, to participate more, and so enhance their power.

While developments in a particular locality depend on a number of factors, including the personalities and calibre of leadership involved, there are some general obstacles to the effectiveness of such multi-agency partnerships as routes to Black political empowerment and as a counter to police institutional racism. First, the strategy of multi-agency partnership assumes a smooth unity of interest from the outset between police, local authorities and local communities, and among the latter, rather than as the outcome of a period of adjustment and interaction, which may at times be robust and confrontational. Police might be initially resistant to challenges to their monopoly of expertise, and might feel able to deploy a hectoring tone to those groups they perceive as lacking significant political power.

Second, if those organs in which sections of the community hitherto socially and politically excluded can begin to formulate needs and demands are cut back by lack of funds, then again the process of accommodation is undermined. Macpherson expressed concern at the reduction and withdrawal of funding and support for community organizations with a 'monitoring' orientation, which, as he perceived it (45.20), might 'represent a tendency of funding agencies to withdraw support from groups perceived to be confrontational'. On a more general level, if the priorities of the new community-safety partnerships include the attraction of private-sector funding and participation, then their aims may be deflected towards those of securing property values in areas attractive to business, in effect 'confining criminogenic communities to their usually depressed neighbourhoods, rather than liberating them from these' (Gilling, 1997, p. 196). If ethnic-minority communities are disproportionately confined to these latter areas, and initially reluctant to get involved with police-led initiatives because of a legacy of racism, with their representative organs starved of funding, then increased interaction and empowerment in relation to police is hindered considerably. There is then little pressure on police to respond to their demands. Power relations remain unchanged, and a legacy of racism remains unchallenged.

Blaming the victims: the summer of 2001 and beyond

Changing these power relations would involve a combination of a massive redistribution of resources to poor communities in general, combined with a real democratic accountability of police to communities (Lea and Young, 1984). In the absence of such changes following the Macpherson report, other, older, tendencies have reasserted themselves such that, in the words of Black journalist Gary Younge, 'on the third anniversary of the Macpherson report into the death of black teenager Stephen Lawrence, the government's understanding of race and racism is regressing towards the pitiful level it was before Stephen's birth in the 1970s' (Younge, 2002). Younge is referring to the response to the riots in northern towns during the summer of 2001 involving clashes between poor White youths and Asians. Violence between poor communities enabled a rearticulation of the problem of racism as the product of the very presence of ethnic-minority communities. The issue became the lack of community cohesion and of understanding between poor communities of different ethnicities, and the responsibility for this was laid at the door of the ethnic minorities and their cultures. The Home Office report (Cantle, 2001) into the disturbances sidelined the issues of econonomic deprivation in favour of cultural conflict, which stressed issues of communication and cultural 'understanding'. It called on all communities, including Whites, to 'improve their knowledge and understanding of other sections and thereby reduce their ignorance and fear'. But it immediately followed this with a call specifically for the 'minority, largely non-White community, to develop a greater acceptance of, and engagement with, the principal national institutions' (Cantle, 2001, p. 19). This sermon, it should be remembered, was being addressed to young Asians, born in the United Kingdom, whose alienation from 'principle national institutions' including, presumably, the police was the product of decades of racism and economic deprivation. As regards crime, the report makes the usual call for a strategy that should 'address all aspects of crime, especially that which is racially motivated', but then immediately follows it with a barbed comment to the effect that 'minority communities must also face the fact that over time they have adopted a toleration of certain types of criminalty' (Cantle, 2001, p. 40). As if generations of poor White communities have not tolerated 'certain types' of criminality! The whole tenor of the report is to blame the minority communities for racial conflict and, more specifically, for harbouring criminality.

Such themes had been articulated in police circles for some time. For example, the above-mentioned HM Inspectorate of Constabulary report, in the midst of a eulogy to police–community collaboration, suddenly broke into a sermon to the Black community to the effect that 'the over-representation of black youths in street robbery, particularly in the inner city . . . [combined with] . . . the perceived lack of tangible support from some black community representatives is an ongoing frustration' (Her Majesty's Inspectorate of Constabulary, 1998, paragraph 2.40.)

In a sense, the whole methodology of the Macpherson report, in particular the tendency to define the problem in terms of the cultural values of the participants, undermined its ability to pre-empt such a deflection. The focus on the failure of police to break down their cultural isolation through ethnic balance and and race-awareness training becomes switched to a focus on the alleged failure of ethnic minorities to integrate themselves into British society. In both cases the effect is to hide the real structural determinants of the situation: in the case of the police, the basis of institutional racism in the control of the socially excluded, and in the case of ethnic-minority communities, the economic determinants of marginality and social exclusion.

It is at this point that the issue of statutory police accountability becomes important. Democratic control remains the only available alternative form of empowerment to those who lack political influence based on the control of economic resources. The establishment of:

> . . . a much more organized and rigorous system of local demo-cratic accountability of the police is vital for . . . creating a political structure in which the most deprived sections of the working-class community can articulate their interests and grievances (which, in large measure, concern policing matters).
>
> (Lea and Young, 1984, p. 231)

Macpherson endorsed (46.33) government proposals to introduce a Metropolitan Police Authority, that is, a local-government body with full powers to appoint all chief police officers and with measures to ensure that membership of the body reflects the ethnic mix of the local communities (Recommendations 3, 4, 6 and 7). He sees this as an important contribution to making the Metropolitan Police 'open and accountable'. But there is no discussion as to what this accountability might mean in practice. Matters such as whether a police authority should be able to determine general policing policy and methods are not discussed. If they were, then a central assumption of the whole Macpherson report might well be brought into question. It might rapidly come to be understood that institutional racism is generated by a central aspect of operational policing relationship itself.

The assimilation of the Metropolitan Police to forms of local governance that have existed outside London for many years does little to change the character of the relationship between police and poor communities alienated from the formal political process. More is probably achieved in this respect by individual innovative local police commanders or local councillors than constitutional arrangements that allow, at the most, a voice for middle-class professionals from the minority communities, who are increasingly distanced from the grievances of the poor.

Reforming stop and search

The second strategy recommended by Macpherson, sometimes known as rule-tightening (Chan, 1997), attempts to ensure that the effects of racial stereotypes reproduced in police occupational culture are neutralized by ensuring that relations with the public are tightly governed by rules and procedures to ensure equal treatment. The aim is to prevent attitudes seen as generated essentially *outside* the law-enforcement relationship from interfering with it. These attitudes and values are understood as generated elsewhere, in recreation and social bonding between officers (hence the often-used term 'canteen culture'). They can be seen as functional for the overall cohesion and morale of the police organization, but dysfunctional from the standpoint of that most important of police tasks, law enforcement.

This type of analysis can be found in the 1983 report conducted by the Policy Studies Institute for the Metropolitan Police, which concluded rather optimistically that the predominance of rule-governed interaction already largely characterized relations between police and the Black community:

> Racialist talk ... helps to reinforce the identity, security and solidarity of the group against a clearly perceived external threat ... when police officers actually come into contact with members of minority groups a different set of needs comes into play; very often the officer is forced to look on the person as a person – as someone whose support is required or who must be manipulated – rather than as a member of a particular ethnic group.
>
> (Smith and Gray, 1983, p. 127–8)

At first sight this situation does resemble certain aspects of police work. In a murder inquiry, for example, there is an incentive to 'get a result'. If detectives refused to talk to witnesses on racial grounds they would deprive themselves of vital sources of information. For Macpherson this view of the essentially dysfunctional nature of police racism is assumed to apply to all varieties of policing. But the existence of rules and procedures in no way guarantees their application in the face of incompetence, racial prejudice, or both. In practice, police officers have considerable autonomy in the way they construct cases for prosecution (McConville *et al.*, 1991). It is well established in other areas of policing, for example domestic violence and sexual assault, that the existence of a set of rules ensures neither equal treatment nor that the police will take a particular incident seriously as a criminal offence and deal with it competently (Gregory and Lees, 1999). The argument is ultimately circular. Rule-tightening will only eliminate the effect of racism or sexism where police culture is already committed to the rigorous application of rules as a matter of substantive policy. Macpherson, however, could only recommend more rule-tightening. He called for performance indicators in the investigation of racist crimes, and issued the usual demands for better coordination and a review of procedures, without specifying what changes should be made (see Recommendations 2 and 18–22). Far more productive would have been a demand for organizational changes to counter the independence and autonomy of the police in the investigation of serious crimes. Suggestions such as the establishment of an independent investigating magistrate, on the model of many continental European jurisdictions, or a District Attorney, as in the United States, with powers to monitor and supervise police investigation, are made from time to time (see, for example, Mansfield, 1993). Such debate is however generally marginalized in the English context. Macpherson was timid and conventional in his recommendations in this area, as in others.

The main object of rule-tightening was with regard to the specific issue of the practice of stop and search, which was was established by Macpherson (6.45) as the key issue in bad relations between police and ethnic minorities and the second area of concern in relation to institutional racism after the Lawrence murder investigation itself. Police practices in this area are clearly an obstacle to the development of good police–community relations of the type discussed above. Witnesses interviewed by Macpherson from the local community confirmed this perception (29.57, 36.12, 37.18). In the hearings conducted outside London, Macpherson recorded that complaints about ethnic bias in stop and search were universal (45.8). Macpherson referred (45.9) to 1997/8 figures that Black people were five times more likely to be stopped than Whites.

Any ethnic bias in the level of stops was automatically to be read as a result of racial stereotyping derived from police occupational culture in the manner described above. Macpherson was entirely uncritical concerning the role of stop and search as such, assuming, like Scarman before him, that it was a key crime-control techique. Just as Scarman saw stop and search as 'necessary to combat street crime' (Scarman, 7.2), Macpherson was adamant (46.31) as to the necessity of stop and search even for non-racist policing:

> ... we have ... specifically considered whether police powers to 'stop and search' should be removed or further limited. We specifically reject this option. We fully accept the need for such powers to continue, and their genuine usefulness in the prevention and detection of crime.

The issue for Macpherson, as for Scarman, was to regulate stop and search in such a way as to minimize the deployment of racist stereotypes by officers when deciding whom to stop. Macpherson called simply for a tightening-up of the procedures introduced by the Police and Criminal Evidence Act 1984 (PACE) whereby stops are recorded and a written record is made available to the person stopped. His innovation was to recommend closing the loophole whereby police could circumvent PACE recording requirements by 'voluntary' stops, or stops under drugs or traffic legislation, in other words by the extension of recording to include all stops.

Macpherson's call for rule-tightening was recently endorsed by the Home Secretary, David Blunkett, who, at the time of writing, was intending to impose two major changes: first, a requirement that police officers give a written record for around 4 million stops a year that fall outside the PACE definitions of stop and search, and for which written records are already statutory; and second, pressure on police forces to ensure that stop and search is targeted and 'intelligence-led', so that stops arise more as a result of hard information about offending rather than as a – largely unproductive – trawl for information (Ahmed and Hinscliff, 2002). As a further confidence building measure in police–community relations, it was announced that police authorities would be enabled to set up panels of community representatives to monitor stop-and-search records against disproportionate stops for ethnic minorities.

Such developments constitute, on the face of it, an admission that stops have hitherto been used in a discriminatory fashion, and have not been targeted in respect of actual criminality. This is indeed the conclusion of substantial research. Since the early 1980s there has been, until very recently, a dramatic increase in stop and search. Between 1986 and 1996 stop and search (under the PACE regulations) rose over nine times in England and Wales as a whole, while the proportion of stops that led to arrest fell over the same period from 17 per cent to 10 per cent (Wilkins and Addicott, 1999, Table A). The unproductive nature of stop and search has been confirmed in further Home Office research (see Miller *et al.*, 2000). If regulated stops under the PACE regulations lead to such low yield in terms of criminal offending, then the hitherto unregulated stops are even less likely to lead to productive arrests of criminal offenders.

However, at this point a crucial issue arises. Stop and search may, contra Macpherson, have other purposes than crime control. It is a mistake to think of the police as an organization dedicated predominantly to crime control. Their historical origin lies in the necessity – from the standpoint of the propertied middle class – to control the 'dangerous classes', that is, the poor, unemployed and homeless (Bittner, 1975). This involved less a concern with the detection of crime than the generalized surveillance of entire social groups and communities. This function of the police is again becoming prominent, with the growth of social exclusion and a substantial underclass of people with high rates of poverty, homelessness, school expulsions, etc. Such people are disproportionately on the streets and attract the attention of the police. The increasing use of stop and search at the same time as a declining proportion of stops leading to arrest suggests a growing importance of the role of general surveillance. As a result of racial discrimination, young Black people are disproportionately concentrated among that population attracting police attention, not because of a concrete suspicion of criminality, but more because of a diffuse notion of dangerousness and disorderliness.

This theme emerges as a by-product of police attempts to deny that a disproportionate stop rate for black people is evidence of racism. It can be argued that while such disparities may exist, they have little to do with racial discrimination by police officers, but rather reflect other factors such as the concentration of the black community – owing to economic discrimination – in particular social classes or geographical areas where the rate of stop and search is likely to be higher in any case (Jefferson, 1991, 1993; Jefferson and Walker, 1993). The Metropolitan Police, in their evidence to Macpherson, argued along these lines. Assistant Commissioner Ian Johnston claimed that:

If we look to people who are likely to be out on the streets, youngsters who are truanting and excluded from schools, who are over-represented in the truanting statistics, enormously over-represented in the exclusion statistics, it is young black children. If you look at who else is out on the streets, it is the unemployed. If you look at the differential rates of unemployed, black people, for a range of reasons, some of which are understandable, some of which are abhorrent are unemployed ... so I wouldn't simply jump to the conclusion that because they are over represented, that that necessarily leads to support for an allegation of racism. What I do agree with is that it is something that needs significant exploration and significant looking in to. ....

(Metropolitan Police, 1998)

This type of argument was reproduced in later Home Office research (MVA and Miller, 2000), which attempted to measure the disproportionality of stops, not for the population as a whole in an area but for the 'available population for stop/search', and found no evidence of disproportionality. However there is an important confusion in this line of reasoning. Black people may well face a high level of stops for the demographic reasons alluded to. Large numbers of White youths of a similar socio-economic background may also be subject to stops. The key question is why they are stopped in the first place. If individuals were stopped purely on the basis of reasonable suspicion of involvement in crime, by reference to criteria other than membership of an ethnic group, then racial disparities in stop and search would simply reflect differential crime rates. But, as research has shown, the actual yield of arrested offenders is very low.

The indicators required by police as a basis for stops are therefore less those of explicit criminality than membership of the underclass. Race is used by the police in precisely this way as a trigger for general surveillance and control. It is not, of course, the only such sign. Being a skinhead or dressing in a certain way, and being in the 'wrong place at the wrong time' will also function. Large numbers of Whites are stopped on the basis of such signs. These signs are reproduced as stereotypes of dangerousness, and they are reinforced in the practical street wisdom and occupational culture of police officers. So when Ian Johnston, in the passage quoted above, implies that the police are not racist in stopping a disproportionate number of young Blacks he is both right and wrong. He is right that demographic factors and racial discrimination in education and employment have placed disproportionately large numbers of blacks in the general social category that attracts police attention. He is wrong in the sense that it is precisely because of this fact that race acts as a useful trigger for stop and search.

This is precisely why such racism is *institutional*. It arises out of the practical operational working of the police, not as an inefficient interference by prejudiced officers. Of course, police focus on Black people is overdetermined. Middle-class Blacks get caught in the net to a much greater extent than middle-class Whites. The boundaries between the underclass and the 'respectable' classes are more sharply drawn for the latter than the former. This is a result of the differential political and economic power of these communities. Racial prejudice among police officers, the association of Black with underclass and disorder, is then reproduced in an occupational culture that legitimizes stop and search as the policing of dangerous populations. But it is not the occupational culture that distorts stop and search; rather, the latter provides the material basis for the occupational culture. It is Macpherson's failure to grasp this dynamic that undermines his whole project. By maintaining that stop and search is important for the control of *crime*, despite its minimal yield of arrests and information, he misses the fact that stop and search, as a form of generalized policing of whole communities and groups, is a major factor in generating police racism however much it is formally regulated by rules.

There was, nevertheless, considerable resistance in police circles to carrying through the implications of the Macpherson report. Police critics appeared to resent any suggestion that stop and search was carried out in a discriminatory way, and furthermore appeared to attribute to Macpherson a position he did not espouse: namely, that stop and search was unproductive from the crime-control standpoint. Police use of stop and search had fallen considerably in the period prior to the publication of Macpherson, partly in anticipation of some of its recommendations, and certain forms of street crime had risen. The two were then portrayed as causally related. In fact, a study commissioned by the Metropolitan Police found 'that the link between the fall in searches and the rise in street crime was weak' (Fitzgerald, 1999, p. 22). This weakness was associated with the fact that the type of street crime most likely to be uncovered by stop and search operations was possession of small amounts of cannabis, while the type that had risen during the period of the fall in stops was street robbery, an offence rarely uncovered by such policing operations.

Policing the powerless

The likely trends of future developments are difficult to discern, because stop and search can, as we have seen, fulfil a number of functions. Reductions in stop-and-search levels appear to be underway, and the general theme of recent reforms seems to be a genuine attempt to reduce the effect of stop and search as a form of generalized surveillance of the socially excluded, and to increase its role as a crime-control mechanism based on information already gathered; a shift from stops based on ethnic and class stereotypes to stops based on 'actual hard evidence as to the likelihood that the person stopped was an offender' (Young and Mooney, 1999, p. 38; see also Young, 1995). The successful implementation of such a reform would mean that disproportionate stops for any particular group would indicate solely the disproportionate involvement of that group in criminality. One consequence might well be an increase in the proportion of stops of young males from poor communities, many of which have high concentrations of Black or Asian people. The issue is not the proportion of different ethnic groups stopped but the reason why they are stopped.

However, there are reasons for scepticism. First, it is one thing to legislate for the recording of stops, it is another entirely to enforce it. The police as an organization is very 'bottom heavy'. There is a high level of autonomy and discretion available to officers on the street. This is underlined by another piece of recent Home Office research, which noted that:

> . . . decisions taken by police officers when dealing with members of the public are marked by 'low visibility', and are thus invisible to supervisors and effectively 'unreviewable'. This . . . remains an enduring problem at the heart of any attempt to regulate how officers behave on the street, and specifically in their use and conduct of stops and searches.
>
> (Bland *et al.*, 2000, p. 9)

The research went on to reveal the fact that in its survey areas up to 70 per cent of stops and searches were not properly recorded by officers (Bland *et al.*, 2000, p. 31). These were stops and searches under the PACE regulations occurring at least 14 years after these regulations came into effect, by which time they might be supposed to have become second nature to police constables. One can only imagine the fate awaiting regulations requiring officers to record *all* stops.

The question of targeting also opens a hornets' nest of problems. The overriding sense is one of *déjà vu*. We have been here before. Just as Macpherson repeated many of Scarman's recommendations, seemingly oblivious of their almost impact-free nature, so solutions to the problems of stop and search by an emphasis on targeting are by no means new. Thus, on a tour of London police stations in October 1982, following the Brixton riots of the previous year, the then Commissioner of the Metropolitan Police, Sir Kenneth Newman, claimed that street robbers would henceforth be pursued in 'a much more professional way' than the large-scale stop-and-search operations that provoked the Brixton riots of 1981. Targeting was precisely what he had in mind. (Kinsey *et al.*, 1986). Yet 20 years later, exactly the same innovations have been wheeled out as a solution. The effect may be, moreover, to reproduce existing forms of institutional racism, as police develop targeting strategies within exactly the same ethnic-minority populations to which more generalized stop-and-search strategies were directed. While actual offenders may be a higher proportion of those now stopped, it might still be ethnic-minority offenders who are disproportionately stopped. Certain areas of cities, predominantly socially excluded and deprived areas, will be designated as disproportionately in need of police attention. In the same vein, targeting might involve a greater perception of the need to recruit the support of the middle-classes within the ethnic-minority communities, some representatives of whom have recently spoken in favour of stop and search as a crime-control mechanism (Burrell, 2002). Targeting might be aimed at reducing the extent to which middle-class Blacks are drawn into the population available to be stopped. Another good reason for reducing stop-and-search levels is the pressure to increase clear-up rates for reported crimes, and therefore to spend less time and fewer resources on practices that are minimally productive in this respect.

On the other hand the pressure to engage in generalized surveillance of the socially excluded as a group, rather than as targeted offenders, is considerable. This is part of a trend toward 'actuarial' social control (Feeley and Simon, 1994; Johnston, 1997, 2000; Lea, 2002), emphasizing the management of risk groups rather than a focus on criminal offenders. Stop and search is, as noted above, well suited to such tasks. The reduction of stop and search under such conditions may presage a withdrawal from proactive policing to forms of 'border patrol' of deprived areas, while police operations targeted against offenders, such as organized criminal gangs, dictate episodic forays into areas of the city that are to all other intents and purposes no-go. Time will tell.

The framework for a solution

Analyses that locate institutional racism primarily in a lack of interethnic contact outside law-enforcement situations inevitably lead to a focus on race-awareness training for White police officers and attempts to change the ethnic composition of police forces – strategies that have made little impact over the decades since Scarman. Macpherson was aware of this, but failed to adopt a more radical policy agenda directed at the structure and organization of policing and the relationship between police and ethnic minorities in the law-enforcement situation itself. The analysis presented here, while not negating the goals of race-awareness or the need to change the ethnic composition of police forces, suggests that their successful achievement might be linked to more far-reaching structural changes in operational policing and in the constitutional relationship of police forces with the various ethnic communities.

The first conclusion is the necessity for a developed system of police accountability, in which elected representatives have the power to determine the general strategies and priorities of policing. This would enable ethnic minorities, despite their lack of economic power and status, to contribute to the setting of police goals and thereby to be taken seriously as a political constituency by police. Such an argument is not new. It was made forcibly during the mid-1980s in the context of the campaign by the then Greater London Council (GLC) for an elected Police Authority for London (see Lea and Young, 1984; Spencer, 1985; Greater London Council, 1985). After the abolition of the GLC in 1986 the debate was sidelined. However, recent political developments may provide an environment in which it is likely to resurface. The creation by the present government of a Metropolitan Police Authority, welcomed by Macpherson, may create an opportunity to rethink the nature of police accountability and, importantly, to link the issue of accountability with that of the elimination of institutional racism.

Here is not the place to develop these arguments further. They will no doubt receive a substantial airing in the coming debate about new constitutional arrangements for the Metropolitan Police. I have sought simply to illustrate that the type of analysis of institutional racism given above leads directly to these agendas of institutional change rather than to the more cultural and attitudinal focus that has been the dominant approach to combating police racism, and which, despite attempts to move in other directions, remained the central focus of the Macpherson report.

Notes

1 References to the main body of the Macpherson report, as well as to the Scarman report, are by paragraph number.

2 The question as to whether institutional racism as a matter of overt policy exists in the United Kingdom is beyond our discussion here. Suffice it to say that as regards policing such racism would exist if, for example, the character of laws which the police are obliged to enforce – such as, for example, legislation governing immigration and the granting of asylum status to refugees – were judged to be discriminatory. For a fuller discussion of this variant of institutional racism see Lea, 1986.

References

Ahmed, K. and Hinsliff, G. (2002) 'Race Row as Blunkett Backs Stop and Search', *Observer*, 10 March.

Bittner, E. (1975) *The Functions of the Police in Modern Society*, New York: Jason Aronson.

Bland, N., Miller, J. and Quinton, P. (2000) *Upping the PACE? An Evaluation of the Recommendations of the Stephen Lawrence Inquiry on Stops and Searches*, Home Office Policing and Reducing Crime Unit, Police Research Series Papers 128, London: Home Office.

Burrell, I. (2002) 'Black Community Split by Call for Stop-and-Search', *Independent*, 5 March.

Cantle, T. (2001) *Community Cohesion: A Report of the Independent Review Team*, London: Home Office.

Chan, J. (1997) *Changing Police Culture: Policing in a Multicultural Society*, Cambridge: Cambridge University Press.

Feeley, M. and Simon, J. (1994) 'Actuarial Justice: The Emerging New Criminal Law', in D. Nelken (ed.) *The Futures of Criminology*, London: Sage.

Fitzgerald, M. (1999) *Searches in London: Interim Evaluation*, London: Metropolitan Police.

Gilling, D. (1997) *Crime Prevention: Theory, Policy and Politics*, London: UCL Press.

Greater London Council (1985) *Reorganisation of the Metropolitan Police*, GLC Police Committee.

Gregory, J. and Lees, S. (1999) *Policing Sexual Assault*, London: Routledge.

Her Majesty's Inspectorate of Constabulary (1998) *Winning the Race: Policing Plural Communities: HMIC Thematic Inspection Report on Police, Community and Race Relations 1996/97*, London: Home Office.

Holdaway, S. (1983) *Inside the British Police*, Oxford: Blackwell.

Jefferson, T. (1991) 'Discrimination, Disadvantage and Police Work', in E. Cashmore, and E. McLaughlin (eds) *Out of Order: Policing Black People*, London: Routledge.

Jefferson, T. (1993) 'The Racism of Criminalization: Policing and the Reproduction of the Criminal Other', in L. Gelsthorpe and W. McWilliam (eds) *Minority Ethnic Groups and the Criminal Justice System*, Cambridge: University of Cambridge Institute of Criminology.

Jefferson, T. and Walker, M. (1993) Attitudes to the Police of the Ethnic Minorities in a Provincial City, *British Journal of Criminology*, 33(2), 251–66.

Johnston, L. (1997) 'Policing Communities of Risk', in P. Francis, P. Davies and V. Jupp (eds) *Policing Futures: The Police, Law Enforcement and the Twenty First Century*, London: Macmillan.

Johnston, L. (2000) *Policing Britain: Risk, Security and Governance*, London: Longman.

Katznelson, I. (1973) *Black Men, White Cities: Race, Politics and Migration in the United States 1900–30, and Britain 1948–68*, London: Oxford University Press.

Kinsey, R., Lea, J. and Young, J. (1986) *Losing the Fight against Crime*, Oxford: Blackwell.

Lea, J. (1986) 'Police Racism: Some Theories and Their Policy Implication', in R. Matthews and J. Young (eds) *Confronting Crime*, London: Sage.

Lea, J. (2002) *Crime and Modernity*, London: Sage.

Lea, J. and Young, J. (1984) *What is to Be Done about Law and Order?* London: Penguin.

McConville, M. *et al.* (1991) *The Case for the Prosecution: Police Suspects and the Construction of Criminality*, London: Routledge.

Macpherson, Lord (1999) *The Stephen Lawrence Inquiry*, Cm 4262-I, London: Stationery Office.

Mansfield, M. (1993) *Presumed Guilty: The British Legal System Exposed*, London: Heinemann.

Metropolitan Police Service (1998) *Evidence to the Lawrence Inquiry, Part II. AC Johnston TR/p. 8694*, London: Metropolitan Police Service.

Miller, J., Quinton, P. and Bland, N. (2000) *The Impact of Stops and Searches on Crime and the Community*, Home Office Policing and Reducing Crime Unit, Police Research Series Papers 127, London: Home Office.

Morgan, R. (1987) 'Police Accountability: Developing the Local Infrastructure', *British Journal of Criminology*, 27(1), 87–96.

MVA and Miller, J. (2000) *Profiling Populations Available for Stops and Searches*, Home Office Policing and Reducing Crime Unit, Police Research Series Papers 131, London: Home Office.

O'Malley, P. and Palmer, D. (1996) 'Post-Keynesian Policing', *Economy and Society*, 25(2), 137–55.

Reiner, R. (1992) *The Politics of the Police*, 2nd edition, Toronto: University of Toronto Press.

Scarman, Lord (1981) *The Brixton Disorders 10–12 April 1981*, Cm 8427, London: HMSO.

Smith, D. (1997) 'Ethnic Origins, Crime and Criminal Justice', in M. Maguire, R. Morgan, and R. Reiner (eds) *The Oxford Handbook of Criminology*, 2nd edition, 704–59, Oxford: Clarendon Press.

Smith D. and Gray, J. (1983) *Police and People in London*, vol. 4, London: Policy Studies Institute.

Spencer, S. (1985) *The Case for Police Accountability in England and Wales*, London National Council for Civil Liberties.

Wilkins, G. and Addicott, C. (1999) 'Operation of Certain Police Powers under PACE England and Wales, 1997/8', *Home Office Statistical Bulletin*, 2(99).

Young, J. (1995) *Policing the Streets*, London: Borough of Islington.

Young, J. and Mooney, J. (1999) *Social Exclusion and Criminal Justice: Ethnic Minorities and Stop and Search in North London*, Middlesex University: Centre for Criminology.

Younge, G. (2002) 'Britain is Again White', *Guardian* (18 February).

Chapter 4

Youth justice in England and Wales

John Pitts

Introduction

In Britain and the United States in the past 20 years crime, committed by children and young people has become a major political issue (Garland, 2001; Pitts, 2001). Increasingly, politicians across the political spectrum have demanded that if young offenders are prepared to 'do the crime', they should also 'do the time' (Simon, 2000) and that, in some cases, they should do this 'time' in the same places as adults. This renewed emphasis on the deeds, rather than the needs, of young offenders poses a fundamental challenge to the idea of a separate youth justice system.

The 'child in trouble' as a 'child in need'

This is not to say that youth justice systems are not concerned with the deeds of young offenders. As with the adult justice systems from which they derive, youth justice systems have always aimed to deter young offenders and to punish them when they offend. However, from their inception, youth justice systems have proceeded from the assumption that children and young people, by dint of their relative immaturity, are less able to control their impulses, less able to understand the seriousness of their offences and less able to foresee the consequences of their actions. Linked to this is the belief that the culpability of many young offenders may be further mitigated by the poverty, cruelty or neglect they have suffered. It is for this reason that, until recently, juvenile courts in Western European and the anglophone countries have dealt with both criminal and child protection issues (Hetherington *et al.*, 1997; Fagan and Zimring, 2000). Thus the 'child in trouble' with the law has also been regarded as a 'child in need' (the Children Act, 1989) and sentencers have been required to demonstrate that the penalties they impose serve to further the 'the best interests of the child'. For their part, the agencies that constitute the youth justice system have been required to provide the requisite therapeutic, educational and vocational services and to minimize the negative effects of the young person's involvement in the system. Thus, Article 3.1 of the UN Convention on the Rights of the Child enjoins signatories (all the nations of the world except the United States and Somalia) to ensure that 'in all actions concerning children, whether undertaken by public or private social welfare institutions, courts of law, administrative authorities or legislative bodies, the best interests of the child shall be a primary consideration'. Although these are the principles that have informed most youth justice systems, they have been adhered to differently at different times, by different agencies, in different regions in the same country and in different countries of the world. Clearly there are conflicting pressures at work within youth justice systems. The desire to punish and deter offenders and protect the public, for example, is not infrequently in tension with the imperative to act in a child's 'best interests'. The way this tension is resolved is shaped in crucial ways by prevailing social attitudes, media pressures and political imperatives.

The origins of the youth justice system of England and Wales

The contemporary youth justice system of England and Wales has its origins in the nineteenth century. The 1854 Youthful Offenders Act brought into being a national network of juvenile reformatories, to which, until the end of the 19th century, children and young people under 16 could be transferred on completion of a sentence in an adult jail. This practice was not abandoned until the turn of the century. Once established, these institutions expanded rapidly. The year 1857 saw the introduction of Industrial Schools for 7–14 year olds convicted of vagrancy (Newburn, 1995). Whereas in 1858, there were 45 reformatories holding around 2000 young people, by 1870 this figure had increased to 65 institutions holding 7000 young people, with even more young people being held in Industrial Schools.

Throughout the 19th century, pressure from politically powerful religious, philanthropic and penal-reform groups concerning the corruption, brutality and indiscipline to which children were exposed in adult jails had grown. In the final decades of the 19th century there was widespread public and media concern about the perceived 'crisis of control' in the industrial cities of Victorian England, and the apparent ineffectiveness of the justice system and other agencies of control to contain it (Garland, 1985).

Then, as now, these developments raised concerns among politicians, the media, the police and the clergy about the weakening of conventional family forms and values, the consequent erosion of informal social controls and the drunkenness, vice, violence and crime to which such anomie gave rise. As a result, in the mid-1890s, Asquith, the Home Secretary, established two departmental committees, the Gladstone Committee and the Lushington Committee, which advocated 'treatment' rather than the punishment of young prisoners and the establishment of 'alternatives to custody'. Then, as now, it was a 'modernizing' government that acted on these radical recommendations, and then, as now, this government argued that the new measures were 'evidence-based', informed by the new sciences of paediatrics, child psychology, criminology and penology. Responsibility for this new form of youth justice was placed in the hands of a new legal and administrative entity, the juvenile court.

The juvenile court and the 'invention of delinquency'

The first ever juvenile court was established in Chicago in 1899. By 1910, separate juvenile courts and a discrete institutional and administrative apparatus for dealing with young offenders had been established in most Western European countries. Platt (1969) has argued that the advent of the juvenile court, with its unique amalgam of science, law and administration, ushered into existence a wholly new kind of human being, the 'juvenile delinquent', the management of whom constituted its *raison d'être*. Before the juvenile courts, he argues, there were only 'young offenders', to whom varying degrees of culpability could be ascribed. Juvenile delinquents, however, were believed to differ in a multiplicity of ways from their non-delinquent peers. It was not simply that they behaved differently. They were different in the way they thought, how they felt, in the beliefs and attitudes they held and, indeed, in their very bio-genetic constitution. Thus, the juvenile court did not simply assume powers to sentence children and young people to a new, distinctively juvenile, range of penalties and facilities, it also shaped its disposals in accordance with

73

the relationships the new sciences of human behaviour had hypothesized between the juvenile delinquent's present demeanour and their future deeds. Not only did the juvenile court assume responsibility for the disposal of 'deviant bodies' (Foucault, 1977), it also recast deviant identities (Matza, 1969).

The development of the youth justice system in England and Wales

In England and Wales, the Children Act (1908) and the Prevention of Crime Act (1908) established a national system of juvenile courts, and the Probation of Offenders Act (1907) introduced community supervision as an alternative to custody. By 1920, approximately 8,000 of the 10,000 people being supervised by probation officers were aged between 8 and 18 years.

The Prevention of Crime Act (1908) placed Industrial Schools and reformatories under the administrative control of the Home Office, and introduced Borstal institutions, named after the village in Kent where the first one was built. Borstals were penal institutions for inmates aged between 16 and 20, staffed by teachers as well as prison officers, and unlike the adult prisons they provided educational and vocational programmes and military training.

The spreading of the net of control

The immediate impact of the reforms of 1907/8 was paradoxical. Although the new system offered a non-custodial penalty in the form of the probation order, it failed to diminish institutional confinement. Between 1907 and 1908 the number of youngsters consigned to juvenile reformatories and Borstals rose steadily, topping 20,000 in the early 1920s. Then, as now, this expansion of custodial confinement coincided with scandals concerning brutality towards inmates (Crimmens and Pitts, 2000). And, as is also the case today, the introduction of new, and apparently more positive, institutional regimes encouraged some sentencers to consign more children and young people to them because of their purported benefits. Thus a system established to create 'alternatives to custody' and vouchsafe the humane treatment of those consigned to custody was, in fact, imposing greater custodial control on a larger number of less problematic subjects. This 'spreading of the net of control' (Cohen, 1979) was exacerbated by the probation order, which placed young offenders under obligatory surveillance, with the ever-present danger of harsher penalties if they did not abide by the conditions of the probation order. These conditions required not only that a young person desist from crime but that they also pursue an honest and industrious life, refrain from associating with other people involved in crime, and report to their probation officer when required to do so. By 1920 over 10,000 people were under probation supervision, of whom 80 per cent were under 21, and some, at least, of the juveniles entering Borstals, reformatories and industrial schools were there as a result of breaches of their probation orders. Importantly, this dual expansion of institutional and community control occurred despite a steadily declining crime rate throughout the first two decades of the twentieth century.

The falling rate of youth crime

Commentators on the political right, like Charles Murray (1994), have speculated that the falling crime rate in the United Kingdom at the start of the twentieth century was a result of the protective and deterrent effects of imprisonment. However, as we note below, marked reductions in the prison population in the 1930s paralleled the lowest UK crime rates of the twentieth century. John Lea (1999) has argued that these low crime rates paralleled the rise of the Labour Party and the trades union movement, which together were instrumental in transforming an inchoate urban proletariat into a powerful political and moral force. As a result, the first half of the twentieth century saw the emergence of a relatively secure, unionized, industrial workforce, whose social well-being was underpinned by the progressive expansion of rights to healthcare, housing, education and material security. These developments generated a reliable workforce, low divorce rates, 'stable' families and 'respectable' working-class neighbourhoods. The greater degree of 'social solidarity', or the dilution of dissent, engendered by these developments appears to have been sufficient to keep crime rates relatively low even during the depression years of the 1930s. It is not that youth crime and disorder, once believed to be a ubiquitous feature of lower-class life, disappeared during this period, but rather that in popular perception, and to a considerable extent in fact, working-class crime came to be concentrated in the 'social margins', among those who had not been incorporated into the organized working class.

Penal modernism

The economic, political and social changes chronicled by John Lea created the conditions for the emergence of what David Garland (2001) has characterized as 'penal modernism'. This, he argues, was a product of a particular historical conjuncture in which a social democratic politics, which viewed offenders as disadvantaged or poorly socialized, strove, through its criminal justice and social policies, to ameliorate the conditions that generated crime. These polices attracted bipartisan political support, born of a confidence in policy-making elites, the application of social science to social and criminal justice policy and the expertise of penal professionals.

A child-centred justice

Arguably, penal modernism found its fullest expression in the 'child-centred' youth-justice policies that emerged between 1933 to 1969. Tim Newburn (1995) argues that the 1930s saw a 'sea-change' in penal affairs in the United Kingdom. Prison populations were substantially reduced and new forms of youth justice were constructed on the foundations laid by the reforms of 1907/8. Although responsibility for youth justice in England and Wales has always been shared between the Home Office and the ministry responsible for health and social services, between 1933 and 1969 the Ministry of Health played a major role in the development of policy. The Children and Young Person's Act (1933) established the principle that young offenders should be dealt with in ways that promoted their 'welfare' and that any necessary 'treatment' should be available to them. The Act also formally abolished capital punishment for those under the age of 18, and consolidated the nineteenth century reformatories and Industrial Schools into a national system of Approved Schools for the treatment of young offenders aged 10–15. The subsequent Children and Young Person's Act (1948) established local-authority Children's Departments as the first professional social-work service for children and young people in the United Kingdom. Children's Departments ran their own residential establishments and employed fostering and adoption officers to find alternative families for orphaned, neglected and abused children and young people. The Criminal Justice Act of 1948 replaced corporal punishment with Attendance Centres, which young offenders attended on Saturday afternoons to learn first aid and do PE, and Detention Centres, which replaced short prison sentences.

The reforms of 1907/8 had established the right of young offenders to be dealt with differently. The reforms of 1933 and 1948 were concerned with elaborating the nature of that difference. The ensuing policies were imbued with ideas about child development derived from Freudian psychoanalysis and, in particular, a concern with the effects of poverty and inequality on healthy development. These policies were, therefore, as concerned with the underlying social and psychological origins of youth crime as with youth crime itself.

'Welfare' versus 'justice'

Perhaps inevitably, this change towards an emphasis on the 'needs' rather than the 'deeds' of young offenders created a widening rift between, on the one hand, Conservative politicians, senior police officers, magistrates and judges, who wished to retain a strong element of retribution in the youth justice system, and on the other, those like academic social scientists and health and welfare professionals who believed that, because the 'welfare' of young offenders should be a paramount consideration, offenders should, wherever possible, be dealt with by experts in the care and protection of children and young people. This argument trundled on into the postwar period, but, in the 1960s, the claims of 'welfarism' were given greater impetus by research that showed that the children who passed through the juvenile courts were overwhelmingly poor, badly educated and, in many cases, victims of violence or abuse (cf. Titmus, 1968). With the election of a sympathetic Labour government in 1964, it appeared that the 'welfarist' argument would prevail.

The 1964 White Paper, *The Child, the Family and the Young Offender*, proposed the replacement of the juvenile court with a family council, composed of health and welfare professionals, which would address the social and psychological problems underlying youth crime. The White Paper had its origins in a report for the Fabian Society by the late Lord Longford (1963), in which he observed that:

No understanding parent can contemplate without repugnance the branding of a child in early adolescence as a criminal, whatever offence he may have committed. If it is a trivial case, such a procedure is indefensible, if a more serious charge is involved this is, in itself, evidence of the child's need for skilled help and guidance. The parent who can get such help for his child on his own initiative can almost invariably keep the child from court. It is only the children of those not so fortunate who appear in the criminal statistics.

The Child, the Family and the Young Offender proposed a radical shift of power, from the police, magistrates, lawyers and judges to psychologists, psychiatrists and social workers. The proposals were vociferously opposed by the Conservative Opposition and as a result, a significantly modified reform package was presented to parliament in the Children and Young Person Act (1969). The 1969 Act retained the juvenile court but restricted the magistrate's power to impose Borstal sentences. It passed responsibility for the supervision of young offenders in the community, and decisions about placements in Approved Schools (re-designated Community Homes with Education [CHEs]), to local-authority social workers. The 1969 Act also introduced a new measure, Intermediate Treatment (IT), which could be utilized formally as a requirement in a Supervision Order, but which also permitted local authorities to establish community-based schemes to 'prevent' youth crime among children and young people deemed to be 'at risk' of offending. It was the intention of the government that, as IT proved its worth, it would replace the Detention Centre and the Attendance Centre. In retrospect, it is evident that the 1969 Act marked the highpoint of the 36-year struggle to construct a child-centred youth justice system, in which a concern for the 'welfare' of the child, their needs rather than their deeds, was paramount.

The net of control spreads wider

1970 saw the election of a Conservative government which, although unwilling to limit the powers of juvenile court magistrates did not oppose the implementation of many of the new provisions introduced by the 1969 Act. Thus, Care Orders, Supervision Orders and Intermediate Treatment were introduced alongside the Fines, Discharges, Probation Orders, Attendance Centres, Detention Centres, and Borstals of the existing system. This expanded hybrid system gave both juvenile-court magistrates and social workers more options than ever before for dealing with young offenders. As we have noted, the Act also decreed that social workers should endeavour to prevent youth crime through early intervention utilizing Intermediate Treatment (IT). By 1977 an estimated 12,000 children and young people were involved in Intermediate Treatment, of whom only about 1,500 were adjudicated offenders. At the same time the police had established specialist

Juvenile Bureaux to deal more cost-effectively with petty juvenile offenders. Between 1965 and 1977 the numbers of 10–17 year olds cautioned by the police (formally reprimanded by a senior police officer rather than being charged and tried in the juvenile court) rose from 3,062 to 111,922. The numbers subject to informal intervention by the police were higher still. However, early informal intervention revealed a tendency to draw youngsters further into the system, as the discovery of new needs and new problems appeared to necessitate the formalization of these interventions. In consequence, ever larger numbers of children began to appear in the juvenile courts, and as the 1970s progressed an increasing proportion of these were receiving custodial sentences. Whereas in 1965 21 per cent of convicted young offenders were sentenced to detention centres and Borstals, by 1977 this proportion had risen to 38 per cent (Pitts, 1988). By the late 1970s residential and custodial institutions for juveniles were not only chronically overcrowded, thereby placing additional strains on an equally overcrowded adult penal system, they were also costing a great deal of money.

The rise of 'progressive minimalism'

Margaret Thatcher's 1979 Conservative government pledged to crack down on youth crime. However, as a result of the youth justice system's unregulated expansion in the 1970s, it was coming apart at the seams. Moreover, youth justice was one of the many areas of government spending perceived to be spiralling out of control, and this was acutely embarrassing for an administration committed to 'small government' and 'good housekeeping' (Scull, 1977). Having been saved from electoral defeat by the Falklands War, the second Thatcher administration, now in the thrall of monetarism, confronted the reality of Britain's fiscal crisis (Scull, 1977). The crisis centred on the inability of the state to maintain existing welfare and crime-control services in the face of rising costs, rising demands on state expenditure – largely from unemployment benefit – mounting political pressure to reduce taxation and a significant reduction in the tax-paying population. As a result, the period between 1982 and 1992 witnessed a sustained attempt to contain and reduce the burgeoning costs of the criminal-justice apparatus.

Politicians normally try to draw public attention to the issue of youth crime when the economy is in trouble. Mrs Thatcher's blood-curdling pre-election rhetoric notwithstanding, during the economic boom of the 1980s the issue of youth crime was placed on the political 'back burner'. This relative depoliticization of the issue enabled successive Conservative Home Secretaries – Douglas Hurd, David Waddington and Kenneth Baker – to pay attention to the advice of their Civil Servants and Home Office researchers, rather than to the tabloid press or the law-and-order rhetoric of their leader. As a result, Conservative responses to youth crime in the 1980s were shaped in significant ways by intellectual developments in the fields of crime and justice in the United Kingdom and United States, and by research evidence. This evidence appeared to be suggesting that both punitive and rehabilitative programmes had a minimal impact on re-offending (Martinson, 1974; Wilson, 1975), and that they sometimes worsened the problems they were intended to solve, through the process of 'labelling'. These findings caused certain injudicious criminologists to conclude that 'nothing works'.

In his essay 'Dilemmas of Intervention', the American sociologist Edwin Lemert (2000) succinctly summed up the key messages from research and practice in the field of youth justice:

Evidence that it (the youth justice system) has prevented crime or lessened the recidivism of youthful offenders is missing, and dour sociological critiques urge that it contributes to juvenile crime or inaugurates delinquent careers by the imposition of the stigma of wardship, unwise detention, and incarceration of children in institutions which don't reform and often corrupt.

(Lemert, 2000, p. 161)

The implications for public policy, Lemert argued, were that some behaviours currently regarded as 'delinquent' should simply be 'ignored or written off as inevitable problems of everyday living and growing up', and that many of the problems defined as delinquency 'should be defined as family, educational, or welfare problems and diverted away from the juvenile court into other community agencies'.

In the light of this mounting body of evidence and his own extensive experience, in the 1970s Jerome Miller, the director of juvenile corrections in Massachusetts, had closed all the state's juvenile institutions and transferred the inmates into community programmes, or indeed into no programmes at all. Follow-up studies indicated that this made little difference to either local crime rates or inmate reconviction rates (Ohlin, 1979).

The child's right to justice

Radicals involved in youth justice believed that a child or young person would only receive justice (as distinct from care, protection or welfare) in a system that recognized the child's right to the protections afforded by 'due process of law'. This right was eventually secured in the United States as a result of an obscure court-ruling in Arizona. On 15 June 1964, 15-year-old Gerald Gault was committed to a State Industrial School for boys until his 21st birthday, because he was found guilty of making obscene telephone calls to his teacher, and his parents appeared unwilling or unable to exert adequate control over him. The American Council for Civil Liberties appealed the Gault case all the way to the Supreme Court, which ruled that in adjudication hearings that might result in young persons being sent to institutions, they had the right to the protections of due process of law. The implication was that a juvenile could not be subjected to longer periods of deprivation of liberty than an adult who had committed the same offence, on the basis of her/his 'welfare' needs. This was, in effect, the moment when a concern with 'children's rights' entered the Anglo-American youth justice arena. The Gault case became an international *cause célèbre* for activists associated with what came to be called the 'Back to Justice Movement'.

By the early 1980s, in the United Kingdom, the Back to Justice message was being articulated by an increasingly influential youth justice lobby, composed of youth justice professionals, penal-reform groups, progressive Home Office and Department of Health civil servants and academic criminologists. They were pressing for the replacement of a 'welfare'-oriented system with a 'justice'-oriented system which accorded with the principles of due process of law, but which also minimized intervention in the lives of young offenders.

Elliot Currie (1994) has characterized the convergence of the *'nothing works'* discourse and the Back to Justice movement as 'progressive minimalism' – a strategy for youth justice reform that attempts to fuse informalism and non-interventionism with the adoption of due process of law in defence of children's rights. Writing in 1977, Andrew Scull argued that whatever the ideological obstacles in the way of such a programme, governments of all political hues, confronted by fiscal crises occasioned by burgeoning state expenditure, would adopt minimalist criminal justice strategies in an attempt to balance the books. Ironically, although Scull was writing about the United States, where his thesis was not borne out, in the United Kingdom it all happened just as Scull had predicted.

Progressive Minimalism in the United Kingdom: the Intermediate Treatment Initiative

In an attempt to reduce the numbers of juveniles held in custody, in 1983, the Department of Health launched the Intermediate Treatment Initiative in which £15 million was granted to non-governmental agencies to develop 4,500 alternatives to custody, over three years, in collaboration with the police and juvenile-court magistrates. Between 1981 and 1989 the numbers of juveniles imprisoned in Young Offenders Centres fell from 7,700 to 1,900 per annum. The parallel reduction in the CHE population during the same period was triggered by severe reductions in local-government funding and growing scepticism about the institutions' effectiveness (Cornish and Clarke, 1975).

Corporatism: the third model of youth justice

The radical reductions in custodial sentencing during the 1980s are not solely attributable to changes in the attitudes of sentencers and their greater willingness to use alternatives to custody, although this clearly played a part. A major factor was a huge reduction in the numbers of children and young people entering juvenile courts. Whereas in 1980 around 71,000 boys and girls aged 14–16 were sentenced by the juvenile courts in England and Wales, by 1987 this figure had dropped to 37,300. This was made possible by the development of local multi-agency diversion panels, composed of representatives from the police, social services, education, the youth service and the voluntary sector. Multi-agency diversion panels developed a range of educational, recreational and therapeutic 'alternatives to prosecution', to which children and young people in trouble could be diverted as a condition of their police caution. Many panels offered robust informal intervention in the spheres of education, family relationships, use of leisure, vocational training and drug abuse. The apparent effectiveness of many of these schemes led to a practice, known as 'cautioning plus', in which youngsters might be cautioned on several different occasions if they and their parents agreed to participate in particular programmes or activities. Between 1980 and 1987 the cautioning rate for girls aged 14–16 rose from 58 per cent to 82 per cent. For boys the figures were 34 per cent and 58 per cent respectively. John Pratt (1989) argues that the advent of the multi-agency diversion panel ushered in a new model of youth justice, 'corporatism', which supplanted both the 'welfare' and 'justice' models, and was triggered, initially, by a desire to manage young offenders more cost-effectively. Multi-agency diversion panels diverted the bulk of young offenders away from the system, thus minimizing its costs. Critics have argued that because corporatism, through the medium of the 'caution plus', elaborates a 'shadow tariff' alongside the formal tariff operating within the juvenile court, it effectively acts as 'judge and jury' without regard to either the rules of evidence or due process of law. While it is true that there is an ever-present danger that informal systems of justice may make greater inroads into the lives and liberties of their subjects than would be the case in the formal system it shadows, there is little evidence, that this has actually happened.

The Conservative government was eager to build on the successes of the multi-agency diversion panels and the alternatives to custody developed as part of the Intermediate Treatment Initiative. It therefore institutionalized many of their practices within the Criminal Justice Act (1991), which was to introduce similar schemes for young adult offenders aged 18–21.

Delinquency management

The minimalist practices enshrined in the 1991 Act, often described as 'delinquency management', shifted the focus of youth justice from the rehabilitation or punishment of individuals to the cost-effective management of entire cohorts or categories of young offenders. Writing of analogous developments in the United States, Feely and Simon (1992) describe the emergence of a 'new penology'. This, they argue, is a politically ambiguous development, representing the convergence of two ostensibly antagonistic intellectual and political currents. As we have noted, the first, progressive minimalism, adopts an essentially optimistic stance, believing that left to their own devices, most youngsters will simply grow out of crime. The second, neo-conservative criminology (Wilson, 1994), is rooted in a far more pessimistic philosophy, which holds that 'evil people exist', and so the best we can hope to do is incapacitate the most serious offenders with exemplary jail sentences and subject lesser criminals, and those on the edge of crime, to cost-effective management and surveillance. Feely and Simon write:

The new penology is neither about punishing nor rehabilitating individuals. It is about identifying and managing unruly groups.

It is concerned with the rationality not of individual behaviour or even community organisation, but of managerial processes. Its goal is not to eliminate crime but to make it tolerable through systemic co-ordination. ... For example, although parole and probation have long been justified as a means of reintegrating offenders into the community, increasingly they are being seen as cost-effective ways of imposing long-term management on the dangerous.

(Feely and Simon, 1992, pp. 453–4)

As we have seen, the government's delinquency management strategy resulted in relatively few young offenders being incarcerated. However, this was a government that had been elected in 1979 on a pledge to 'restore the rule of law'. It was therefore necessary to cloak governmental pragmatism with the trappings of toughness, not least because by the late-1980s a rising crime rate and growing media and parliamentary concern about violent youth crime was placing the government under pressure.

The justice model

The practical consequence of these political manoeuvres was the emergence, in the late 1980s, of what came to be called the 'justice model' as the rehabilitative model of choice in both adult and youth justice systems. The justice model was sold to the key political, professional and media constituencies as a tough, confrontational, non-custodial response to offending. It was 'targeted' at more serious young offenders' in individualized 'offending programmes', the duration of which was determined by the length of the prison sentence to which it was to be an alternative.

However, just as the 1969 Children and Young Persons Act had marked the high water mark of 'welfarism', so the 1991 Criminal Justice Act signalled the rapid decline of 'progressive minimalism'.

The origins of penal populism

Whereas progressive minimalism held sway in the United Kingdom until the early 1990s, in the United States, from the early 1980s, it found itself in retreat from an ascendant radical right wing. The presidency of the liberal Jimmy Carter (1977–81) paralleled the emergence of the religious Right as a significant political force, and it is, in part, as a result of its influence that youth justice in the United States today has such a strongly retributive character. By the mid-1980s most US states had passed laws restricting the jurisdiction of the juvenile courts and reallocating specified groups of offences and offenders to adult criminal jurisdictions (Feld, 1988; Szymanski, 1987; Wilson, 1994). These changes were justified on the basis that juvenile courts offered inadequate retribution for serious crimes committed by juveniles, no effective deterrence and little community protection via incarceration in secure facilities (Feld, 1987; Wolfgang, 1982).

In this vein, Attorney General Edwin Meese, a personal friend of Ronald Reagan, had argued against the wisdom of diverting 'status' offenders, juveniles apprehended for under-age drinking, curfew busting, etc., from secure institutions since these were, he believed, the same young people who either 'went missing' only to become involved in prostitution, 'hustling' and drug dealing, or were drawn into the pornography industry. These preoccupations were expressed via substantial federal grants for 'juvenile intelligence' and 'enhanced prosecution' programmes for the juvenile bureaux of state police forces.

The most obvious outcome of these developments was a growth in juvenile incarceration in the United States between 1979 and 1989 of 103.5 per cent. 'Minority youth' constituted 93 per cent of this increase. By 1985 two-thirds of the nation's training schools were officially deemed 'chronically overcrowded' (Krisburg and Austin, 1993). In the same year Meese called for the execution of teenage killers (Lilley *et al.*, 1995).

These developments mark the advent of what has been described as 'penal populism'. Penal populism is usually contrasted with 'penal elitism', which, Mick Ryan argues, 'had its heyday in the two and a half decades after 1945. . . . (and) is often attributed with defending and promoting liberal, humane and welfarist policies against the demands of a more punitive public culture.' (Ryan, 1999, pp. 3–4) The defining characteristic of penal populism is that policy ends and policy means must accord with the dictates of an invariably retributive 'common sense' rather than the imperatives of 'experts' and criminal-justice professionals. New policy initiatives are no longer justified by reference to the criteria of these 'experts'. Now the experts are called upon to advise on the means whereby populist policy goals may be realized, rather than the ends to which policy should strive. In an earlier period, growing penal populations were represented as a shameful error on the part of the authorities because they were both wasteful and

85

inhumane; latterly a rising penal population is celebrated as a political achievement (Currie, 1985; Simon, 2000).

Penal populism in the United Kingdom and the renaissance of youth imprisonment

Record rises in the crime rate at the end of the 1980s and youth riots in out-of-town housing estates in 1991 and 1992 were to force the government to defend its minimalist policies on youth crime. But it was the murder in 1993 of two-year-old James Bulger by two truanting ten-year olds that put youth crime unequivocally back on the 'front page'. As a result, the key reforms embodied in the Criminal Justice Act (1991) were abandoned. In March 1993, only five months after the newly implemented Act had abolished custody for children under 15, Kenneth Clarke, the Conservative Home Secretary, promised to create 200 places for 12 to 15 year old persistent offenders in new 'Secure Training Centres'. This volte-face signalled a new era, in which crime in general, and youth crime in particular, were to be moved back to the centre of the political stage. In 1994 a new Home Secretary, Michael Howard, set about toughening the probation service by allowing direct recruitment of junior officers from the armed forces and from the ranks of former police officers. In October 1994 he told the Conservative Party's annual conference that 'prison works, it ensures that we are protected from murderers, muggers and rapists – and it makes many who are tempted to commit crime think twice'. Howard's period in office marked a key moment of transition in the English justice system in general, and youth justice in particular, from 'penal modernism' to 'penal populism'. In this period the issue of crime was moved out of the depoliticized space it occupied under modernism to become a 'hot' political issue. In the process, policies forged by political and professional elites gave way to those that resonated with 'popular' retributive sentiments. The 'victim', not the perpetrator, now emerged as the central object of penal policy and, increasingly, being 'for' the victim meant being 'against' the offender. In this changed ideological climate prison became a tool of incapacitation rather than rehabilitation, while community supervision became, first and foremost, risk management. Garland (2001) has argued that during this period we witness a move away from a modernist vision of the perfectibility of man to a darker, neo-classical vision of self-seeking man contained by a strong family, a strong community and a strong state, and constrained by fear of the penalty. Clearly the courts were now being sent a very different message by the government, and between 1993 and 1998 the number of young offenders under sentence in penal establishments rose by nearly 60 per cent, from 5,081 to 8,500.

Hard Labour

Following the Labour Party's defeat in the 1992 General Election, Party strategists turned their attention to the United States, where Bill Clinton and his team had 'reinvented' an apparently defunct Democratic Party and built, and then held together, a political constituency that would elect it. This new constituency of the centre, the argument ran, was 'post-political', in that it had rejected both right- and left-wing dogmatism, preferring governments that administered the state in accordance with the dictates of common sense, administrative and technical competence, and value for money. This was, however, a constituency which, next to job security, was most concerned about the threat of criminal victimization posed by an expanding 'underclass' in the 'unemployed ghettos' of the inner city.

For Clinton, 'youth crime' in general, and the implicit promise to contain the threat posed by socially and economically marginal African-American and Latino 'ghetto youth' to those in the social and economic 'mainstream', proved to be a kind of electoral glue, which sealed an otherwise socially disparate political constituency.

New Labour, which, like the US Democrats, had spent the best part of the previous 20 years in a political cul-de-sac, recognized that if it was to revive its electoral fortunes it must bury its image as the natural party of penal reform and seize the mantle of law and order from the Conservatives. In the wake of the murder of two-year-old James Bulger, Labour mounted a full-scale attack on the Tory law-and-order record, orchestrated and led by their new shadow Home Secretary, Tony Blair. Under the Conservatives, Blair claimed, crime in general, and youth crime in particular, was running out of control. The Conservatives had not only created a moral vacuum in which crime flourished, but also shown themselves to be incapable of forging the radical measures needed to contain crime. Labour, Blair maintained, would be 'tough on crime' and 'tough on the causes of crime', and, in the ensuing debate, the Labour Party deployed the entire lexicon of 'get tough' soundbites in an attempt to wrest the political initiative from the Conservatives' grasp (Chapman and Savage, 1999).

In July 1994 Tony Blair became leader of the Labour Party, and Jack Straw became Shadow Home Secretary. Straw's job was to retain the political initiative that Blair had seized in the furore surrounding the Bulger case. Straw's task now was to plant firmly in popular consciousness the idea that New Labour was the 'natural party of law and order', while stressing that Labour offered not a radical departure from, nor a reversal of, the Conservative's stated objectives on youth crime, but rather a policy that integrated popular Conservative law-and-order themes with vastly improved economy, efficiency and effectiveness.

New Labour's youth justice strategy was translated into law in record time. Its legislative intentions were embodied in the *No More Excuses* White Paper, a title deliberately chosen to signal the Labour Party's abandonment of its traditional role as the party of penal reform. Following a brief consultation period in 1997, the White Paper became the Crime and Disorder Act on 31 July 1998. It had taken Harold Wilson's government five years to get the Children and Young Persons Act (1969) onto the statute books. Mrs Thatcher, her law-and-order bluster notwithstanding, took three years to enshrine her ideas in the Criminal Justice Act (1982). New Labour enacted its law in 14 months. The speed of the legislative process attested to the political centrality of youth crime and youth justice policy to New Labour's thinking.

The Crime and Disorder Act (1998) epitomized the New Labour project. That the ideas it embodied came from across the political spectrum, though mainly from the political Right, attested to New Labour's new-found 'toughness'. The criminal justice provisions promised the victims of crime a voice in the outcome of criminal cases, while the new civil measures offered to 'empower' 'middle England' by handing it the legal and administrative means to re-establish order and civility in its 'communities'. The entire system was to be robustly managed at a local level, to ensure that it all 'joined up' and offered 'best value' to the public. Moreover, it was now subject to central government audit; and God help the laggard local authority or hapless police chief whose performance was found wanting. The political message was clear, and it was pre-eminently a message to the Conservative voters who had switched their loyalties to Labour in 1997 that New Labour could be trusted on law-and-order.

The Crime and Disorder Act (1998)

Jack Straw described the Crime and Disorder Act as 'the most radical shake-up of youth justice in 30 years'. The Act required chief executives of local authorities to bring into being Youth Offending Teams (YOTs), modelled on the multi-agency diversion panels of the

1980s, and staffed by personnel seconded from the police, the probation service, education services, social services and the health service. YOTs had to produce a Youth Offending Plan specifying how the team would organize and discharge its functions, and how it would liaise with other statutory and voluntary bodies. The Act created the Youth Justice Board of England and Wales to oversee the development of the YOTs, specify the standards of efficiency and effectiveness to be achieved by them, and assume control if they were under-performing. The government hoped that, in this way, comparable standards would be achieved throughout England and Wales. These changes represented a significant move towards a national system of youth justice in England and Wales. The Youth Justice Board also assumed responsibility for the rationalization and modernization of 'the secure estate', comprising the remaining local authority CHEs and secure units, prison department Young Offender Institutions, which dealt with youngsters aged 15–18, the three Youth Treatment Centres run by the Department of Health, and the new Secure Training Centres for 12–15 year olds which the government planned to introduce.

The structure of the 'new youth justice' (Goldson, 2000) was derived in large part from the recommendations in the Audit Commission report on the youth justice system, *Misspent Youth* (1996). *Misspent Youth* was primarily concerned with whether or not the youth justice system of England and Wales offered 'value for money'. Its authors brought extensive experience and expertise in economics and social policy to their task and, in consultation with psychologically orientated criminologists in Britain and the United States, they deliberated on the origins of youth crime and the likely impact of a range of interventions on young offenders. They concluded that:

> The current system for dealing with youth crime is inefficient and expensive, while little is being done to deal effectively with juvenile nuisance. The present arrangements are failing the young people – who are not being guided away from offending towards constructive activities. They are also failing victims – those who suffer from young people's inconsiderate behaviour, and from vandalism and loss of property from thefts and burglaries. And they lead to waste in a variety of forms, including lost time, as public servants process the same young offenders through the courts time and again; lost rents, as people refuse to live in high crime areas; lost business, as people steer clear of troubled areas; and waste of young people's potential.
>
> (Audit Commission, 1996, p. 96)

The central messages in *Misspent Youth* were that we should be intervening earlier, before the actual commission of offences if necessary, and that we should be targeting young persons' offending behaviour.

Youth crime and the family: science and politics

How the family came to be a central focus of New Labour's youth justice strategy offers a salutary example of the ways in which governments employ social science. Economic management, crime and the family were the three key areas in which New Labour had seized the political initiative from the Conservatives in the run-up to the 1997 General Election. In the 1980s and 1990s, 'welfare-dependent', 'underclass' families had become a key focus for a newly emergent neo-liberal intelligentsia and right-wing communitarians (Etzioni, 1995). Theorists like Murray (1994) and Dennis (1997) in the United Kingdom had argued that the problems of youth crime could be traced back to the children of the urban 'underclass'. However, New Labour was committed to 'evidence-based' policy, and evidence about the existence of an underclass, with a different set of cultural values, and the role of underclass families in fostering youth crime was in short supply.

In *Tackling the Causes of Crime* (1996), a discussion document produced by the Conservatives, eight 'key risk factors' associated with youth offending were identified: 'parenting', 'truancy', 'drug abuse', 'lack of facilities', 'homelessness', 'unemployment', 'low income' and 'economic recession'. These 'risks' are similar to those cited in the Audit Commission's *Misspent Youth* (1996), which also derived its evidence from the findings of the Cambridge Study of 411 South London boys undertaken by David Farrington and Donald West between 1961 and 1985 (West and Farrington, 1973). However, in *Misspent Youth* these risk factors are divided into 'foreground' and 'background' factors. Familial and developmental factors occupy the foreground, while factors such as family income, employment and the socio-economic status of the neighbourhood are relegated to the background. The 1997 *No More Excuses* White Paper drew on *Crime and the Family*, a pamphlet written by three New Labour insiders (Utting, Bright and Hendrickson, 1993), which, in turn drew on the Cambridge Study data. Despite Farrington's observation (2000) that it is not possible to distinguish between those risk factors which are causes and those which are effects, *Crime and the Family* asserted that 'the tangled roots of delinquency lie, to a considerable extent, inside the family'. In consequence, the *No More Excuses* White Paper proceeded to reduce the multiplicity of risk factors originally identified by West and Farrington to three main groupings: parenting, schooling and peers, with the key risk factors identified as 'being male', 'poor parental discipline', 'criminal parents' and 'poor school performance'.

These claims are remarkable because a significant body of contemporary research, utilizing huge databases, suggests that neighbourhood of residence has as significant an impact on serious juvenile offending as the quality of parenting (Jones *et al.*, 2000); that 'risk factors' will operate quite differently in different cities and, indeed, in different neighbourhoods; that in certain well-resourced, higher socio-economic status neighbourhoods, all predictions of future chronic delinquency based on a risk-factor assessment failed to materialize and that offending by children and young people with the lowest individual risk factors occurred significantly more frequently in the lowest socio-economic status neighbourhoods (Wikstrom and Loeber, 1997). Nonetheless, in an interview with the *Observer* (1 February 1998), Jack Straw felt able to assert that:

> . . . all the serious research shows that one of the biggest causes of serious juvenile delinquency is inconsistent parenting. We need to bring parenting out as a public issue so people feel able to talk about it. It is not easy, but one of my tenets in politics is that we should try the difficult issues.
>
> (Straw, 1998, p. 10)

Thus, by 1995, New Labour's emergent 'family policy' had more or less converged with its 'criminal justice policy'. Indeed, the advent of the Parenting Order in the 1998 Act must be seen against the backdrop of New Labour's high-profile commitment to the rejuvenation of the family as an 'effective caring and controlling social unit', and the pre-eminence the government gave to what Straw described as family forms characterized by 'two participating parents'. As Tony Blair declared in his speech to the 1995 Labour Party conference, 'a young country that wants to be a strong country cannot be morally neutral about the family'.

The 1998 Act marked a reaction against both 1960s' welfarism and 1980s' progressive minimalism. The measures it introduced focused on the criminal deeds of young offenders rather than on their social or psychological needs. As the title of the White Paper which preceded the Act, *No More Excuses*, suggests, the idea of youth crime as a product of poverty, social inequality or psychological disadvantage was supplanted by an emphasis on individual and family responsibility. The theme of responsibility was underscored by the abandonment of the principle of *doli incapax*, a defining feature of the juvenile jurisdiction in the United Kingdom from its inception. *Doli incapax* holds that in their dealings with children below the age of 14 who have broken the law, the courts must proceed from the assumption that, by dint of their immaturity, and even though they may have known that they were doing wrong, children do not have criminal intent and do not fully understand the consequences of their actions for themselves or their victims. As a result, the onus is upon the prosecution to demonstrate criminal intent. In the case of 14–17 year olds, by contrast, the onus is on the defence to demonstrate the absence of criminal intent. The change of emphasis in the 1998 Act aimed to send the message that considerations of responsibility, culpability and retribution were henceforth to have a much higher priority in the youth justice system. The minimalist strategies of the 1980s and 1990s had aimed to divert youngsters in trouble out of the system, in order to deal with them informally within mainstream services. The 1998 Act abandoned both diversion and normalization in favour of a strategy aiming to bring both first-time offenders and troublesome youngsters below the age of criminal responsibility within the ambit of the criminal justice system. Whereas welfarism and progressive minimalism strove to minimize the stigma associated with involvement in the youth justice system, the 1998 Act employs stigma as a deterrent strategy. Indeed, a central theme in the *No More Excuses* White Paper is that more young offenders should be brought before the courts earlier, and more swiftly, and that the anonymity traditionally afforded to juvenile offenders could, in certain cases, be waived if the magistrate deemed this to be in the public interest.

Systemic logic

The Criminal Justice Act (1998) provided both a stage upon which New Labour could demonstrate its political grit and an opportunity to remedy the administrative shortcomings of the existing system. However, the reworking of priorities, and the incorporation of new system elements which the Act required paid scant attention to the fact that a new *system*, which like all bureaucratic systems had a logic of its own, was being brought into being.

For example, it seemed to have occurred to no one that if the YOTs, which were modelled on the multi-agency youth diversion panels of the 1980s, were inserted into a system that aimed to draw far greater numbers into it, rather than divert them out, then the system would be overwhelmed by the new influx, forced to offer its new clientele a substantially reduced service, or require a significant increase in funding. Nor did anybody appear to have considered that early induction into the system might, through a combination of stigmatiz-ation, deviancy amplification and administrative drift, accelerate young people's progress through it.

The youth justice system brought into being by the 1998 Act allowed formal pre-emptive intervention with populations previously beyond the reach of the youth justice and child protection systems, via Child Safety, Anti-Social Behaviour, Child Curfew and Parenting Orders. This brought a new, younger, population into the purview of the criminal justice system. The requirement that all first offenders be dealt with formally, the ending of police discretion with regard to repeat cautioning, and the replacement of the caution with one Reprimand and one Final Warning, meant that this larger number of children and young people in trouble entering the system exhausted this diversion-ary option at a younger age and an earlier stage in their offending careers.

The Act repealed the Absolute and Conditional Discharge, disposals previously imposed in 28 per cent of cases, and replaced them with the *Referral Order*. Thus, having been found guilty of an offence, a young person is referred to a Referral Panel, with a professional and lay membership, which will determine the nature of the penalty to be imposed and the type of programme a child or young person should pursue. Any prosecution flowing from a breach of the Absolute or Conditional Discharge required that the young person in question should re-offend, that the offence should be detected, that s/he should be apprehended, charged, prosecuted and found guilty. As with the introduction of the Probation Order in 1907, a breach of a *Referral Order*, by contrast requires only that the youngster fail to attend a session of their 'programme'. As evidence from a similar scheme operating in Denmark indicates, this is very likely to result in a higher number of young people re-appearing in court.

The Act introduces two new 'community penalties' to add to the existing Supervision Order: an Action Plan Order and a Reparation Order. These intensive, 'evidence-based', community penalties are designed to deter young offenders who have not been deterred at an earlier stage. The architects of the Act presumed that the proven efficacy of the 'evidence-based' programmes, which underpin these penalties, would ensure that only a handful of the most intractable offenders would persist beyond this stage. (The shortcomings of these measures and the flaws in the evidence which supports them are discussed at length in Pawson and Tilley, 1997; Matthews and Pitts, 2000; Pitts, 2001). Indeed the whole logic of the 1998 Act is predicated on the success of these measures. These community penalties were to be the means whereby custody would be averted and the juvenile custodial population reduced. Such was the government's confidence in these measures that the Act specified that a community penalty could be imposed on only two occasions. In fact, over 50 per cent of young people sentenced to community penalties re-offend and, taken together with breaches of other conditions of these Orders, community penalties appear to be accelerating many young people's progress towards imprisonment.

The 'fast-tracking of 'persistent' and/or 'serious' young offenders, introduced by the Act, is having a similar effect. This means that offenders appear more frequently and, as a result, their charges are dealt with separately, thus increasing the likelihood that they will attract a custodial sentence. The issue of the definition of seriousness and persistence in the Act is itself contentious. Hagell and Newburn (1994) discovered in their research into this group of young offenders that the 'serious' are seldom persistent and the 'persistent' seldom serious. As a result, secure training centres and youth jails are tending to attract growing numbers of persistent minor offenders who, while fulfilling the administrative criteria for persistence, pose a minimal threat to the public and, more than anything else, require help to cope with their usually chaotic lives rather than a spell of imprisonment.

Pressures towards increased use of custody have also been intensified by the extension of the power of the Youth Courts to remand children and young people directly into secure and penal establishments, the unequivocal signals sent to magistrates by the expansion of secure and custodial provision, and the Home Secretary's observation, in Spring 1998, that 'prisons are a demand-led service; if the courts want to impose custodial sentences, it is my job to provide the cells'. A promised 400 additional places in Secure Training Centres, the 'three strikes' sentencing strategy for repeat juvenile offenders introduced in June 2001, and the *de facto* one-strike, 'breach' conditions introduced in the Criminal Justice and Court Services Bill (2000) all attest to the growing centrality of penal incapacitation to New Labour's youth justice strategy.

Locking up children

In Spring 2002 Britain had more children and young people under lock and key than at any time since the youth justice system was brought into being in 1908, and more than any other Western European country. There were also more children, young people and parents under the supervision of youth justice personnel. Between 1995 and 1999 the number of children and young people sentenced to some form of custodial confinement in England and Wales (excluding those held under the Mental Health Act 1983) rose by approximately 30 per cent, from 5,863 to 8,492. These figures are the more remarkable because this period has seen a steady decline in the crime rate. Not only were more young people being held in custody, they were also being held for longer. Between 1989 and 1999 the average custodial sentence for 15–17 year-old boys increased from 5.6 months to 10.3 months. For girls the increase was from 5.5 months to 7.1 months.

Most Young Offender Institutions (YOIs) are underfunded, over-crowded and mismanaged. Even in the better institutions, only 30 per cent of young prisoners receive education. At Feltham YOI during 2002 only 10 per cent of inmates were attending education classes, despite the fact that in the system generally 54 per cent of inmates score below level one (GCSE standard) in reading ability. Sir David Ramsbotham, the recently retired Chief Inspector of Prisons, found that over 50 per cent of young prisoners on remand and 30 per cent of those serving a sentence have a diagnosable mental health problem. These problems are compounded by widespread drug abuse, violence and intimidation. Self-harm is at record levels. In the past 10 years, 22 boys aged 15–17 have taken their own lives in YOIs in England and Wales, and one has been killed by a cell-mate. Among 18–20 year olds, the figure for successful suicide attempts during the period is 65. A recent Chief Inspector's report on Feltham YOI noted that 'the boredom and isolation of spending long hours in a cell was overwhelming'; the regime there was, he said, 'rotten to the core'.

The future of youth justice

Since the 1970s the distinctiveness of the youth justice systems in the United Kingdom and the United States has been progressively eroded (Fagan and Zimring, 2000). In the 1970s and 1980s, progressive minimalists successfully established the 'child's right to punishment' rather than treatment. In the 1990s penal populists introduced a range of penalties that aimed to hold young offenders to their responsibilities, replaced rehabilitation with correctionalism, and repackaged youth imprisonment as a valuable correctional resource.

It is ironic that the social and political conditions accompanying the erosion of the distinctive youth justice systems on both sides of the Atlantic are similar in many ways to those that pertained at its birth. In the first decade of the twenty-first century we once again confront unprecedented levels of migration, burgeoning social and economic polarization, family breakdown and rising levels of street crime, particularly in the poorest urban neighbourhoods (Pitts and Hope, 1997; Pitts, 2001). Meanwhile sociology points to changing class relations and a population, variously described as the 'socially ex-cluded' or an 'underclass', which, to all intents and purposes, has fallen through the bottom of the class structure.

However, whereas 100 years ago social-scientific ideas, pressures from interest groups and the priorities of modernizing governments led to social and institutional reform, the contemporary orthodoxy appears to point to the need to inculcate self-control into the offspring of an impoverished 'underclass'. The victims of crime have emerged as a significant political lobby and, like the proponents of restorative justice, they demand that the victim be given a voice and the perpetrators be held to account. For their part, modernizing govern-ments appear to be far more concerned with the cost-effective management of the 'risks' posed to the populace by young offenders than their social needs.

This is not to suggest that the problem of youth crime can be solved simply by the restoration of an adequately resourced youth justice system. As we have seen, the problem of youth crime in late Victorian England was not solved by the creation of a separate system of youth justice. The major factor influencing the falling crime rate in the early part of the 20th century was the alleviation of poverty by sustained political action and economic intervention, and the gradual narrowing of the gap between the 'haves' and the 'have-nots'

If we compare different societies, or the same societies over time, it is evident that there is a strong relationship between the degree of 'social justice' or 'social inclusion' pertaining in a society and the nature and volume of youth crime. Between 1987 and 1994, for example, Sweden, the European Union country with the lowest income differentials, experienced the second lowest annual rise in its crime rate (0.4 per cent per annum). Meanwhile, England and Wales, with the highest income differentials, experienced the second highest annual rise in its crime rate (4.4 per cent per annum). This, and many similar examples, have led social theorists and criminologists to locate the origins of crime in general, and youth crime in particular, in the experience of 'relative deprivation' (Merton, 1938; Cloward and Ohlin, 1960; Lea and Young, 1988; Young, 1999).

To addess contemporary problems of relative deprivation and social exclusion will require sustained social and economic intervention on the part of government. However, the imperatives of the free market and the fiscal constraints placed on national governments by the financial markets (Hutton, 1995), the IMF, and the European Central Bank (Bordieu, 1998) have meant that governments lack both the means and the political mandate to protect society from the social dislocation generated by globalization, and the ability to embark on economic and social reform on a scale sufficient to ameliorate the problems of crime, income polarization and social exclusion. In these circumstances, modern, centre-left, governments have tended to focus on social and criminal justice policy rather than robust economic intervention, aiming to change the behaviour of individuals rather than their social and economic circumstances.

The fact that the youth justice system alone cannot make a dent upon the social and economic factors that ultimately determine the nature, level and distribution of youth crime does not mean that it can do nothing constructive however. If linked effectively with high-quality educational, health, housing and welfare provision, it can make an impact upon the lives of children and young people who become involved in crime. Indeed, the Crime and Disorder Act 1998, in establishing the Youth Offending Teams, created an entity well-suited to this task. Moreover, other recent government initiatives in the areas of education, training, employment, drugs and leaving care are beginning to flesh-out the kinds of provision with which YOTs could connect. However, the potential of the YOTs and the band of supportive services being developed around them is, as we have noted, all too often undermined by the politicization of youth crime and our responses to it, political pragmatism and managerial rigidity. The past two decades have seen a welter of new youth justice legislation, far too much of it cobbled together in a hurry by Home Secretaries with an urgent political need to demonstrate their toughness. This is the legacy of penal populism, a political fashion that threatens to undermine such positive potential as lies within the new youth justice system.

References

Audit Commission (1996) *Misspent Youth: Young People and Crime*, London: The Audit Commission.

Bourdieu P. (1998) Acts of Resistance: Against the New Myths of Our Time, Cambridge: Polity Press.

Chapman, S. and Savage, P. (1999) 'The New Politics of Law and Order: Labour, Crime and Justice', Powell M. (ed.) New Labour, *New Welfare State: the Third Way in British Social Policy*, Bristol: The Policy Press.

Cloward, R. and Ohlin, L. (1960) *Delinquency and Opportunity*, London: Routledge & Kegan Paul.

Crimmens, D. and Pitts, J. (2000) *Positive Residential Practice, Learning the Lessons of the 1990s*, Lyme Regis: Russell House Publishing.

Currie, E. (1991) 'International Developments in Crime and Social Policy' NACRO, *Crime and Public Policy*, London: NACRO.

Dennis, N. (1997) (ed.) *Zero Tolerance – Policing a Free Society*, London: Institute of Economic Affairs.

Etzioni, A. (1995) *The Spirit of Community*, London: Fontana.

Fagan, J. and Zimring, F. (2000) *The Changing Borders of Juvenile Justice*, Chicago: Chicago University Press.

Farrington, D. (2000) Explaining and Preventing Crime: The Globalisation of Knowledge, *Criminology*, Vol. 38, No. 1, February 1-24.

Feeley, M. and Simon, J. (1992) 'The New Penology: Notes on the Emerging Strategy of Corrections and its Implementation', *Criminology*, 30(4), pp. 452-74.

Feld, B. (1988) 'The Juvenile Court Meets the Principle of the Offense: Legislative Changes in Juvenile Waiver Statutes', *Journal of Criminal Law and Criminology*, 78, pp. 471-533.

Foucault, M. (1977) *Discipline and Punish: the Birth of the Prison*, London: Allen Lane, Penguin Books.

Garland, D. (1985) *Punishment and Welfare: A History of Penal Strategies*, London: Gower.

Garland, D. (2001) *The Culture of Control*, Oxford: Oxford University Press.

Goldson, B. (2000) (ed.) The New Youth Justice, Lyme Regis: Russell House Publishing.

Hagell, A. and Newburn, T. (1994) *Persistent Young Offenders*, London: Policy Studies Institute.

Hetherington, R. (1997) *Protecting Children: Messages from Europe*, Lyme Regis: Russell House Publishing.

Hutton, W. (1995) *The State We're In*, London: Jonathan Cape.

Krisburg, B and Austin, J. (1993) *Re-inventing Juvenile Justice*, London: Sage Publications.

Lea, J. and Young, J. (1988) What Is To Be Done About Law and Order, London: Penguin.

Lemert, E. (1970) *Social Action and Legal Change: Revolution within the Juvenile Court*, Chicago: Aldine.

Lilley, R., Cullen, F. and Ball, R. (1995) *Criminological Theory*, London: Sage Publications.

Merton, R. (1938) Social Structure and Anomie, *American Sociological Review*, 3, 672-82.

Matthews, R. and Pitts, J. (1998) Rehabilitation, Recidivism and Realism: Evaluating Violence Reduction Programs in Prison, *The Prison Journal*, Vol.78, No.4, Dec. pp. 390-405, Sage Publications, C/A.

Matza, D. (1969) *Becoming Deviant*, Englewood Cliffs, New Jersey: Prentice Hall.

Murray, C, (1994) Underclass: The Crisis Deepens, London: Institute of Economic Affairs.

Newburn, T. (1995) Crime and Criminal Justice Policy, London: Longman.

Ohlin, L. (ed.) (1979) *Prisoners in America*, Englewood Cliffs NJ: Prentice Hall.

Pawson, R. and Tilley, N. (1997) Realistic Evaluation, London: Sage.

Platt, A. (1969) *The Childsavers*, Chicago: Chicago University Press.

Pitts, J. (2001) The New Politics of Youth Crime: Discipline or Solidarity, Basingstoke: Palgrave.

Simon, J. (2000) From the Big House to the Warehouse: Re-thinking Prisons and State Government in the 20th Century, *Punishment & Society*, Vol. 2, No. 2, April, 213-34.

Szmanski, L. (1987) Statutory Exclusions of Crime from Juvenile Court Jurisdiction, unpublished manuscript, Washington, National Center for Juvenile Justice.

Utting, W., Bright, J. and Hendrickson, P. (1993) Crime and the Family, Improving Child Rearing and Preventing Delinquency, Family Policy Studies Centre, Paper No. 16 London.

West, D. and Farrington, D. (1973) Who Becomes Delinquent?, London: Heinemann.

Wilson, J. J. (1994) *The Future of the Juvenile Justice System: Can We Preserve It?*, Paper presented at the 21st National Conference of Juvenile Justice, Boston.

Wilson, J. Q. (1975) *Thinking about Crime*, New York: Basic Books.

Wolfgang, M. (1982) 'Abolish the Juvenile Court System', *California Laywer*, 17, pp. 12-13.

Young, J. (1999) *The Exclusive Society*, London: Sage Publications.

Chapter 5

It's the family, stupid: continuities and reinterpretations of the dysfunctional family as the cause of crime in three political periods

Jayne Mooney

> Strong families are the centre of peaceful and safe communities. Parents have a critical role in teaching their children the difference between right and wrong . . . Respect is all important, and this is missing in families that behave dysfunctionally.
>
> (Home Office, 2003, p. 8)

So states the recent White Paper *Respect and Responsibility: Taking a Stand against Anti-Social Behaviour* (March 2003). Here the Labour Government places the family as the most fundamental bulwark in the control of crime and anti-social behaviour. During the preceding year the newspapers were full of the problem of street crime, of the youths who committed these crimes and the poor parenting which supposedly caused it. One columnist spoke of 'feral children' (literally wild beasts), who stalk the inner city estates, and praised the Prime Minister Tony Blair's suggestion that the state benefits for single mothers should be withdrawn if, as Bruce Anderson puts it, 'they fail to keep their brats under control' (the *Independent*, 29 April 2002). Meanwhile, a woman was sent to prison for allowing her children to truant, and the government has allocated £90 million to help schools develop the electronic tracking of pupils in order to halt truancy, while the Metropolitan Police have proposals to create a database of potential young offenders including those youngsters – some as young as six – who have never committed crimes. Once again, the focus of government is on the family and family breakdown as the cause of crime.

In May 1997 the New Labour government was elected by a landslide. A major focus in its policy, through a series of legislative Acts, has been crime as a major problem in society and the family as the key building-block of a civilized society. In this chapter I want to suggest there is nothing new in this, and trace both the differences and continuities in the attitudes of governments from the 1960s onwards, highlighting three separate moments: first, the social democratic ascendancy of the period up until the Conservative election of 1979; second, the radical neo-liberalism of the Conservative years of Thatcher and Major; and, finally, the present New Labour government. But, as an introduction, it will be useful to contrast the way in which radical criminology views the role of the family in the genesis of crime with that of right-wing or establishment criminology.

The central tenet of a radical criminology, as its name suggests, is a criminology that deals with the root causes of crime and which locates these in the class-based and patriarchal nature of contemporary societies. This also locates crime in the nature of market capitalism: in its unequal class structure and in the rampant individualism that the market engenders; that is, within a class structure which systematically frustrates the meritocratic ideals that serve to legitimate the system, and within the core values of a competitive individualism that shape and guide people's anger and frustrations. Furthermore, radical criminology locates crime within a patriarchal system, where the hegemony of dominance of men over women, when threatened, results in violence and aggression against women. As Anthony Giddens points out in *The Transformation of Intimacy* (1992) such hegemony was particularly threatened by the massive entry of women into the labour market in the postwar period and women's increased level of autonomy.

In contrast, the historic role of establishment criminology (in its many varieties, from positivism to control theory) is to ignore the causes of crime in the wider structure of society and to locate it within the microstructures of society (the family, the school) or the individual's genetic or psychological predisposition. Juvenile delinquency, for example, is blamed on maladministration in controlling the young (whether in the schools or the family) and on the inherent nature of individuals, perhaps influenced by events earlier in life. Thus, establishment criminology takes attention away from criticism of the wider society while reversing the direction of causality: it is not a problematic society that causes delinquents but delinquents who cause problems for society. Solve the problem of delinquency, solve the problems of administration and predisposition, and you have solved the problem of crime. In this equation the family has been the perennial fulcrum of analysis, its key role usually taken as obvious. For radical criminology such 'obviousness' is severely questioned. First of all, it must be noted that the family is a prime site of crime. In my own study a full half of violence has been found to occur within the family (Mooney, 2000): it should not be thought automatically that 'crime' is something out there that occurs outside of the sanctuary of the family. Second the institution of the family is very frequently a cause of crime. I have mentioned Giddens's notion of violence occurring as a threat to patriarchal dominance. The 'strong' family may well be the repressive family, to both women and children, where violence breaks out in an attempt to maintain authority. In such a situation the break-up of the family often results in the lowering of violent crime. In this context it should be seen as a crime-prevention strategy not a delinquency engendering one. Furthermore, the strong traditional family that uses violent child-rearing techniques may well create notions in children that violence is a major way to solve problems, a belief that fits well with much wider cultural values portrayed in the cinema and television. Third, the family is often a fundamental and necessary building block of successful organized-crime networks. Organized crime needs the strong family. The extended family is a haven of trust in a divided society and is scarcely an inhibitor of corporate crime, where often the needs of the family over the rest of society is used as a rationale by offenders. There is, of course, the residual rational kernel of the 'weak family leads to crime' thesis, which holds that the disorganized family (of whatever shape or structure) may contribute to community disintegration and to crimes of disorganization (in contrast to crimes of organization and control as discussed previously), such as vandalism, petty theft and so on. Here it must be admitted the argument is on surer footing; but the problem of establishment criminology is that, given its underlying axiom of ignoring the wider structure, it puts emphasis on the family as if it were separate from the wider society. It commits what Elliot Currie (1985) calls 'the fallacy of autonomy'. For crime does not spring fully fledged out of the weak family, but is a product of the criminogenic nature of a wider society of which the family is part.

Thus, to summarize, radical criminology believes that certain types of crime are uncontrolled by family socialization, others are augmented by successful socialization, while crimes of disorganization are facilitated by a weak family structure although engendered by the criminogenic nature of the wider society. The problem, in the latter instance, is not that the role of the family should be ignored but rather that in establishment criminology it is overstressed and decontextualized. Let us now look at the three periods mentioned above in this light.

The Social Democratic Labour administration

Crime in the postwar period up to the 1990s was viewed in the context of a well-established welfare state, full (male) employment and constantly rising living standards. In this scenario politicians of both major parties, but particularly those within the Labour Party, saw crime as a marginal phenomenon, a product of dysfunctional families who had been untouched by progress and prosperity. It was a temporary phenomenon, and one that trained social workers would eliminate by targeting that minority of families whose child rearing was insufficiently capable. As Gordon Hughes states:

> By the 1960s in the UK ... it was argued that deprivation or lack of opportunity could no longer be considered to be at the heart of the social problem of delinquency. Instead the source of the problem was viewed as residing within the pathological character-istics and dynamics of certain 'problem families' and in the transmission of 'inadequacies' from one generation to the next. Delinquency was thus seen as a temporary problem residing in certain working-class families left behind in the post-war social democratic prosperity. In turn, the new quasi-professions of the welfare state, such as health visiting and social work, were seen as being crucial in tackling this problem. It was their task to educate families in child-rearing and to rehabilitate the residue of young people that came under the jurisdiction of the criminal justice system. The family therefore had to be reformed if delinquency was to be tackled.
>
> (Hughes, 1998, p. 47)

Crime was viewed, therefore, as a marginal phenomenon of a successful welfare state where, given these terms of reference, it was 'obviously pathological' and the product of dysfunctional families. The role of the welfare state was to intervene and integrate.

For the first decade and a half of the postwar period the crime rate fluctuated but rose only marginally; however, from the 1960s onwards the crime rate rose remorselessly each year. The Conservative and

Labour governments of this period were faced with a recalcitrant and sizeable phenomenon. Yet the family remained the key institution used to explain criminality. The pivot of this explanation shifted from the dysfunctional family to the broken home, the growth in divorce and illegitimacy paralleled the growth in crime, and it was then but a short step to presume that the one caused the other.

The Conservative years

The Conservative administration, 1979–1997, was characterized by a neo-liberalism which trumpeted the ascendancy of the market. Crime was located firmly in the individual rather than in society. Thus, Michael Howard, then Home Secretary, said in 1993,

> We have to recognise where crime begins. I don't mean that we should listen to the woolly-headed theories that society is at fault. . . . Of course not – we can leave that message to others. We must do more to teach children the difference between right and wrong. . . . It must start at home. And it must also be taught in our schools. . . . Above all, it must be taught by example.
>
> (speech to House of Commons, June 1993)

By 1991 the number of crimes known to the police in England and Wales passed the 5 million mark. The previous ten years had seen the largest numerical increase in recorded crime since records began. It would not have taken much mental agility to correlate such a quantative leap with the economic recession and a period of Conservative government which was intent on deepening the market society. But it was not in the market place but in the family that commentators chose to find the cause of such an increase in crime. For example, in the furore about youth crime that followed the James Bulger[1] murder, Peter Lilley – a senior government minister – made it clear that the crime wave was, in his view, unrelated to the recession. Meanwhile the Prime Minister, John Major, categorically stated that to seek the causes of crime in the wider society was futile. Instead, he said we should look at the problems of the family, and rather surprisingly he blamed socialism – by this he meant the welfare state. In this context the figure of the single mother became the focus of all the hostility that the Conservative Party held towards the welfare state. She was presented as a welfare-dependent scrounger, who had chosen to get pregnant to gain priority in council-housing lists over the respectable married poor.

It was remarkable that, in order to avoid putting any blame on the economy, the Conservatives blamed the ills of society on its most deprived members.

The focus, once again, was on the family, and crime was conflated with juvenile delinquency. But the crime rate was enormous, and the notion of a few dysfunctional families scarcely fitted the bill. A more substantial case, therefore, was needed, but again one that would not touch the wider inequalities of society. So, the neo-liberal explanation was that the welfare state had created a dependency culture of single mothers and feckless fathers, which had, in turn, created a maladjusted population. Thus, the social democratic diagnosis is reversed – the welfare state causes, rather than prevents, delinquency. And free will, and thus responsibility, enter the equation: the feckless underclass chooses not to work and consequently generates a culture that schools its children in delinquency.

Thus the Conservative years sought to exclude rather than include. The Conservatives sought to roll back the welfare state, and conjured up the notion of an underclass, which was demonized and blamed for the troubles of society. And for Conservatives private crime-prevention measures became a major strategy against crime; the public were held as responsible for crime control. Indeed, there was an element of returning crime-control to the community. Overall, the Conservative years represented a period when the crime rate rose seemingly inexorably year by year. It was an era where the state very understandably tended to disclaim responsibility for such a recalcitrant problem. In contrast the situation for New Labour in the period that followed was that of declining crime rates and a situation where the 'the sovereign state' would claim, in a very precise way, to be in control of crime rates (see Garland, 2001, Young, 2003).

New Labour

The New Labour government was first voted in, in 1997, on a manifesto in which crime control was a central pillar of policy. This was in contrast to past Labour administrations, where crime and delinquency were distinctly minor concerns. Furthermore, the maintenance and shoring up of the family was a matter that permeated so many policy statements. Tony Blair is famous for his couplet 'tough on crime, tough on the causes of crime', and the last line of this, for many, signalled that the Labour administration would once and for all locate the causes of crime in the deep structure of society. But this was not so: in practice, the first line of the couplet meant punishment and the maintenance of a large-scale prison system, the second located the causes of crime within the family and poor parenting. The key research influence was the work of David Farringdon who, in a 1995 article with Michael Tonry, prioritized above all 'developmental prevention' as the major strategy to combat crime; that is, intervention in the family and the school to ensure that the development of the child occurs in a way that is 'normal' and ipso-facto non-delinquent. As they noted, 'the central insight is Shakespeare's that the child is father to the man. . . . Developmental prevention is the new frontier of crime prevention' (Farringdon and Tonry, 1995, p. 10).

The New Labour administration took on board much of the Conservative rhetoric about underclass and fecklessness, but these notions have been incorporated into its central policy motif, 'social inclusion' (see Young and Matthews, this volume); that is, it views the underclass as socially excluded, and therefore what is necessary is to incorporate its members fully into society. Thus, New Labour's intention is to return the single mother to work (often in ways that would seem financially absurd), and to tackle head on problem families and estates rather than leave them to their own devices. Thus, the first policy decision in office was to set up the Social Exclusion Unit to coordinate the process of social inclusion. The forceful nature of such inclusionary policies, both in terms of inclusion in the workforce and inclusion in the family (witness the Social Exclusion Unit's proposals (1999) on teenage pregnancies), has strong echoes of Clinton's awesomely entitled 'The Personal Responsibility and Work Opportunity Act of 1996'.

But it cannot be overstressed that genuine social inclusion should not be confused with coercive inclusion in the labour market at poverty wages or forcefully created families backed by the threat of hostel accommodation for single mothers. And there cannot be any doubt that such measures are not perceived by the people concerned as inclusionary measures but as exclusionary ones, which confine them not to the middle of society but to the margins.

The stress of New Labour is on creating a responsible citizenship by a proactive state. In this attempt, they contrast both with social democratic Labour (which talked of citizens' rights, playing down individual responsibility, and advocating state intervention) and Conservatism (which talked of the responsibilities of the citizen and attempted to reduce state intervention). But the continuity throughout, despite fundamentally different political philosophies, has been in the idea of the weak family as the key to the crime problem. The wider structural factors are explicitly denied. Thus, at a Nexus Conference on the Third Way held in London, Jack Straw (Home Secretary 1997–2001) talked of how good schools occur in poor areas because of good head teachers and that poverty does not link with crime because many impoverished parents have good parenting skills. Time and time again the rising statistics of one-parent families, teenage pregnancies and divorces are placed against the rise in crime and the 'obvious' conclusions drawn.

The most profound change that has occurred in the social structure since World War II is the massive entry of women into the labour force, although concentrated in low-pay, low-status occupations. If this has been accompanied by a rise in the level of aspirations and possibilities for women, and a greater ability to deal with marriages or partnerships that do not work out, well, all to the good. The levels of domestic violence against women scarcely suggests there is no justified reason for the break-up of many families, even when it is economically disadvantageous.

The greater flexibility in family relationships scarcely explains the crime rate. The 5 million crimes reported to the police every year in England and Wales, with an estimated 10 million or more unreported, cannot conceivably be blamed on that fraction of single mothers who are on state benefits and have adolescent sons. Further a new scenario has developed, for since 1995, two years before New Labour came to power, the crime rate has been falling for the first time since the 1950s. During a period where the number of single mothers and broken families continued to increase, the crime rate did not continue upwards but did exactly the reverse. At the present time the crime rate is at the level it was in the 1980s, and remains a massive problem of course. But what is important to stress is that the weakening of the family cannot explain the change in direction. Indeed, as 'broken' homes and single parents continue to proliferate, the crime rate has dropped. Yet the New Labour government, as Jock Young has emphasized (in this volume), has not credited this fall on the wider structural factors of prosperity, a drop in unemployment and economic stability but has perversely insisted, once more, on continuing to blame the family for the crime that remains.

So there we have it: governments at all three political moments described have attempted to disconnect the wider social and economic situation from the facts of crime, locating the weak family as the prime cause of criminality. Yet the supposed weakness of the family, although a constant theme, is recast with each political change, seen as isolated patches of dysfunction in social democracy, welfare-dependent and excluded under neo-liberalism, and welfare dependent yet redeemable through work and self-discipline under New Labour. Nowhere are the deep inequalities that stretch through our society mentioned, nowhere is class or patriarchy – the wider structural problems – allowed to enter the equation.

Let us return to basics and examine how market forces dominate and disrupt the basis of people's lives. It transforms the poor, who deserve more, into an underclass of undeserving poor. So many of the factors which are said to lead to delinquency are a product of the predicament of poverty; it is not a wilful fecklessness that generates the predicament in the first place. It is not the sins of the past that lead to underachievement in school but children in their teens realizing the future holds little in store for them. As one of the kids on a North London housing estate put it:

> Although I'm not saying I commit crimes, if you just look at some of the flash cars that can be seen in this area, you can see why crimes are committed. People need money, clothes and food. They are bored and even if there are things to do, you still need money and the dole does not pay that much. When we leave school we can only look forward to unemployment. ... Sometimes, it is exciting to commit crimes, especially when you get away with it.
> (Mooney, *Miranda Estate Survey*, 1994)

Academic achievement is of little significance if schooling has no purchase on the future. And how do you hold the children in school once the penny has dropped that there is little to gain from staying in school? To say that underachievement and truancy correlate with delinquency, and all are closely associated with family poverty is correct; but to imply a line of causality from family to school performance to delinquency is a nonsense. For it is the poverty engendered by the wider society that dominates both the past and the future of the children and adolescents involved. To mistake the symptoms for the causes is to reverse causality and to distract attention away from the severe social problems we face.

Postscript: criminalizing disorder and claiming precognition

The recent White Paper *Respect and Responsibility: Taking a Stand against Anti-Social Behaviour* (Home Office, 2003) represents the culmination of New Labour's concern with law and order and its reinterpretation of the family as the cause of crime and anti-social behaviour. First of all it clearly recognizes that the crime rate in England and Wales has declined, yet it insists its response is not to reduce expenditure on crime control (see Young, this volume) but to widen the net of behaviour to be controlled by the criminal-justice system. Thus, anti-social behaviour (noisy neighbours, harassment, drunken and abusive behaviour, vandalism, litter, etc.) becomes criminalized, and a multi-agency system of control, including a larger and elaborated police service, is set up in order to tackle it. Deviancy is therefore defined up (see Moynihan, 1993), and lessened tolerance of deviation from the norm is embraced as part of what is seen as an important 'cultural shift' (Home Office, 2003). Indeed, the White Paper notes tellingly that despite falling crime rates public fear remains high, and it claims that not only is this a problem in its own right but is a function of incivilities. So, anti-social behaviour as engendering fear of crime is seen, in part, as a rationale for pressing on and expanding the social-control apparatus. What is interesting here is that this is the very reverse of social democratic Labour. Then, likewise, the boundary between crime and anti-social behaviour was blurred and to an extent obviated. But in the case of the earlier Labour administrations the aim was to decriminalize – particularly juvenile delinquency – placing both delinquency and incivilities into a category of anti-social deviant behaviour. Now the reverse is occurring, and incivilities are being criminalized. Also, the White Paper, as one might expect, views the family as the central institution in the control of crime and as the main site of the teaching of 'rights and responsibilities' in order to produce a 'something for something society'. But conversely a *few* dysfunctional families are seen as contributing largely towards the problem of anti-social behaviour. For this reason a wide range of controls are proposed including: Parenting Orders to compel parents to be responsible for their children, coupled with fixed penalty fines for non-compliance; intensive support schemes for families, including residential 'options' for parents – perhaps as a 'requirement' attached to a Parenting Order; parenting contracts for parents who permit their children to truant; Intensive Supervision and Surveillance Programmes (ISSP) for young offenders, of twelve-months' duration.

Furthermore, the success of developmental psychology in impressing policy makers and reinforcing the family as the prime site of intervention can be seen in the forthcoming (at the time of writing) Green Paper, *Children at Risk*, where not only is developmental support focused on the family but a precognitive assessment of the risk of child delinquency is proposed.

The White Paper makes some reference to the discourse of social exclusion/inclusion and the wider problems of area, employment and deprivation. But such inclusionary discourses place crime in a wider structural context only to give way easily to the focus on individuals and their families (see Young and Matthews, this volume). It is this lack of balance that is seen throughout the politics of the postwar period, and which is reproduced in a particularly repressive form today.

Notes

1 James Bulger, aged two, was abducted from a shopping centre in Liverpool, in 1993, and subsequently murdered by two 10-year-old boys.

References

Anderson, B. (2002) 'The Time for Sentimentality is Over. Let Us Tame These Feral Children', the *Independent* (29 April), 12.

Currie, E. (1985) *Confronting Crime*, New York: Pantheon.

Garland, D. (2001) *The Culture of Control*, Oxford: Oxford University Press.

Giddens, A. (1992) *The Transformation of Intimacy*, Cambridge: Polity Press.

Farringdon, D. and Tonry, M. (1995), 'Strategic Approaches to Crime Prevention', in D. Farringdon and M. Tonry (eds) *Building a Safer Society*, Chicago: University of Chicago Press.

Home Office (2003) *Respect and Responsibility: Taking a Stand against Anti-Social Behaviour*, Cmnd 5778, London: Stationery Office.

Hughes, G. (1998) *Understanding Crime Prevention*, Buckingham: Open University Press.

Mooney, J. (1994) *Miranda Estate Survey*, London: Middlesex University, Centre for Criminology.

Mooney, J. (2000) *Gender, Violence and the Social Order*, London: Macmillan.

Moynihan, C. (1993) 'Defining Deviancy Down', *American Scholar*, 62 (Winter), 17–30.

Social Exclusion Unit (1999) *Teenage Pregnancy*, London: Stationery Office.

Young, J. (2003) 'Searching for a New Criminology of Everyday Life', *British Journal of Criminology*, 43(1), 228–42.

Chapter 6

Drugs: the great cannabis debate

Catriona Woolner and Betsy Thom

Drugs and society: a 'love-hate' relationship

It is difficult to find a place or a time when drugs, in some form or other, were not in common use in society. Alcohol, tobacco, opiates, hallucinogenic drugs, cannabis and other substances have been used medicinally, recreationally and as part of religious and secular ceremonies from the earliest times. Awareness of the pleasures and benefits of drug use in its various forms has not prevented people from observing the personal and social harms that can accompany drug use. Most societies have imposed rules about who is allowed to use a particular substance, for what purposes, on which occasions and in what ways. For example, in some societies, access to alcohol was denied to certain groups of people – usually women, slaves and servants – on the belief that alcohol use might lead to rebellious behaviour or to neglect of responsibilities and duties (Heath, 1990).

But what is most striking about the history of drug use is the way in which different drugs have been defined as either 'good' or 'bad', and how perceptions of drugs have changed over the centuries. Tobacco, condemned by King James I of England (James VI of Scotland) as 'harmful to the brain, dangerous to the lungs', nevertheless became a legal, socially acceptable and economically important substance, which has been seriously challenged only in the last 50 years (Royal College of Psychiatrists, 2000). Opium and its derivatives, laudanum and morphine, were widely available in nineteenth-century England and were used recreationally as well as to treat a wide range of medical ailments. Opinion about the balance between benefits and harms began to change towards the end of the century, hardening into formal legislative restrictions and the prohibition of the substance by the beginning of the 20th century (Berridge, 1999).

How do we explain the shifting perceptions and conflicting social responses to different drugs? To what extent is the definition of a drug as 'dangerous', 'acceptable', 'unacceptable' or 'useful' and its classification as 'legal' or 'illegal' based on scientific 'fact', emerging from rigorous research on the dangers and harms of particular substances, rather than on cultural traditions and customs, assumptions and prejudices, religious beliefs, economic and political interests or moral judgements? If we look at the history of any drug we will see that all of these factors have a role to play in the 'love–hate' relationship between drugs and societies (see, for example, Berridge, 1999; Gootenberg, 1999). However, in an era when scientific fact is often held up as the gold standard by which decisions are taken regarding health, social welfare and social order, it is instructive to consider the following comment on the current distinction between licit and illicit substances:

> It is based largely on the assumptions, prejudices, customs and above all economic interests of the Western European and North American nations who were the dominant influence on the League of Nations in the 1920s and 30s, and who determined the attitudes and policies of the United Nations in the aftermath of the Second World War. Alcohol and tobacco were then widely used by the citizens of the nations of Western Europe and North America. The most powerful of these countries – the USA, the UK and France – also had a huge economic investment in these drugs, and their cultural and economic dominance allowed them to export their attitudes, their customs and their chosen drugs to the rest of the world. . . .
>
> (Royal College of Psychiatrists, 2000, p. 33)

Drugs such as opium, cocaine and cannabis, favoured by other, less powerful, nations and less dominant cultures were, consequently, proscribed, placed on the 'dangerous substances' lists and removed from free trade.

While the global picture may be determined by the economic interests of powerful nations, we still need to consider why attitudes towards the use of a particular drug change within a country. Again, we need to ask questions about the role of scientific knowledge about the drug, the part played by vested interests, the power of different groups of people to promote their definitions of the drug as 'good' or 'bad', the influence of the media or the links between fashions – for instance, those associated with youth cultures – and the use of the drug. We could take almost any drug – including our daily drugs such as coffee and tea – and show how responses to drugs and drug use are influenced by a complex web of many factors, shifting as social and historical circumstances change. However, for the purposes of this chapter, we will concentrate on cannabis, a drug that has been hotly debated over the last few decades.

A great deal has been written about cannabis, much of it factual and some of it positively fanciful. In 1890, writing in the *Lancet*, Russell Reynolds said it was 'one of the most valuable medicines we possess' (cited in Schofield, 1971, p. 17), while in the 1930s it was described by US Federal Bureau of Narcotics Commissioner Harry Anslinger as 'the most violence-creating drug on this planet' (quoted by Blanchard, 1994). So what is this drug that is considered both beneficial and evil to humankind?

In the remainder of this chapter we will describe cannabis, its uses as both medicine and recreational drug, and the events that led to its prohibition. We will consider why, at this time of writing, the British Home Secretary is considering the reclassification of cannabis from a Class B to a Class C drug, and discuss the future implications of relaxation of the law in relation to the drug in terms of decriminalization or even eventual legalization.

'C' for Cannabis

What is cannabis?

Cannabis is a plant, of the herb variety, which has been cultivated for thousands of years in Asia and the Middle East both for its fibre and as a drug. 'Therapeutic uses were described in Indian medical texts before 1000BC and in the Chinese herbal *Rh-ya* in the fifth century BC.' (Brown, 1995, p. 253). It is referred to by many names and nicknames, but generally speaking 'hashish' refers to the sticky resin (cannabis resin) secreted by the leaves and flowers of the female plant, and 'ganja' to the dried flower tops of the female plant (grass). As with the names of many plants, cannabis originates from the Greek, being 'the Greek word for "hemp", from which the word "canvas" is derived, after the plant's fibrousness' (ibid., p. 99). Indeed, it is for its fibre that cannabis has been widely grown throughout the world for hundreds of years, when hemp was used in the manufacture of rope, twine and material for clothing, sails, 'and the rough fabric that covered westward-bound American pioneer wagons' (Grinspoon, 1971, p. 11).

Cannabis is a very vigorous plant that grows best in hot, dry conditions. Both male and female plants are necessary for cultivation, as it depends on the wind for pollination, no birds or insects being attracted to it. So vigorous is the plant that 'it still grows wild in countries where systematic efforts to eradicate it have been going on for centuries' (Gossop, 2000, p. 105). This may account for the popular nickname 'weed'.

The active ingredient that distinguishes cannabis as a 'drug', as opposed to other common and widely used herbs, was identified in 1964 as tetrahydrocannabinol, or THC (Blanchard, 1994). It is unique as a drug because, as noted by Gossop, 'It defies attempts to precise pharmacological classification since its effects are so various. Under different conditions it can act as a stimulant, as a sedative, as an analgesic or as a mildly hallucinogenic drug' (Gossop, 2000, p. 106).

Cannabis, therefore, is a naturally occurring plant, which has been around for thousands of years and grows well in the wild and under cultivation. Its commercial and practical uses have made it a very attractive plant for humankind over many centuries.

Palliative and recreational uses

'It is believed that in 2737BC the Emperor Shen Nung wrote a book which gave accurate pharmacological details about the hemp plant . . . [he] prescribed it for "female weakness, gout, malaria, constipation and absent-mindedness".' (Schofield, 1971, p. 17). Thus, nearly 5,000 years ago, it is believed that the medicinal benefits of the cannabis plant were recognized and recorded. That is to say that long before the testing of drugs on animals, prior to administration to human beings, was ever considered, cannabis was already in use on what we would today call 'human guinea pigs' with positive palliative results. Gossop notes that it 'probably first reached Europe more than a thousand years ago following the Muslim invasion of Spain' (Gossop, 2000, p. 105), and by the mid-19th century 'it was welcomed as a valuable therapeutic agent. Walton (1938) reported: "During the period from 1840–1900 there was something like over 100 articles published which recommended cannabis for one disorder or another".' (Schofield, 1971, p. 17; Grinspoon, 1971, p. 242), and according to Gossop, 'the *American Dispensatory* of 1851 recommended extracts of hemp as a treatment for gout, rheumatism, tetanus, convulsions, depression and delirium tremens.' (Gossop, 2000, p. 115).

Latterly, in the closing decades of the 20th century, the medicinal benefits of cannabis returned to the forefront of debate, following a period in the wilderness. It had been used less and less 'and eventually removed from the British Pharmaceutical Codex in 1954. One reason for this was the fear that patients might become addicted, but this cannot be justified' (Schofield, 1971, p. 18), and for a number of reasons, which we shall explore, it had been 'removed from the *U.S. Pharmacopoeia* and *National Formulary* in 1941' (Grinspoon, 1971, p. 242).

One interesting influence on the American medical profession's abandonment of cannabis treatment for the many ailments it appeared effective in treating was the introduction, from Britain in 1856, of the hypodermic syringe (Grinspoon, 1971, p. 247). This was not the first time that developments in Britain had an immediate and significant effect on the relationship between cannabis and American society. In the seventeenth century the British navy had an ongoing and urgent need for the by-products of hemp: ropes, sails and rigging. It had had a regular supply of hemp from the Dutch East Indies, but this was interrupted by conflict with the Dutch, and it was decreed that Britain's colony in America should grow its hemp. 'By 1630, hemp had become a staple of the colonial clothing industry' (Schofield, 1971, p. 17). According to Gossop, in 1630 'the government of Virginia awarded bounties to those producing cannabis and imposed penalties on those who produced other crops' (Gossop, 2000, p. 105).

The arrival of more durable synthetic materials in the manufacture of rope, twine and fabric have long since replaced hemp, an organic material that naturally breaks down under normal climatic conditions. Cotton replaced hemp products in the manufacture of clothing, due in part to the development of the Lancashire cotton industry. Steam replaced sail in shipping, and rail replaced the wagon train for those venturing westward. And thus the cultivation of hemp for commercial purposes died out.

Returning to the realm of medicine, Grinspoon argues that the arrival of the hypodermic syringe heralded an increased use of opiates in the United States, 'for the water-soluble opiates could now be conveniently administered through this route with fast relief of pain; hemp products are insoluble and cannot be administered parenterally'[1] (Grinspoon, 1971, p. 247).

As a recreational drug, cannabis is most usually smoked in Europe and the United States, but it can also be eaten in confections or drunk in teas, like most other herbs. In the form of 'grass', the leaves and flower heads are dried and smoked either 'neat' or mixed with tobacco in a joint or 'spliff'. Hashish, or cannabis resin, comes in solid, block form and is heated and crumbled, then added to tobacco in a hand-rolled joint, or smoked neat in a pipe. Medicinally, other methods of administration are being explored, possibly because smoking has long since been recognized as a dangerous activity, and the introduction of a new palliative substance that is most effective when smoked (Zimmer and Morgan, 1997, p. 19) would be unpalatable to a public being encouraged to stop smoking tobacco with state-sponsored publicity campaigns displaying the warning 'Smoking Kills'. For example, asthma patients, for whom early research with cannabis held out considerable hope, would now consider it an extreme contradiction to be encouraged by their GP to *smoke* as a palliative alternative to using a synthetic spray. Zimmer and Morgan note that:

> Smoking is a highly unusual way to administer a drug. Many drugs could be smoked, but there is no good reason to do so because oral preparations produce adequate blood concentrations. With THC this is not the case. Inhaling is a better route of administration than swallowing. Inhaling is about equal in efficiency to intravenous injection, and considerably more practical.
>
> Other than its illegality, the primary drawback of smoking marijuana is that it deposits irritants in the lungs. With prolonged high-dose use, this could cause pulmonary problems. ... However, with short-term use, there is little risk of lung damage. For terminally ill patients, the potential harm from smoking is of little consequence. Other THC delivery systems – for example, suppositories and aerosol sprays – have not been proven effective, but should be studied further. Given currently available options, smoking marijuana is the most efficient and effective way to deliver THC. It is also potentially the cheapest.
>
> (Zimmer and Morgan, 1998, pp. 20–1)

In the past it was often claimed that smoking tobacco was a route, or gateway, to smoking cannabis, though this has never been proved. Ironically, though, it may be that smoking cannabis mixed with tobacco could actually result in the development of an addiction to tobacco.

As noted, the effects of cannabis on the individual user vary from one to another and even in the same person at different times. The potency of the drug also varies and, for example, it has been noted that the potency of resin produced by plants grown in hot, dry conditions is superior to that grown in a temperate climate. Its illegality has made it difficult to research its effects on human subjects, although much research has been carried out on animals and on human cells in petri dishes (Zimmer and Morgan, 1997). With the current revival of interest in its medicinal value, the research is improving, and it is now known that the effects of cannabis vary from species to species, so that its effects on rats in a laboratory cannot be extrapolated to human beings, however much its detractors would like to convince us otherwise (see, for example, Stuttaford, 2001, and for a critique of this position, Zimmer and Morgan, 1997).

In his pathbreaking 1971 study of drug users, *The Drugtakers*, Jock Young noted that cannabis's 'net effect is initial stimulation of the central nervous system associated with sensations of pleasure, followed by sedation, drowsiness and sleep' (Young, 1971, p. 15): obviously a far cry from Anslinger's depiction of the drug as 'the most violence-creating drug on this planet' (see above). Gossop notes that:

> The drug is often used in connection with activities which are themselves highly pleasurable – eating, listening to music, watching a film, having sexual intercourse, meeting friends etc. Cannabis is used as a means of intensifying the level of enjoyment. To this extent it is accurately described as a recreational drug.
>
> (Gossop, 2000, p. 107)

With regard to long-term effects, a number of expert studies, dating back to 1894, have shown no evidence of serious, long-term side effects from moderate use of cannabis, but research is still ongoing, and it is hoped that contemporary research, benefiting from a subject population of countless long-term moderate and heavy users of the drug, will confirm or deny the findings of these expert studies once and for all. A lethal dose of cannabis for human beings, based on research using cats, is about one and a half pounds for a 12-stone man (Young, 1971, p. 16). While we have already asserted that research on animal subjects cannot be extrapolated to human beings, it is clear from the evidence that a human lethal dose is very high indeed, and according to Gossop, 'cannabis is one of the least toxic drugs known to man, and there is no evidence that anyone has ever died as a direct result of taking an overdose of it' (Gossop, 2000, p. 108).

Cannabis is also used in religious ritual and 'has been associated with Rastafarianism where the use of ganja is seen as an aid to spirituality' (Murji, 1999, p. 52), and Gossop notes that 'those who worship the Hindu deity Shiva have used bhang[2] in their religious practices' (Gossop, 2000, p. 105).

Prior to the 1960s, cannabis use was restricted to a minority, and 'the traffic in cannabis had been for many years linked with ports and dockland districts and was destined mostly for seamen, musicians and immigrants' (Schofield, 1971, p. 53). Young noted that in the 1960s there was:

> ... an unparalleled growth in use, occurring largely amongst young people. ... Both in America and Britain use of this drug is increasingly associated with white middle-class youth and particularly students who often embrace a new form of bohemianism which has been popularly termed hippie.
>
> (Young, 1971, p. 11)

Basing his figures on arrest rates for possession, Young estimated a growth in use between 1960 and 1969 of approximately 45 per cent per annum. Further, the ratio of white to black people arrested for possession also changed dramatically from 45:55 in 1963 to 73:27 in 1967 (Young, 1971, p. 12). While urging caution in the interpretation of such statistics, Young nevertheless concluded that 'there has been a considerable increase in use and that this is concomitant with the spread of use to young white offenders' (ibid., p. 13). Gossop notes that the growth of use in the 1960s 'was probably as much the result of American cultural influences as of any other single factor' (Gossop, 2000, p. 106).

By the end of the 20th century cannabis use had become 'normalized' in Britain, and indeed in most of the Western world. Normalization is the process whereby activities previously considered as deviant no longer attract negative responses from the wider society (see Rock, 1973, p. 84). So, for example, whereas certain types of behaviour in women, such as smoking, or attending pubs and clubs, was considered deviant, say, 50 years ago, such behaviour is not now regarded as deviant, having become 'normalized'. With reference to the normalization of cannabis use, Professor Howard Parker and his colleagues at the Social Policy Applied Research Centre of the University of Manchester conducted a study of adolescent recreational drug use and found that cannabis was the second favourite drug of the adolescents in their study, alcohol coming first, and then followed by ecstasy and tobacco (Parker, Aldridge and Measham, 1998, pp. 70–71), and Gossop notes that although the popularity of cannabis use in Britain has had its ups and downs, 'its use has now become virtually normalized for many people' (Gossop, 2000, p. viii).

We will turn now to the reasons why this substance, whose medicinal benefits have been recorded through the ages, came to be prohibited, yet which at the same time became 'the most widely used drug in all age groups' in Britain (Home Office, 2001).

Prohibition

Rather surprisingly, given the popularity of the drug today, the prohibition of cannabis in Britain, on 28 September 1928, was something of a non-event. There was no debate in parliament, no lobbying for or against, no letters in *The Times*, and it hardly raised a whimper. It was prohibited under the 1925 Dangerous Drugs Act, 'controlling "Indian Hemp and all resins and preparations based thereon" [which] had been passed after Britain signed the 1925 Geneva International Convention on Narcotics Control, organised by the League of Nations' (Blanchard, 1994). At that time, as noted above, recreational use of cannabis was restricted to a minority, and its use in medicine had been overtaken by other developments, including the hypodermic syringe. There was, therefore, no public outcry in support of cannabis, nor indeed any real opposition to its use.

Although the Geneva Conference was convened primarily to discuss problems of opium misuse, the subject of cannabis was proposed by delegates from Turkey and Egypt, the Egyptian delegate being particularly vociferous in denouncing the drug as a social evil (see Blanchard, 1994; Schofield, 1971, pp. 44–45). Considering it inappropriate to include total prohibition of cannabis in an international convention until more was known abut the drug, Britain initially abstained from the vote, but in the end signed the agreement, together with 57 other nations. The United States did not sign, they were not members of the League of Nations, and when the US proposal for a worldwide ban on opium was rejected, the US delegation 'walked out of the conference, before cannabis was mentioned' (Blanchard, 1994). The result was that cannabis was not banned in the United States until Anslinger's 1937 Marijuana Tax Act.

In 1961, under the auspices of the United Nations, the Single Convention on Narcotic Drugs superseded all previous drugs treaties, and drugs were classified in accordance with their perceived harmfulness. Cannabis was classified with opiates and cocaine as 'having strong addictive properties' and/or being 'a risk to public health'. Schofield wrote that the Single Convention 'is a strange document. The preamble refers exclusively to addictive drugs, but their own expert advisers had noted that cannabis was not addictive' (Schofield, 1971, p. 45).

The 1961 Single Convention is a very important piece of international legislation, allowing for cooperation between nations to combat the harms caused by dangerous, addictive drugs. International agreements of any kind are hard won, involving painstaking discussion and research, and it would be folly indeed to jeopardize the beneficial purpose of such an agreement by unilaterally deciding to declassify one drug. Yet according to Schofield, Article 46 of the Convention 'states that any signatory may denounce it unilaterally after six months' notice. [and] It is also open to any country to propose amendments' (Schofield, 1971, p. 47). The mechanism to reclassify cannabis among less harmful drugs therefore exists within the Convention.

During the mid-1960s, in order to bring Britain's drugs policy into line with the Single Convention, an Advisory Committee on Drug Dependency (ACDD) was formed, and a sub-committee, chaired by Baroness Wootton, began to investigate the legal position with regard to cannabis. The Wootton report was published in 1969, after it had been leaked to the press, with the result that the then Home Secretary, James Callaghan, had already signalled his disagreement with it even before it was released.

One of the report's conclusions was that 'in terms of *physical* harmfulness, cannabis is very much less dangerous than the opiates, amphetamines and barbituates, and also less dangerous than alcohol. ... Psychosis or psychological dependence ... do not seem to be frequent consequences of cannabis-smoking' (ACDD, 1968, p. 17), although on the latter point the report did stress that not enough was known about long-term effects and that more research was needed.

By the 1960s, however, support for cannabis had grown considerably, and in 1967, sponsored by the Beatles, a full-page advertisement appeared in *The Times*, 'signed by 72 prominent people including some of Britain's best-known artists and writers, two Nobel Prize winners, two MPs, journalists, doctors and the Beatles' (Blanchard, 1994). In the parliamentary debate that followed the publication of the Wootton report, James Callaghan expressed the view that the Wootton Committee had been influenced by the pro-cannabis lobby, which he viewed as 'another aspect of the permissive society and he was glad that his decision had enabled the House to call a halt to the advancing tide of permissiveness' (*Times Parliamentary Report*, 28 January 1969, cited in Young, 1971, p. 200). The Wootton report became the latest in a long line of such expert studies on cannabis (listed below) to be 'rejected and the combined medical, psychological, police and judicial experience of the committee ignored out of hand. It did not fit the facts as the politicians and the popular press saw them' (Young, 1971, p. 201).

1894 Indian Hemp Drugs Commission: 'the moderate use of hemp drugs is practically attended by no evil results at all'

1925 Panama Canal Zone report: 'there is no evidence ... that it [cannabis] has any appreciably deleterious influence on the individual using it'

1944 LaGuardia Commission Report (New York): 'there is no direct relationship between the commission of crimes of violence and marihuana'

1969 The Wootton report (Britain): 'there is no evidence that in Western society serious physical dangers are directly associated with the smoking of cannabis'

1970 LeDain Commission Report (Canada): 'physical dependence to cannabis has not been demonstrated and it would appear that there are normally no adverse physiological effects ... occurring with abstinence from the drug, even in regular users'

1972 National Commission on Marihuana and Drug Abuse (USA): 'existing social and legal policy is out of proportion to the individual and social harm engendered by the drug'

1972 Baan Commission (Holland): 'Cannabis does not produce tolerance or physical dependence. The physiological effects of the use of cannabis are of a relatively harmless nature'

1977 Commission of the Australian Government: 'One of the most striking facts concerning cannabis is that its acute toxicity is low compared with that of any other drugs. ... No major health effects have manifested themselves in the community'

1982 National Academy of Sciences Report: 'Over the past 40 years, marijuana has been accused of causing an array of anti-social effects including ... provoking crime and violence ... leading to heroin addiction ... and destroying the American work ethic in young people. [These] beliefs ... have not been substantiated by scientific evidence'

1995 Dutch Government Report: 'everything that we now know ... leads to the conclusion that the risks of cannabis use cannot ... be described as "unacceptable" '

(adapted from Zimmer and Morgan, 1997, p. xvi)

Thus, despite a considerable body of evidence that cannabis is not a 'dangerous drug', the 1971 Misuse of Drugs Act, which came into effect in April 1973, classified cannabis in category B, together with amphetamines. Class B drugs carry a maximum penalty of up to 14 years for cultivation or for allowing premises to be used for supplying them, and the 1971 Act created a new offence of possessing cannabis with intent to supply. For mere possession you could get a five-year prison sentence. This Act also established the Advisory Council on the Misuse of Drugs (ACMD), whose purpose was to inform government policy in relation to illicit drug use. In 1979 the ACMD proposed that cannabis should be reclassified to category C, and that penalties for possession should be relaxed, so that prison was no longer an option for first-time cannabis offenders. The proposal was ignored (Blanchard, 1994).

It is the view of Sean Blanchard, of the Independent Drug Monitoring Unit, that the laws prohibiting cannabis exist 'because of official apathy, racism, and the manic waffle of a few professional anti-drug campaigners. . . . Official policy is to reduce both the supply of and demand for all illegal drugs. It has failed miserably, and done great damage to hundreds of thousands of people' (Blanchard, 1994). For example, in 1997 Gossop notes that:

> . . . more than 86,000 people in Britain were arrested and convicted of cannabis offences. Nearly two thousand people were expensively (and probably quite pointlessly) locked up in prison for this reason. Every year more people are imprisoned for cannabis offences than for heroin offences.
>
> (Gossop, 2000, p. viii)

So what has changed?

On 6 July 2001, the former deputy leader of the Conservative Party, Peter Lilley, threw down the gauntlet to his party leadership contenders on the issue of reforming the law in relation to cannabis. Lilley himself was calling for legalization, on the grounds that existing laws forced cannabis users 'into the arms of hard drug pushers. It is that link I wish to break.' (BBC News Online, 2001). After a General Election defeat, which resulted in the resignation of their leader, William Hague, the Conservatives were in disarray, and there was considerable confusion as to the future direction of their policy. Shadow Home Secretary, Anne Widdicombe, was in no doubt about her position vis-à-vis cannabis, warning that if it were to be legalized, the 'drug barons' would not disappear, but would 'put a huge amount of effort into marketing hard drugs and probably targeting ever younger age groups' (ibid.). Other leading Conservatives in contention for the leadership, such as Michael Portillo and Kenneth Clarke, were more cautious, welcoming a debate and declaring themselves open to 'new thinking' (ibid.). That the Conservatives were interested in cannabis at all may be attributable to the fact that the turnout among young people in 2001 marked an all-time low for a General Election, causing all political parties to consider ways and means of bringing the younger generation of voters into the political process. As Parker *et al.*'s (1998) research suggests, entering the cannabis debate could be one way of demonstrating a willingness to engage with issues that mainly affect young people. This view is corroborated by recent research for the Joseph Rowntree Foundation (2002), which concluded that 'the main benefits of reclassification would be non-financial, in removing a source of friction between the police and young people'. Meanwhile, the message from the Labour government was that 'cannabis is dangerous, it does cause medical problems, cancer, hallucinations – therefore the position has not changed' (ibid.). That was in July 2001.

On 23 October 2001, the newly appointed Home Secretary, David Blunkett, issued a press release, in which he announced his intention to 'seek advice from scientific and medical experts on the Advisory Council on the Misuse of Drugs (ACMD) on their assessment of the arguments for re-classifying cannabis from Class B to Class C' (Home Office, 2001). Blunkett made clear that it was not his intention to 'go soft on drugs'. He stated that 'We need to warn young people that *all* drugs are dangerous, but class A drugs such as heroin and cocaine are the most harmful. We will only be successful at delivering this message if our policy as a whole is balanced and credible' (ibid., emphasis added). It is clear from the statement that the Home Office's intention was to concentrate on the *drugs business*, that is the dealers and traffickers thought to amass massive profits from the trade: 'the Proceeds of Crime Bill will allow us to seize more cash out of the hands of criminals and channel it back into our communities' (ibid.). Blunkett also said that the intention was 'to get drug misusers out of the Criminal Justice System and into treatment' (ibid.), signalling a return to the rehabilitative ideal of treatment rather than punishment, or *inclusion* rather than *exclusion*, and a definite move away from the 'prison works' rhetoric of former Home Secretaries.

As acknowledged in the Home Office press release, reclassification does not mean decriminalization, nor does it mean legalization: 'cannabis would remain a controlled drug and using it a criminal offence' (ibid.). Reclassification means moving cannabis from the status of a Class B drug to Class C. As noted above, under the 1971 Misuse of Drugs Act, certain drugs were categorized from A to C in accordance with their perceived harmfulness. Class A drugs are those perceived to be most harmful, and include cocaine, heroin, opium, morphine and other narcotics, LSD and injectable amphetamines. Class B includes amphetamine sulphate (also known as 'speed'), cannabis resin, and cannabis. Class C drugs are those perceived to be the least harmful, including mild amphetamines, tranquillisers and anabolic steroids.

The net effect of reclassifying cannabis as a Class C drug is largely to do with penalties. In practice, it will no longer be possible for police to arrest anyone caught smoking cannabis. In addition, 'Most people caught in possession will face no legal action, although the maximum penalty will be two years in jail (reduced from five). To prosecute, police will be required to produce a court summons; few will bother' (Jeffery, 2001).

The penalty for simple possession, as opposed to possession with intent to supply, would therefore change upon reclassification, from a prison term to a fine or caution. Since cautions are widely used, albeit informally, for cannabis possession in many areas (Joseph Rowntree Foundation, 2002), the net effect would therefore appear to be 'no change'. However, since it is widely held that in ethnic-minority communities the police have hitherto justified their powers to stop and search in terms of discovering possession of small amounts of cannabis, the reclassification has potential for considerable change. Murji, for example, has argued that:

> The widespread use of cannabis, or perhaps the idea that use was common, meant that drugs often became a source of conflict between the police and black people, especially when the police were seen as exceeding their powers of 'stop and search' and using drugs as an excuse to harass many young black men for no obvious reason other than their blackness.
>
> (Murji, 1999, p. 52)

Taking account of the obvious alienation of the 'black community' in the aftermath of the Stephen Lawrence inquiry, with its identification of 'institutional racism' in the Metropolitan Police, we can perceive a situation in which police relations with the public could do very much better without further alienation caused by the stopping and searching of individuals for possessing a fairly innocuous substance like cannabis.

As noted, reclassification does not mean decriminalization. Decriminalization means that there is no sanction against possession and use, while legalization would mean that cultivation, processing, supply, possession and use are all legal. This may be a step too far; perhaps it is better for us to crawl before we attempt to walk. After all, what could it do to a Home Secretary's career to be the one who 'went soft on drugs'?

However, with a burgeoning interest in cannabis as a therapeutic drug in the treatment of a variety of ailments, particularly HIV, multiple sclerosis and cancer, the legal position regarding recreational use of cannabis is becoming increasingly untenable. Sufferers of these illnesses have taken part in television documentaries where they have effectively admitted to crimes in relation to a Class B drug, for which they should, technically, be arrested and imprisoned: they have admitted to procurement, possession and use of a drug that carries the penalty of a prison sentence. They have not been arrested, nor have they been charged. The truth is that the public outcry from such an arrest, charge or conviction, would in fact be far more injurious to a serving Home Secretary than the charge that he had 'gone soft on drugs'. The contradiction here, however, between tolerating certain users and convicting, even imprisoning, others makes a mockery of the law in relation to cannabis. For any law to be effective it must have the support of the majority of the population, for, as noted by Schofield, 'any law which acts more like a lucky dip than an enforcement policy is a questionable law, especially when a particular segment of the population (e.g. coloured immigrants) are more likely to be caught' (Schofield, 1971, p. 57).

It could be argued that the war on terrorism, following the tragic events in New York on 11 September 2001, is exacting a huge toll on the Exchequer and the proposed relaxation of the law in relation to cannabis has purely pragmatic intent, i.e., any reduction in the cost of processing offenders on convictions for a drug that has become so normalized as to be the second favourite among adolescent drug users (Parker *et al.*, 1998), and is 'the most widely used drug in all age groups' (Home Office, 2001), would free up funds that could be put to more immediate and effective use for the benefit of the whole population. It has been reported, for example, that during Police Inspector Brian Paddick's controversial six-month pilot scheme in Lambeth, where 'police informally caution people caught in possession of cannabis and then let them go ... police gained 1,400 hours of working time and a significant rise in arrests for Class A drugs was recorded' (Paton Walsh and Hinsliff, 2002). Furthermore, recent research for the Joseph Rowntree Foundation (2002) found that 'the financial costs of policing cannabis amount to at least £50 million a year (including sentencing costs), and absorb the equivalent of 500 full-time police officers'.

Apart from this purely pragmatic and fiscal explanation for the apparent U-turn in government policy between July and October 2001, could it be that we are now entering a more inclusionary phase in British politics? Is it not possible that, at long last, politicians are actually listening to their expert advisors, monitoring public opinion and responding positively to the views of the electorate?

Or, is it just as simple as this: in 1971, Michael Schofield predicted that in the future jurors who had themselves tried, and maybe were still enjoying cannabis, would be called upon to convict offenders on cannabis offences. There is no doubt that this prediction has been borne out. Even the former president of the United States, Bill Clinton, has admitted trying cannabis as a student (although he did not, apparently, inhale). The most recent one-page advertisement in a national newspaper included the signatures of some very successful, well-heeled members of the community; could it not just be that we have arrived at the time when most people in positions of high office – as opposed to a few jazz musicians in an earlier age – have tried and continue occasional use of cannabis and *know* beyond all shadow of doubt that this has not ruined their lives?

In 1971, according to Schofield, some of the arguments against legalisation included:

1. It may be less harmful than alcohol and tobacco, but it is still a non-therapeutic drug, so why legalise it?

2. Legalisation would be in breach of an international convention.

3. We should not appear to be condoning its use.

4. '. . . public opinion is not yet ready for any liberalization in the law' (Schofield, 1971, p. 55).

On the first point, it now seems clear that cannabis is indeed considered by the medical profession to be a therapeutic drug. On the second, Schofield has demonstrated that the mechanism exists within the 1961 Single Convention on Narcotic Drugs for reclassification to take place (see above). The third point has to do with more general social concerns in 1971, amid fears that growing permissiveness among young people represented a real threat to British society, although as noted by Schofield, 'the permissive society has its drawbacks, but the repressive society has many more' (Schofield, 1971, p. 168). On the last point, it could be that public opinion *is* now ready, and that the Exchequer could not only save money on processing cannabis offenders, but could also create revenue through the taxation of cannabis.

On balance, it appears likely that the current Home Secretary has studied the evidence of the harmfulness of cannabis, its recent revival as a palliative substance and the contradiction between that use and its classification as a 'dangerous drug', and also the economic implications at a time when resources are stretched to the limit. In any event, any relaxation of the penalties imposed for possession and supply of a drug that Baroness Wootton's report of 1969 asserted was 'less dangerous than alcohol' (see above) is likely to be welcomed by considerable and diverse sections of the population.

Notes

1 Parenterally = 'administered or occurring elsewhere in the body than the mouth and alimentary canal' (Pearsall, 1998, p. 1348).
2 bhang = 'the leaves and flower-tops of cannabis, used as a narcotic' (Pearsall, 1998, p. 169).

References

ACDD (1968) *Cannabis: Report by the Advisory Committee on Drug Dependence*, London: HMSO.

BBC News Online (2001) ' "Legalise Cannabis" says Lilley', *UK Politics*: www.news.bbc.co.uk.

Berridge, V. (1999) *Opium and the People: Opium Use and Drug Control Policy in 19th and early 20th century England*, London: Free Association Books.

Blanchard, S. (1994) 'How Cannabis was Criminalised', Independent Drug Monitoring Unit: www.idmu.co.uk.

Brown, D. (1995) *The Royal Horticultural Society Encyclopedia of Herbs and Their Use*, London: Dorling Kindersley.

Gootenberg, P. (ed.) (1999) *Cocaine Global Histories*, London: Routledge.

Gossop, M. (2000) *Living with Drugs*, 5th edition, Aldershot: Ashgate.

Grinspoon, L. (1971) *Marihuana Reconsidered*, Cambridge, MA: Harvard University Press.

Heath, D.B. (1990) Anthropological and Socio-cultural Perspectives on Alcohol as a Reinforcer, in W. M. Cox (ed.) *Why People Drink*, New York: Jardner, pp. 263–90.

Home Office (2001) 'Blunkett to Focus on the Menace of Hard Drugs', press release 255/2001, 23 October.

Jeffery, S. (2001) 'Reclassifying Cannabis', *Guardian* (25 October) (www.guardian.co.uk).

Joseph Rowntree Foundation (2002) 'The Policing of Cannabis as a Class B Drug', *Findings* (March).

Murji, K. (1999) 'Culture, "Race", and Drugs', in N. South (ed.) *Drugs: Cultures, Controls and Everday Life*, London: Sage.

Parker, H., Aldridge, J. and Measham, F. (1998) *Illegal Leisure; The Normalization of Adolescent Recreational Drug Use*, London: Routledge.

Paton Walsh, N. and Hinsliff, G. (2002) 'Drug Laws Revolution Set for UK: Cannabis on NHS under Radical Scheme', *Observer* (17 February).

Pearsall, J. (1995) (ed.) *The New Oxford Dictionery of English*, Oxford: Oxford University Press.

Rock, P. (1973) *Deviant Behaviour*, London: Hutchinson.

Royal College of Psychiatrists and the Royal College of Physicians (2000) *Drugs Dilemmas and Choices*, London: Gaskell.

Schofield, M. (1971) *The Strange Case of Pot*, London: Penguin.

Stuttaford, T. (2001) 'Cannabis Kills', *Times*, section 2 (31 July), 2–3.

Young, J. (1971) *The Drugtakers*, London: Paladin.

Zimmer, L. and Morgan, J.P. (1997) *Marijuana Myths/Marijuana Facts*, New York: Lindesmith Centre.

Chapter 7

Urban regeneration and crime reduction: contradictions and dilemmas

Lynn Hancock

Since New Labour's General Election victory in 1997 a number of initiatives have been introduced or redeveloped to regenerate those neighbourhoods experiencing deprivation on a range of indicators. Reducing crime and involving local communities form important parts of their remits. These include the (new) Single Regeneration Budget (SRB) the New Deal for Communities (NDC), and, more recently, a package of initiatives included in the National Strategy for Neighbourhood Renewal, informed by reports and research findings from various Policy Action Teams working under the auspices of the Social Exclusion Unit (SEU). A common theme running through these initiatives, and indeed others preceding them, is that they are to be put into effect by partnerships involving local authorities, other statutory bodies, and the private, voluntary and community sectors.

These developments signify some considerable improvements in central government's approach to urban renewal, but questions remain about whether the major problems that undermined previous efforts to regenerate communities, and reduce crime, will persist under these initiatives. This chapter outlines some of the contradictions and dilemmas that become evident when considering the relationship between urban regeneration and crime in the contemporary period. It will show why it is simplistic to assume that urban regeneration will necessarily reduce crime and disorder, particularly in declining and distressed neighbourhoods. The discussion is, in part, based on empirical work preceding the most recent policy developments,[1] though many observations remain significant for academic criminologists and practitioners in the contemporary urban policy setting. In this vein, a number of issues (theoretical and policy-orientated), which require further research in the current period, are outlined.

How can we explain the failure of earlier initiatives?

The report of Policy Action Team 17, *Joining It Up Locally*, highlighted (DETR, April 2000:10) some of the principal reasons for the failure of earlier regenerative efforts. These included that: communities were not adequately involved or empowered; initial joint strategies were not translated into sustained joined-up working; too much attention was driven by central funding rather than local needs; and central government policies and practices made local joint working difficult.

There are a number of mechanisms the government has put in place to address these problems. A 'Community Empowerment Fund' was established by the government in the summer of 2001, and a sum of £36 million was committed over three years for the 88 most deprived localities in England, to develop effective community- and voluntary-sector involvement in regeneration at a variety of levels (DTLR, 2001a). In this way, the government accepted that community groups needed a source of funding of their own, particularly in the most disadvantaged localities. The National Strategy envisaged that one of the principal routes for community involvement would be via Local Strategic Partnerships (LSPs), though it is hoped that the development of community networks will facilitate community- and voluntary-sector involvement in a range of forums.

LSPs are intended to ensure that joint strategies are translated into joined-up practice across different initiatives and services and in response to local priorities. They are forums in which key organizations and interests, including the public sector, businesses, local community groups, including hard-to-reach groups, and voluntary sectors are to be brought together. Responsibility for developing a strategy for the renewal of the economic and social fabric of a given locality lies with the LSP. In addition, 'neighbourhood management' is being piloted in selected eligible authorities, containing some of the most disadvantaged neighbourhoods, to better coordinate and manage local service delivery (DTLR, 2001b).

Central funding has undergone further shifts. A Neighbourhood Renewal Fund has been established to target resources on the most deprived neighbourhoods, and a Neighbourhood Renewal Unit – based in the Office of the Deputy Prime Minister, but expected to bring together the work of several departments – has been set up to monitor and coordinate locally based regeneration activities. Regional Development Agencies (RDAs) are to be given a single budget for regeneration and more freedom to respond to local priorities albeit within the overall targets set by government, and subject to the scrutiny of Regional Chambers. Monies allocated through RDAs will replace those secured through the SRB national bidding schemes. There will be no more SRB rounds following the completion of SRB Round 6 schemes. In addition, the government has approved the establishment of a small number of Urban Regeneration Companies (URCs) set up by partnerships involving the local authority, the RDA, English Partnerships, private-sector and other key agencies (DETR, 2001) in a small number of areas. The government's guidance suggests that the number of these will remain limited since they are (human and public) resource intensive. Their role is to secure private-sector investment that is sustainable in the long term, in a given sub-region. Government provides no additional resources; instead, partners are expected to target and prioritize their resources in these localities for 10–15 years to bring about sustained renewal (DETR, 2001).

The government has recognised the limitations of tight deadlines for regeneration initiatives in some localities. Some of these problems were highlighted by the national evaluation of City Challenge programmes, commissioned by DETR, which found that 'in areas of very high unemployment, it may not be realistic to expect to achieve fundamental changes [as a consequence of the programme as a whole] in the short term'. Moreover, 'the appropriate time-scale should be determined by local circumstances, not fixed, and in some cases it may need to be 10–15 years or even longer' (DETR, 1999: 2). NDC programmes also recognized the need for longer time-frames. And, indeed, the 'New Commitment to Neighbourhood Renewal: A National Strategy Action Plan' is very much a long-term strategy. Its stated aim is to close the gap between the poorest neighbourhoods and the rest of the country over the next 10 to 20 years (SEU, 2001). The objectives – to improve health, education, housing and the physical environment, and reduce crime and unemployment, in a joined-up way – are to be commended. But it is also worth noting, for our present purposes, that Challenge-funded anti-crime initiatives were the *least* successful as far as the delivery of their stated objectives were concerned. Lack of strategic direction was regarded as being a key reason for this finding, though it was felt that crime and disorder partnerships established under the Crime and Disorder Act 1998 would help to overcome these problems (DETR, 1999).

In a number of ways these developments *may* signify that the government has the political will to address the problems of distressed and high-crime neighbourhoods. A number of authors (Donnison, 1995; Pitts and Hope, 1997, for example), however, have highlighted 'political will' at local *and* national level to be of great significance in addressing crime and its root causes in these neighbourhoods: as Donnison noted, 'purely technical solutions will not work. Initiatives which are to put these things right must be launched by political leaders who have the authority to change public priorities and focus resources in new and sustained ways on such areas' (Donnison, 1995: 1.73).

But the developments *may* go some way towards strengthening local community networks and relationships, and connect marginal communities to sources of power, influence and resources beyond the locality, which has been argued to be so important for ameliorating conditions in high-crime communities (see Hope, 1995; Pitts and Hope, 1997). However, there are many practical problems that can thwart these efforts. For example, while there may be new 'pots' of funding for local bodies and authorities to tap into, overall levels of funding for agencies in some areas are in decline, and public services are often expected to make year-on-year 'efficiency gains'. Demands for agencies to meet the myriad targets now required by regulating authorities can undermine efforts to prioritize activities traditionally lying outside agencies' core business (Hough, 2002), militate against 'joined-up working', and distort what agencies regard as their main concerns. But there are also other fundamental problems that will need to be addressed, including, not least, the assumptions underpinning the connection between urban renewal and crime reduction.

What is the presumed relationship between regeneration and crime reduction?

Government, and other commentators, have long argued that the nature of the relationship between urban regeneration and crime is as follows: reducing crime is a prerequisite for achieving regeneration (Social Exclusion Unit, 2001). As the aforementioned evaluation of City Challenge stated:

> Crime and its effects were a significant barrier to regeneration because of their impact on the willingness of residents and businesses to stay and get involved in the problems of the area and their adverse impact on the views of potential investors.
>
> (DETR, 1999, p. 7)

Indeed, the aims of the Safer Cities programme at its launch (in 1988) were to (a) reduce crime, (b) lessen the fear of crime and (c) create safer cities where economic enterprise and community life could flourish (Crawford, 1998, p. 52). In part this reflected the Thatcherite government's wider ideological commitment to stimulating an 'enterprise culture' through which urban regeneration would be achieved (Keat and Abercrombie (1991) in Crawford, 1998a). The current government's National Strategy makes it clear that addressing crime and disorder to facilitate a context in which local economies are stimulated remains a priority. Though the strategy and supporting documentation from Policy Action Team reports also recognize that factors other than crime and disorder have undermined poor neighbourhoods, or have furthered a spiral of decline. Nevertheless, the point to note is that although crime and disorder *can* impact on the desirability of an area its potential to attract inward investment, and that these problems may promote outward migration, the nature of these connections is by no means mechanical (Taylor, 1991). In order to make sense of the relationships involved it is worth considering some of the factors that influence neighbourhood transitions.

Taub *et al.* (1984) examined some of the key processes in the North American context. Though there are some important differences to consider when we examine these from a British perspective, their study provides a useful summary of the 'drivers' of change in urban localities (see also Skogan, 1990). First there are the *ecological facts* – such as potential sources of employment, levels of housing-market demand, quality of housing, and other local amenities; they shape the social and economic context of areas (Taub *et al.*, 1984, pp. 182–3). Second are the *corporate and institutional decisions* – of banks, universities, insurance companies and so on, because they can 'buttress or abandon a neighbourhood' (Taub *et al.*, 1984, p. 183); they not only contribute to the ecological make up of the locality, but play other important roles too, for example as a lobbying force on government, or as supporters of community organizations. Conversely, their decisions to move away from a neighbourhood can have a devastating, negative multiplier effect. Third, community organizations can influence levels of satisfaction in a neighbourhood, which in turn influence individual households' moving decisions. Dissatisfaction, concerns about crime or fears of abandonment, for example, can set in motion a series of events that can trigger further deterioration. What is important is that these factors interact with one another (Taub *et al.*, 1984). The impact of crime is not direct: perceptions of safety play an important part in residents' evaluations about the likely future of their area – economically and socially – and in turn these affect investment decisions. However, the influence of crime can be offset, or reduced, by the presence of other conditions or amenities (ecological facts), which increase residents' tolerance levels (Taub *et al.*, 1984, p. 170). In this way corporate and other agencies' decisions can have a symbolic as well as material role in determining the direction of neighbourhood change.

All this suggests a rather different analysis than the perfunctory link between crime and urban decline, as implied in government policy, would suggest. In fact, we know relatively little about workers' and businesses' decisions to move away from, to, or remain in particular localities (see Levi, 2001), or the relative importance of different factors, including crimes and fear of victimization, when decisions such as these are made. An absence of schools with a good reputation for high educational achievement *may* be more important for upwardly mobile parents. It is clear, however, that the associations are too crude when we consider areas where different economic pressures are brought to bear on urban neighbourhoods. Where the wider urban or regional context is characterized by economic growth, for example as in parts of London, a more sophisticated analysis is perhaps required. The presence of crimes may not necessarily present barriers to inward investment on behalf of individual households or other interests; the significance of the 'trade-offs' that Taub *et al.* (1984) refer to is of particular relevance here. For example, the role of appreciating house-values may tip the balance in favour of moving to or staying in a neighbourhood despite evidence of relatively high rates of crime and disorder (Taylor, 1991). That said, in regions where economic development is slower and more precarious, but where amenities remain or are brought to neighbourhoods, trade-offs are also struck by those willing to stay or move to localities despite relatively high levels of crime and/or disorder (see Hancock, 2001). All in all, a more complicated picture is suggested. Furthermore, while the assumption that crime must be addressed in order to facilitate urban renewal can be questioned, so too can the idea that economic and social investment in a locality will bring about an automatic reduction in crime, as shown below.

Building community capacity?

Failure to involve local communities adequately has been regarded as one of the major problems to undermine earlier attempts to regenerate distressed localities, as noted in the earlier stages of this chapter. Some initiatives afforded only token status to resident involvement or, where commitment was present at the local level, extraneous factors undermined community confidence in the involvement process and/or the impact community groups could achieve as part of these arrangements. This is seen clearly in Power and Tunstall's (1997) study of 13 localities that experienced serious disorders during 1991–92. Regeneration initiatives had been present for a number of years in some localities. But 'involvement' of residents was not enough to protect localities from serious and violent disorder. Indeed, some residents felt that the manner in which regeneration had been pursued had been 'directly provocative'. They described how: physical improvements were prioritized over local jobs; outside contractors benefited rather than local small businesses; and short-term remedies were favoured, rather than long-term strategic action to address deeply entrenched social and economic problems. Consequently, economically marginal young men's prospects failed to improve, and their stake in the locality failed to be restored. Though residents had some involvement and, in some cases, influence upon these programmes, many externally funded initiatives were 'driven' by external constraints. They were insensitive to the complexity of local problems (Power and Tunstall, 1997).

Current arrangements place much more emphasis on 'involving communities' and on the 'hard-to-reach groups'. Indeed, there have been some innovative attempts to involve local people in the elections for community representatives on partnership boards under the New Deal for Communities. As a consequence, turnouts in some elections have been recorded as being in excess of 50 per cent in some localities, far more than can usually be expected in local-government elections (Benjamin and Humphries, 2001). In Bradford, local people normally excluded from the formal political process were strongly encouraged to become involved. Young people (15-year olds) and non-British citizens were given rights to vote, and voting papers were translated into the most common community languages. Seeing visible change in the locality was argued to be pivotal for getting people involved, and marked the difference between this ballot and an earlier one in the locality (Benjamin and Humphries, 2001). Whether the involvement of 'hard-to-reach' groups can be sustained, however, remains an open question in a context where other aspects of partnership work and funding allocations are regarded with suspicion, as discussed below. Indeed, suspicion surrounding the allocation of funding to particular groups, and beliefs that 'others' were benefiting, were seen as contributory factors in the urban disorders that took place in Bradford during the summer of 2001 (Home Office, 2001a). Furthermore, the involvement of such groups may be difficult to maintain in areas where 'fundamental change' may take a long time to be realized, in city regions lagging behind in their economic development, with the implications for further depopulation and/or disinvestment.

It is in this setting that the appropriateness of government's commitment to public–private partnerships as a mechanism for achieving urban regeneration can be questioned. Paul Humphries' account (2001) of the disastrous consequences of a public–private housing partnership in Hull, which was expected to repair and upgrade 1,200 pre-war houses on the Gipsyville estate, illustrates some of the key problems. For example, the local authority was felt to have rushed into arrangements with a private property developer attracted by the income to be generated through the sale of land and its share of the profits from the sale of new dwellings. In so doing, critics argued, the council failed to assess the financial risks associated with the deal. The scale of demolition carried out was also felt to be unwarranted. However, what is important for the present discussion is that the initiative went disastrously wrong because of the collapse of the housing market, driven by a weak local labour market and depopulation. Against more powerful interests the local community was marginalized in the decision-making process, though local people bore the consequences. Residents were moved out of Gypsyville as council homes were demolished to be replaced by mixed-tenure developments. As the remaining properties were to be refurbished using the profits from the public–private partnership – profits that did not materialize – the houses remained derelict. The Hull public–private partnership was established in 1995, but this approach remains an important force behind urban renewal. Furthermore, while the current government appears committed to 'involving' communities and including local people in decision-making processes, the tensions among the different interests involved are too often downplayed or ignored.

Regeneration managers, like Ministers in government, often assume (or present the view) that there is agreement among partners about the way in which regeneration should be pursued. Research carried out in 1996–98 in Merseyside, however, showed an absence of consensus between (and sometimes within) community-based groups and regeneration partners (see Hancock, 2001). Powerful local-interest groups often dominate regeneration agendas, while other voices are rendered silent, especially where regeneration projects seek to attract inward investment. In some cases, community representatives who express criticism of a particular approach are regarded as naive or out of touch. For example, one SRB-funded project manager commented: 'many people feel that jobs in the arts and in cultural industries are not as important as jobs in manufacturing; they should be regarded in the same way'. Though this view ignores the inferior *quality* of employment opportunities often found in service industries in the region.

The national evaluation of City Challenge found that poor levels of community involvement were related to weak partnership performance (DETR, 1999). In the Merseyside study there was evidence to suggest that some costly decisions could have been avoided by listening, if not according more influence, to local people. The following quotation illustrates some of these points, to which we will return:

> City Challenge was located in this area. It was a complete rip off! Public money was used to do up [a bar] on ... Street. Private money had been used to do it up only one or two years before that. They promised to create short-term jobs as part of the refurbishment and permanent jobs as a result of the investment, but it has closed down now. It doesn't seem viable. The regeneration projects seem to bend over backwards to accommodate projects where external funding can be obtained, at the expense of the residents' views or any proper consideration about viability. They're the pits! There are jobs for professionals ... some people in this street are self-employed. For working-class people most of the jobs available are low paid, temporary, with little notice of being made redundant or laid off. They often involve anti-social hours. Poor quality jobs, if any. It's the pits!
>
> (Owner-occupier, residents' association in Earleschurch)

Many community group members in the Merseyside study said that the needs of their communities were not being addressed by local regeneration initiatives. In general they often regarded non-local people, or those who were not in greatest need, as being the main beneficiaries. Most did not simply reject regeneration out of hand; in most cases they recognized there were *some* benefits, mainly associated with environmental improvements. But few residents expected significant numbers of jobs to be created; few regarded the kinds of provisions being developed (arts and leisure industry developments) to be 'for' local people:

> There are lots of good things happening now but there's a need to make sure that things are approached democratically. There has been a great deal of nepotism going on ... the large number of

consultancies and the public money spent on consultancies and the lack of money that is used for visible projects in the area is a scandal. There have also been problems of openness and of democracy. It's a 'money go round'.

(Representative of the mixed-tenure, community-wide
association in Earleschurch)

Our needs are not being met at the moment. Although, that is not to say they won't be in the future. People are quite quick to criticize. The residents' association goes to the [project's] meetings. I represent them there as the Chair. We can't make decisions though; we only act in an advisory role. We are consulted about grants to organizations and businesses, especially about properties. Some are really silly – there are clearly no employment opportunities or possibilities – people just want the grants. My personal opinion is that these projects face a lot of criticism but it is really too early to say that it is not a good thing – things do not happen overnight. They are not doing enough for ordinary people though.

(Chair, local authority tenants' group, Edgebank)

In this case the respondent's last point referred to the development of museums, art galleries and other cultural amenities. But the same point was made regarding housing regeneration, particularly shared-ownership housing, private developments and other schemes of a non-social nature, which were being developed in the mixed-tenure inner areas. These were to have ramifications for some of the social and spatial divisions that emerged in these localities and for reconfiguring patterns of victimization. For now, we can note that regeneration managers acknowledged that the provisions were not really aimed at local people; rather, the aim was to attract visitors from beyond the town. Residents were expected to benefit from the employment opportunities created, as part of a 'trickle down effect'. In addition to being critical of some of the regeneration partnerships, it is also worth noting that all community groups in the inner areas were critical of their local authorities, which raises questions about the latter's ability to form durable partnerships with these communities. Representatives felt their respective local authorities neglected their area and that any improvements they managed to secure from the local authority were achieved only after a prolonged period of pressure and lobbying.

Not only were there divisions between community groups and regeneration partnerships, and/or local authorities, but lines of fracture became evident within the communities themselves. Some residents were clearly able to benefit from employment opportunities. Others, especially young men lacking educational qualifications, were being left behind, their relative deprivation becoming more marked in this context. The following quotations from the Earleschurch neighbourhood illustrate the point:

> Jobs! There isn't any. Education has failed people in the area – so people do not see what opportunities that exist or if they do they don't think it's for them. And there are students and ex-students who move out despite wanting to stay, because there are not the opportunities for them. For local people there's not much hope. Most work is low-paid and part-time.
> (Representative of the mixed-tenure, community-wide association in Earleschurch)

> The mushrooming of cafés, restaurants, bars etc. has created a boom in part-time, low-paid jobs with little security. You could say that job availability is getting worse *and* better. It depends on what you mean by jobs (respondent's emphasis).
> (Male owner-occupier, Earleschurch)

The amount of job creation that regeneration managers and other commentators claimed was taking place, however, needs to be subject to some critical appraisal. Funding bodies' arrangements for monitoring of employment outputs brought about as a consequence of local projects was problematic; processes both within grant-making partnerships and/or between these and contractors and/or subcontractors were recognized as being in need of improvement. When estimates of the numbers of jobs created for local people were made on an areal basis, there was anecdotal evidence to suggest that capital projects tended to overestimate the numbers of jobs created. There was no central database, and in this context there was the potential at least for employment outputs to be counted more than once. Employment figures, perhaps not surprisingly, were very much a delicate topic, a political issue.

The problems posed for community cohesion and the role of urban regeneration arrangements as a compounding factor in this process were key concerns for the Cantle report, which reported on 'Community Cohesion' following urban disorders in towns in the north of England during the summer of 2001 (Home Office, 2001a). Many of those who gave evidence were troubled by the damaging impact of communities having to compete with each other for scarce resources. Many groups felt that decisions lacked fairness and transparency, which resulted in 'suspicion across communities that "other" areas were being favoured in the allocation of resources' (Local Government Association *et al.*, 2002, p. 17).

Will neighbourhood regeneration reduce crime and disorder, particularly in declining and distressed localities?

Can the *National Strategy*, though LSPs, provide the necessary 'strategic' direction to overcome the problems that have dogged attempts at urban regeneration in the past? This question is especially significant in a context where partnerships are expected to coordinate wider ranges of interests and work together to address the myriad problems found in distressed localities, including crime and disorder. The question raised earlier in this chapter regarding the assumed relationship between regeneration and crime reduction will need to be addressed, and the theories, and, or assumptions regarding these relationships, for the most part, will need to be addressed through empirical work on this topic in this contemporary setting. What follows, however, are some insights into these processes from the Merseyside study (Hancock, 2001) and related literature, which illustrate some of the dilemmas associated with the relationship between regeneration and crime reduction.

The first point to note is that there is now a growing body of evidence about the difficulties associated with multi-agency crime-and-disorder reduction partnerships, both pre-dating and following their statutory status granted in the Crime and Disorder Act 1998, which we need not rehearse here (see Phillips, 2002; Crawford, 1997, 1998a, 1998b; Gilling, 2000). Suffice it to note that one of the key problems has been lack of 'strategic direction'. The new LSPs may help to provide this, but some of the (albeit limited) early evidence regarding their operation is not encouraging. It suggests that multi-agency urban-renewal partnerships are beset with some of the problems that have been associated with these modes of service delivery historically. For example, voluntary-sector participants in Birmingham complained about their LSP, notably because of inadequate community consultation and because funding had been diverted to fill the gaps left by cuts or shortages in other budgets (Harward, 2001). Indeed, the Cantle report noted that the review team was 'implored' to draw attention to the overall level of funding that agencies received. While many agencies welcomed new funding sources, they also drew attention to the fact that overall funding was reducing in some areas, particularly as far as youth provision was concerned (Home Office, 2001a, 5.5.4).

The second point concerns the unintended effects of economic regeneration I have alluded to but not yet discussed. Here we are concerned with the kinds of regenerative initiatives that are encouraged in city regions that are struggling to regenerate. The problems are often the consequence of the difficulties that partnerships face in encouraging economic diversity. The development of the arts, leisure and, in particular, the night-time economy is one of the primary ways in which multi-agency regeneration partnerships envisage the regeneration of cities. Hobbs *et al.* express this and its attendant problems succinctly:

> . . . the bulk of investment in the night-time economy is centred on the 'business of pleasure' (Bailey 1986) and is characterised by a flow of capital aimed at the development of licensed premises. That the focus of this capital is predominantly upon city centre sites is, we found, typically lamented by the police yet largely welcomed by the town planners, whose primary aim is to regenerate the city and preserve the city centre as a focus for public usage.
>
> (Hobbs *et al.*, 2000, p. 708)

These authors note, however, that town planners are concerned that few planning applications come from other sectors of the economy (commercial, residential or retail sectors) in city centres examined in their study. As the respondent in the Merseyside study (quoted above) observed, 'regeneration projects seem to bend over backwards to accommodate projects where external funding can be obtained'. For residents who are confronted with the accompanying physical and social disorder that accompanies these developments it is not surprising that a level of cynicism emerges about partnerships' interests or the mode and method of regeneration. The following quotation takes us to the crux of the problem:

> There is a lot of litter from the clubs – discarded curry and chip papers and other take away food. There are also problems with bottles and people urinating in the gardens because of the pubs and clubs around the area.
>
> (Professional woman representing a mixed group of renters and owner-occupiers, Earleschurch.)

Edgebank also contains a high number of social meeting-places and pubs in the locality itself, which have been strongly associated with a high number of (recorded) assaults in the evening and night-time. It is therefore of little surprise to find that the police in Hobbs *et al.*'s study bemoaned these developments: 'From our case study of Eastville, police statistics reveal that 66 per cent of all city centre violent crime, recorded during the last three years, occurred over the weekend period. Of this violence, at least twenty nine per cent was recorded as occurring within or directly outside licensed premises' (Hobbs *et al.*, 2000, p. 706). Furthermore, they note how in this setting age-groups are increasingly segregated; these facilities are aimed primarily at young people, encouraged to drink by special offers to attract customers in the face of intense competition. Fear of crime increases among those whose lifestyles are not associated with contemporary hedonistic youth cultures.

Thomas and Bromley's (2000) study in Swansea and Cardiff illustrates these trends in more detail. Their study showed that most Swansea residents rarely visited the town centre in the evening. Of those who did, there were marked variations according to age and social class between those who visited on a weekly or more frequent basis (17 per cent of their sample), or less frequently, monthly or fortnightly (21 per cent). Theatre-going and eating-out attracted people from the older age-ranges, while cinemas, pubs and clubs attracted their custom from the younger sections of the population (under 30 years). The former activities attracted people from the more affluent and professional social classes, while pubs and clubs were cited as the main reason for visiting Swansea town centre for those in social classes IV and V and those who were unemployed. Moreover, those visiting restaurants and theatres did so less frequently. The most frequent visitors to the town centre were those going to pubs and clubs. What is significant about the frequency of visits is that those who visited the most were the least concerned about their safety, and the more infrequent visitors the most fearful (Thomas and Bromley, 2000). Clearly, there are important debates, regarding definitions of 'fear of crime' and the socio-spatial conditions that give rise to fearful responses, which are pertinent to any consideration of these issues, as these authors acknowledge. However, what is more important for our present purposes is that there are, as Thomas and Bromley (2000) and Hobbs *et al.* (2000) note, implications for the segregation of city-centre spaces in the night-time.

Thomas and Bromley (2000) suggest that the problems raised by their findings need to be addressed through strong and focused planning and development, since they emerge from the decentraliz-ation of retail, commerce and leisure businesses to the urban fringe and the suburbanization of middle-class housing developments. They suggest a number of ameliorative measures in the interim, including: encouraging a wider range of city-centre activities; a stronger residen-tial function; improvement to access, including public transport; strategies aimed at managing people's perception of risk; and 're-imaging' the city. They acknowledge, however, that these strategies are accompanied by a number of problems that will need to be addressed, as well as considerable cost implications, which mean they are unlikely to revitalize city-centres in the short-term. The problems of attracting other amenities have already been noted. Where 're-populating' city-centres has been pursued (or has occurred), as in some parts of Merseyside, some of its effects have had adverse consequences, and it is to these issues that we now turn.

Housing regeneration and economic activity: spatial divisions

In Earleschurch many residents felt that private developments and public–private housing partnerships (including shared ownership) were furthering a process of uneven gentrification and polarization. The existing general housing stock, mainly converted flats for small households, most commonly controlled by housing associations, had been deteriorating in relation to modern standards. Furthermore, the changing housing needs of the population in these areas (notably a growing demand for family accommodation) was difficult to address under the funding regimes in place, which drove down capital grants and increased the need for private income in the 1980s and 1990s. Some housing-association managers lamented the loss of their associations' traditional role as community-based, locally focused regenerators and made strenuous attempts to improve their stock and develop other functions that would support the wider needs of their tenants (including mediation and employment training schemes). However, national housing policies often acted as a constraint on these activities in this period. Where the socially rented stock was improved, this often meant rent increases, which, though covered by increased housing benefit payments for those receiving them, created the danger of binding tenants into a poverty trap. As a consequence of these processes some residents, particularly the social and private renters, felt marginalized, perhaps understandably given that most did not benefit from the small-scale improvements that housing associations were able to bring about at the time of the research. Put briefly, this neighbourhood was becoming more divided in terms of its social composition and affiliation (see Hancock, 2001).

Those areas experiencing the greatest 'gentrification' were located in the west part of Earleschurch, in the few streets where the houses remained as single-family dwellings. In part because these houses remained intact, and therefore cheaper to convert, they were attractive to private developers, to housing associations seeking to develop properties for sale or shared ownership, or for purchase by more affluent groups. Though this trend remains patchy, and confined mostly to these particular streets, there were other private developments on cleared spaces in the neighbourhood, and there was evidence to suggest that, in combination, these developments were redefining the social composition of the neighbourhood. Community groups commented how the western side of Earleschurch had 'different interests' to the remainder of the area, especially the eastern part of the neighbourhood. The eastern side had seen some environmental improvements during the course of regeneration initiatives through the 1990s, including improvements to a social-housing scheme; but the bulk of improvement and economic investment (public and private) was concentrated in, or on the periphery of, streets in the west. This separation of interests became manifest in a debate over which regeneration partnership to join and about whether the areas should be split down the middle to reflect divergent interests. The alternatives were to join a partnership with a clearer remit to address the needs of the town centre or to join one concerned with the more residential (and more impoverished) area lying to the southeast. The outcome was a decision to keep the area as one and to join the latter partnership. Nevertheless, community members and other commentators remember the conflict that surrounded these negotiations.

Those sub-areas of Earleschurch that had experienced some regenerative activity and the bulk of housing renewal were, on the whole, the same areas that had experienced improvements in the economic activity of residents between the 1981 and 1991 censuses. Hancock (2001) discusses these processes in more detail. Suffice it here to note that in 1991 unemployment was lowest in the southwestern part of the neighbourhood (though still relatively high at 28.9 per cent), and unemployment among young people was also the lowest there at 32 per cent of 16–24 year olds, according to the small area statistics. The population had increased in this part of the neighbourhood, against the general trend of decline between 1981 and 1991. In the eastern part of the neighbourhood, in contrast, male unemployment was high, particularly among the unskilled. Indeed, economic activity among men declined by 18.2 per cent in the northeastern corner of the locality (though women's economic activity increased by over 7 per cent). Limited though the data for employment was following the 1991 census, it nevertheless suggested that these trends had continued, as other measures such as housing-benefit claimant rates indicated.

The experience of victimization was closely connected to the fortunes of the various subsections of Earleschurch and the social and spatial divisions that had been emerging in Earleschurch since the 1980s. In the areas that had witnessed gentrification a variety of crimes were reported at a much lower rate than in those areas that had experienced decline (or a mixture of decline and renewal, as was commonplace in the middle of the neighbourhood). I explore these issues in the next section, again focusing on the Earleschurch neighbourhood, whose experience of regenerative activity is longer, and in this context offers insights into the current debates that this chapter has been concerned to explore.

Spatial divisions and victimization

Earleschurch as a whole experienced persistently high rates of property crimes (especially burglary and robbery) according to command and control data. In 1992–94 calls regarding burglary were two and three-quarter times the regional average. But residents in the eastern part of Earleschurch reported the greatest amount of property burglary and robbery, neighbour disputes and both minor and serious disorder. By 1997 command and control data showed that property crimes (particularly theft of property and street robbery) remained key problems in this neighbourhood. Residents in the west were also experiencing an increasing number of property crimes, according to both police and non-police data (for example, data from the local Victim Support scheme). That said, residents in streets on the west side were also more willing to report their lower level of victimization to the police. Moreover, the streets in the southwestern corner, the area that has experienced the greatest amount of gentrification, had the lowest rates of reporting as far as property crimes in general, assaults, and neighbourhood disputes were concerned (half the regional average or less for each type of crime). Despite under-reporting, the figures for these offences in the eastern side were several times higher than the regional average. For example, in the northeastern part of the neighbourhood, property-crime calls between 1992 and 1994 accounted for

24.6 per cent of calls, against a neighbourhood average of 13.4 per cent. Towards the southeast of the neighbourhood robbery calls were nearly ten times the regional (Merseyside) average, and assaults more than four and a half times. The districts in the middle were more complicated; there were no clear patterns, but robbery was reported at a consistently higher rate across the centre of the neighbourhood.

There is considerable evidence from ethnographic work, data from the police and Victim Support, to suggest that these patterns underplay the significance of the social and spatial divisions that have emerged in this neighbourhood. The ethnographic work suggested that people living in the east were more likely to mistrust the police and were therefore less likely to report crimes directly to them. Victim Support reported that many cases they dealt with originated from victim, rather than police, referrals. Residents talked about the 'stigma' associated with having a police car parked outside their homes; people were afraid of being called 'a grass'. In any case, many residents felt that there was little to be gained from reporting to the police. Only a very small minority of the population in that part of the locality had insurance, because of the prohibitive level of premiums (according to a Victim Support survey). Middle-class professionals were more likely to call the police and 'argue their case', and they were more likely to have home-contents insurance.

Though residents in the most disadvantaged sections of the neighbourhood were the most victimized there was some evidence to suggest that middle-class residents faced increasing rates of victimization. Some respondents suggested that theses groups were targets for 'resentment crime'. As one put it:

> I used to like it [around here] because of all the 'culture' on the doorstep. . . . And the laid back atmosphere. At the same time as all these positive things it can be a bit mad, there's a lot of angst about, there is violence and arguments in the street – the potted plants that I put out got trashed. There is a lot of theft, most of it petty, and a lot of break-ins but these result more in a sense of violation than involving the theft of large amounts of money or property. There are a lot of angry people. People get their cars scratched. All these things make the area unpleasant. Sometimes I feel very positive about the area, at other times I feel negative. It is a bit like the glass half-full, glass half-empty scenario. At the moment I feel bad things.

She continued:

Urban regeneration and crime reduction: contradictions and dilemmas

Bottles are quite often broken on the outside wall [of the house]. The cars have been scratched as I said before. 'People hate success'. People like to bitch about things and complain – they like to blame. It is ok if you don't show success. There are people down the road who are very middle class but the outside of their house looks quite run down – they are ok – they try to blend in. The business next door has been targeted, they have a lot of problems. . . .

(Woman aged 20–30, Earleschurch)

Regeneration: inclusion and exclusion

Local arts and cultural-industry representatives, and their supporters, were aware that visitors to the area were worried about damage to their vehicles; though, publicly, respondents were keen to discuss the positive aspects of the area and the actions being taken by local businesses to reduce fear of crime. From the mid-1990s there were efforts to put in place some of the mechanisms for reassuring the visiting public, which Thomas and Bromley (2000) have suggested. These included improving access, through the provision of coach transport at a nominal cost (and in some cases without charge), providing security through car watching, and campaigns to 're-image the city'. Nevertheless, respondents from arts and cultural-industry pressure groups indicated that worries about 'car parking and car crime' were 'almost an obsession', as one put it. Anecdotal evidence suggested that older people, particularly from the more affluent surrounding districts, were affected the most, as Thomas and Bromley's research demonstrated. Other suggestions made by these authors, such as the development of a broader 'mix of activities' aimed at attracting these social groups (older and more affluent), need to be treated carefully. Such developments are often felt to be at the expense of facilities available for the less affluent, and particularly the economically marginal, sections of the local population, as we have seen.

The problem was most clearly expressed in the case of one community group based at a local authority housing estate near Edgebank[2], where activists were concerned about the enduring problems faced by young people gaining access to affordable, legitimate, local activities and facilities. The chair of the association put it thus in 1997:

There are still problems – the availability of cheep beer and the kids drinking it on the street is a problem. There is a need for more facilities for kids. There's no youth club in the area. . . . The council used to own a football pitch but this has been lost to the tennis centre which the kids can't use – it's £11 for each half hour!

Another local authority tenants' association chair from Edgebank made a similar point:

There has been quite a lot of rejuvenation around [the neighbourhood] and elsewhere in [the town]. The [project] promised to use local labour, but we will wait and see. Some of the other schemes didn't use local labour. They brought in people from outside – from Rochdale and elsewhere. Lots of people are angry about it. Unemployment has always been a problem for people – it hasn't changed while I've been here. . . . Some of the projects are quite good, they are improving the image of the area and that was needed. The latest [SRB funded project] is going too much 'up market' though – trying to bring in a load of 'arty stuff'. There isn't enough mixed facilities – facilities that can be used by local people as well as bring people in from outside.

Complaints about the lack of use of local labour were frequent in this research, and the regeneration initiatives and other bodies made strenuous efforts to reassure local people about employment practices: contracts awarded would include appropriate clauses to ensure local labour would be used. However, two key points need to be borne in mind. First, as I have indicated, obtaining data regarding employment outputs and measures were problematic at the time the empirical work was taking place. Second, other commentators have noted that once local people obtain sound employment they leave distressed areas; moves are enabled because the housing market is fluid. The consequence for the locality of origin is that economic activity indices remain the same (Blackman, 2000). A further point to note is that there were a number of initiatives funded by City Challenge, various SRB rounds and European Union monies that were indeed concerned with widening access to opportunities for local people. However, often these centred on education and training, and local people were sceptical about their value in a context where there were few 'real' employment opportunities (see Hancock, 2001). Limited local employment opportunities caused considerable unease for other commentators, who recognized that better qualifications and training can lead to further outward migration if local opportunities remain limited, in a context where the regional or national economy is growing (Merseyside Economic Assessment, 1996).

Conclusion

The new policy framework for the regeneration of disadvantaged communities contains a number of positive developments. Notable among these are the longer time-frames in which projects can be expected to bring about change, and the commitment to providing a source of funding for 'community empowerment'. The worries accompanying the latter development are associated with the bureaucracy that may be encountered accessing these funds, as the Cantle Report (Home Office, 2001a) acknowledged, and that many funds are limited to the 88 most deprived local authorities in England. The framework also recognizes that distressed communities have a range of problems that need to be addressed in a holistic manner. The difficulty faced here is dealing with the myriad interests that will be brought to partnerships, and reconciling them in policy terms. This is particularly the case in regions that suffer from underdevelopment and uneven development, weak labour markets and sluggish housing markets, as the experience of the public–private partnership in Hull has shown. Public–private partnerships remain a key plank of government policy, as do measuring performance and achieving value for money in the core activities of those agencies brought to the partnership tables, though the ways in which these measures undermine intra-agency and multi-agency work are increasingly being recognized.

Local people will need to be assured that investment is for their benefit. In this respect, while the policy recommendations (both in the long and short term) made by Thomas and Bromley are useful, it is important that they reflect local nuances and are inclusive. In part, the government has recognized some of these problems. The Ministerial Group on Public Order and Community Cohesion (Home Office, 2001b), in its response to the urban disorders in Bradford, Burnley and Oldham in the Summer of 2001, promised to review the Neighbourhood Renewal Unit's (NRU) funding mechanisms to improve transparency. Moreover, the government has pledged itself, and the NRU, to making 'community cohesion' a fundamental part of all its programmes and policies (Home Office, 2001b), and has set up a Community Cohesion Unit to facilitate this work. Whether government spokespeople and policy-makers will be alert to the hazards associated with the implications and contradictory rhetoric accompanying other social policies, especially when set alongside criminal justice and, in particular, policing responses, remains to be seen.

Many regeneration initiative managers in Merseyside, like the arts and cultural industries' pressure groups referred to above, were keen to improve the images of their respective localities; arts and leisure-led regeneration was being hindered because of people's fear of crime. Potential investors were perceived to be discouraged by perceptions that the area was a site of violent crime. In this context, high-profile policing responses to address crime, disorder and the fear of crime received widespread support from local authorities, regeneration partnerships, and the media. Some community groups and other commentators in the inner areas expressed concern about these developments and sensitivity toward those who were targeted for police attention, but public support for tougher police action was regarded as being widespread. Police commentators argued the need to take tough action to reassure the public 'in the interest of regeneration'. Hancock (2001) discusses the implications of one such initiative in particular. Suffice it here to note that the most marginal sections of the community bore the brunt of police action and the 'demonizing' rhetoric that accompanied these developments.

Of course, it is important to recognize that achieving community cohesion, regenerating disadvantaged and distressed areas, and reducing crime is never going to be easy or quick. There are also the difficulties associated with striking a balance between raising local expectations enough yet not so much that they cannot be achieved. Moreover, should policies and initiatives fail, further disaffection and cynicism, particularly in those areas that have experienced numerous regenerative efforts over recent years, is more than likely. What is clear, however, is that the idea that 'community-led' means 'when we want your opinion we will give it to you', or that 'NDC means New Deal for Consultants' (in Jones, 2001), must be avoided under the new framework.

Much of the empirical evidence on which parts of this chapter are based precedes the publication of the National Strategy and its related initiatives. While, in many respects, the observations are relevant to the current context, there is clearly a need for further research in this area. A future research agenda needs to include a thorough evaluation of these policies and the manner in which they have been experienced and perceived by local people. The relationships between urban regeneration and crime, the ways they are characterized, and the transitions experienced by residents in urban communities deserve further examination. Some North American research has suggested that rapid social change in urban communities is associated with increasing levels of disorder, while slower transformations can have positive effects in this regard, though the precise mechanisms and mediating forces have not been the subject of systematic research (see

Taylor, 1991). Given the problems highlighted above, concerning the deeply entrenched problems of distressed communities in regions lagging behind in their development in the United Kingdom, rapid change seems unlikely. Nevertheless, the mechanisms, processes and effects of British urban change, including the impact of regeneration initiatives on rates of victimization, need to be the subject of more research. In particular, an examination of changes in patterns of victimization in areas experiencing regeneration and gentrification is needed. The empirical work discussed in this chapter shows that intra-community divisions became more sharply drawn, victimization concentrated among the more economically vulnerable, while there was some evidence to suggest that incoming, more affluent, residents were experiencing increasing crime rates in the Merseyside neighbourhoods, particularly in Earleschurch. We need to understand the mechanisms that underpin these processes in a greater variety of contexts, including urban neighbourhoods in regions experiencing economic growth.

Notes

1 The research was funded by the Leverhulme Trust, Keele University and Middlesex University through the Leverhulme Special Research Fellowship Scheme 1996–98. Hancock (2001) discusses the methodology employed. The study was centred on two main neighbourhoods, located relatively close to their respective town centres. Each had economic, physical and social-regeneration initiatives ongoing at the time of the research. 'Earleschurch' in particular had been part of, or on the periphery of, nationally funded urban regeneration activities from the early 1980s. They contained a mix of housing tenures. Other neighbourhoods forming part of the study had also undergone or were undergoing improvement, in some cases funded from non-local government sources, but they were controlled by the local authority. In these cases, regeneration projects were present at the time of the research or had been operating in the vicinity over recent years. The names of the regeneration initiatives have been omitted, where local names were adopted, and the localities have been given pseudonyms (Earleschurch and Edgebank are the names given to the main neighbourhoods) to protect the anonymity of the areas. The primary reason for this is to avoid further stigmatization of what are high crime areas and to counter the damaging and lasting effects of stigmatization for their residents.

2 See Hancock (2001), Chapter 6 (Case Study B), for further discussion.

References

Benjamin, A. and Humphries, P. (2001) 'Grassroots a Votes Winner: Polling Changes Boost the Turnout for New Deal Project Elections', *Guardian, Society* section (23 May).

Blackman, D. (2000) 'Economic Growth Hampers Regeneration', *Guardian, Society* section (19 December).

Crawford, A. (1997) *The Local Governance of Crime: Appeals to Community and Partnerships*, Oxford: Clarendon.

Crawford, A. (1998a) *Crime Prevention and Community Safety: Politics, Policies and Practices*, London: Longman.

Crawford, A. (1998b) 'Delivering Multi-agency Partnerships in Community Safety', in A. Marlow and J. Pitts (eds) *Planning Safer Communities*, Lyme Regis: Russell House.

Donnison, D. (1995) 'Crime and Urban Policy: A Strategic Approach to Crime and Insecurity', in C. Fijnaut, J. Goethals and I. Walgrave (eds) *Changes in Society, Crime and Criminal Justice in Europe*, The Hague: Kluwer.

DETR [Department of the Environment, Transport and the Regions] (1999) Regeneration Research Summary, *City Challenge – Final National Evaluation*, 27: www.regeneration.detr.gov.uk/rs/02799/index.htm.

DETR [Department of the Environment, Transport and the Regions] (April 2000) report of National Strategy for Neighbourhood Renewal Policy Action Team 17, *Joining It Up Locally*, www.regeneration.detr.gov.uk/.

DETR [Department of the Environment, Transport and the Regions] (2001) *Urban Development Companies (URCs) Development of Guidance and Criteria*, *www.regeneration.dtlr.gov.uk/urcdev/index.html*.

DTLE [Department for Transport, Local Government and the Regions] (2001a) *Community Empowerment Fund – Preliminary Guidance*, www.regeneration.dtlr.gov.uk/neighbourhood/cef/.

DTLR [Department for Transport, Local Government and the Regions] (2001b) *Neighbourhood Management: Invitation to Participate in a Pathfinder Round*, www.regeneration.dtlr.gov.uk/nminvite/.

Gilling, D. (2000) 'Policing, Crime Prevention and Partnerships', in F. Leishman, B. Loveday and S.P. Savage (eds) *Core Issues in Policing*, 2nd edition, Harlow: Pearson Education.

Hancock, L. (2001) *Community, Crime and Disorder: Safety and Regeneration in Urban Neighbourhoods*, Basingstoke: Palgrave.

Harward, E. (2001) 'Consultation Hiccups as Birmingham LSP Misfires', 22 August newstartmag.co.uk/news241.html.

Hobbs, D., Lister, S., Hadfield, P., Winlow, S. and Hall, S. (2000) 'Receiving Shadows: Governance and Liminality in the Night-time Economy', *British Journal of Sociology*, 51/4, 701–17.

Home Office (2001a) *Community Cohesion: A Report of the Independent Review Team*, chaired by Ted Cantle, London: Home Office [the Cantle Report].

Home Office (2001b) *Building Cohesive Communities: A Report of the Ministerial Group on Public Order and Community Cohesion*, London: Home Office.

Hope, T. (1995) 'Community Crime Prevention', in M. Tonry and D.P. Farrington (eds) *Building a Safer Society: Strategic Approaches to Crime Prevention*, Chicago: Chicago University Press.

Hough, M. (2002) 'Rubbing Along Nicely Together? Frictions in Crime Reduction Partnerships' paper presented to the Community Safety Five Years On conference held at ORT House, Camden Town, London (19 March).

Humphries, P. (2001) 'Private Grief', *Guardian, Society* section (23 May).

Jones, J. (2001) 'Give Them the Money', *Guardian, Society* section (29 August).

Levi, M. (2001) 'Business, Cities and Fears about Crimes', *Urban Studies*, 38(5–6), 849–68.

Local Government Association, Department of Transport Local Government and the Regions, Home Office and Commission for Racial Equality (2002) *Draft Guidance on Community Cohesion*, London: Home Office.

Matthews, R. (1992) 'Replacing Broken Windows: Crime, Incivilities and Urban Change', in R. Matthews and J. Young (eds) *Issues in Realist Criminology*, London: Sage.

Merseyside Economic Assessment (1996) www.merseyworld.com.m.tec/mea.sect7.html.

Phillips, C. (2002) 'From Voluntary to Statutory Status: Reflecting on the Experience of Three Partnerships established under the Crime and Disorder Act 1998', in G. Hughes, E. McLaughlin and J. Muncie (eds) *Crime Prevention and Community Safety: New Directions*, London: Sage.

Pitts, J. and Hope, T. (1997) 'The Local Politics of Inclusion: The State and Community Safety', *Social Policy and Administration*, 31(5), 37–58.

Skogan, W.G. (1990) *Disorder and Decline: Crime and the Spiral of Decay in American Neighbourhoods*, New York: Free Press.

Social Exclusion Unit [SEU] (2001) *A New Commitment to Neighbourhood Renewal: National Strategy Action Plan*, www.cabinet-office.gov.uk/seu/2001/Action%20Plan/contents.htm.

Taub, R.P., Taylor, D.G. and Dunham, J.D. (1984) *Paths of Neighbourhood Change: Race and Crime in Urban America*, Chicago: Chicago University Press.

Taylor, R.B. (1991) 'Urban Communities and Crime', in M. Gottdiener and C.G. Pickvance (eds) *Urban Life in Transition (Urban Affairs Annual Reviews*, 39) Newbury Park, California: Sage.

Thomas, C.J. and Bromley, R.D.F. (2000) 'City Centre Revitalisation: Problems of Fragmentation and Fear in the Evening and Night-time City, *Urban Studies*, 37(4), 1403–29.

Chapter 8

The politics of policing: managerialism, modernization and performance

Denise Martin

Introduction

Over the past two decades the police service has experienced a number of reforms and changes. A turning point in the recent history of police reform was the election of the Conservative Party in 1979 and its determination to achieve value for money from public services, including the police. In order to pursue the three E's – efficiency, effectiveness and economy – the Conservatives embarked on a programme of managerial reform. An underlying feature of these reforms was the emphasis on improving the performance of the police service by introducing a performance management framework, which included the use of performance indicators designed to improve services to the public and extend the accountability of the police service. Under the Conservative government this objective was, however, compromised by the aspirations to ensure value for money and to control crime, which intensified rapidly throughout the 1980s. The reliance on performance indictors to measure efficiency was to create a series of tensions between the police and the community.

When New Labour came to power in 1997 it emphasized the need for 'modernization'. Such an approach would involve the introduction of local partnerships to control and prevent crime and disorder, while providing a public service that would focus on not only efficiency but also on enhancing the quality of public service. The aim of this chapter is to consider police service reform under the Conservatives and New Labour, paying specific attention to the performance culture and how it has played a major role in the direction the police service has taken in recent years.

Policing in Britain: the Conservative era

After a turbulent period in the winter of 1978–1979, the Conservatives, led by Mrs Thatcher, entered an 18-year period in power. The Conservatives stressing their 'New Right' agenda, rejecting the post-war consensus of Keynesian economic policies and a strong welfare state. They argued that the economic crisis in the 1970s was due to the dominance of the state over private enterprise and too high a level of public spending. Keynesian-style polices, they believed, stifled the market, which needed to be strong in order for Britain to be competitive in the global marketplace. Additionally, widespread dependence on the state was seen to diminish individual responsibility. Services provided by the state, particularly those public services such as health and education, were viewed as inefficient, bureaucratic and self-serving. As a result, the Conservatives embarked on a programme of privatization and public-sector reform, with the overall objective of providing more cost-effective services.

No public service was safe from reform. However, while other public services, including education, were experiencing reductions in spending and were presented as failing in their functions, the development of the police service followed a much more complex and contradictory path (McLaughlin and Murji, 1997). The Conservatives presented themselves as the party of 'law and order', and while they were determined to reduce public spending they emphasized that they would spend 'more on fighting crime while they economised elsewhere' (Conservative Party, 1979, p. 19). The new government was keen to quell 'rising crime, public disorder and industrial unrest which had merged to form a society under siege from the forces of lawlessness' (Savage, 1990, p. 89). To demonstrate their commitment to law and order and the police service, the Conservatives immediately introduced the recommendations of the Edmund Davies Committee (Committee of Inquiry into the Police, 1978). This involved an improved pay package for police officers as well as the introduction of generous allowances and benefits. Also, expenditure on policing increased by 41 per cent in real terms between 1986/7 to 1993/4 (Home Office, 1995).

This initial wave of financial support for the police was seen as creating a bond between the police and the Conservatives. However, this relationship was to go through a series of ups and downs throughout the 1980s. Despite early financial gains, the police, like other public services, were about to experience the beginnings of the managerial reform agenda. New Public Management (NPM) is the term frequently associated with the new modes of managerialism that were introduced into the public sector at this time. NPM is best described as 'a summary description of a way of reorganising public sector bodies to bring about their management and reporting closer to a particular perception of business methods' (Dunleavy and Hood, 1994, p. 9). The Conservatives favoured managerialism, as they believed that the introduction of techniques borrowed from the private sector would alleviate inefficiency and produce value for money. Public services, by emulating the management style of the private sector, would, it was believed, be able to provide an adequate service with the resources that were available. A number of traits are associated with NPM and many of these have been influential in changing the police and other public-sector organizations. The characteristics of NPM have been outlined by Hood (1991, p. 4), and include:

- 'hands on' professional management in the public sector, where those at the top of the organization are provided with responsibility to manage

- explicit standards and measures of performance, where definite quantitative targets are set to measure success

- emphasis on output controls, where resource allocation is linked to successful performance

- shift to disaggregation of units in the public sector

- shift to greater competition in the public sector, including the use of contracts and tendering, for example, Compulsory Competitive Tendering (CCT)

- stress on private-sector styles of management practice, for example, flexibility in hiring and rewards

- stress on greater discipline and parsimony in resource use.

Most of the above strategies were introduced into the police service during the 1980s. However, as suggested above, this was not a straightforward process, and other developments that arose during the decade prevented the government from fully introducing NPM into the police service. The first attempt at introducing managerialist ideals came as early as 1983, with Home Office Circular 114/83. The Home Office circular insisted that police forces must take account of economy, efficiency and effectiveness. It required police forces to take into consideration public priorities and to think more carefully about whether they were meeting their objectives (Home Office, 1983). Subsequent Home Office circulars also encouraged an analysis of budgets and activities, and required forces to provide evidence of effectiveness using quantifiable indicators (McLaughlin and Murji, 1997).

Despite the early attempt to introduce NPM, subsequent events directed the government's focus away from the pursuit of reform. The miners' strike in 1984/5, and the determination of the Conservatives to defeat the miners, meant that the government needed the support of the police. Furthermore, there was a certain realization that it would not be easy to apply rational management techniques to policing because of a number of factors, including the discretionary power provided to those in the lower ranks of the organization (McLaughlin and Murji, 1997). Other difficulties included establishing clear objectives, because the different functions carried out by the police service including crime prevention, a social service role, order maintenance and law enforcement. Further outbreaks of disorder in inner-city areas across Britain in the mid-1980s increased the government's reliance on, and support for, the police.

By the end of the decade, however, this support began to wane. There were a number of incidents and reports that put the police service at the forefront of political and public debate. Controversy surrounding police operations and accountability became major issues following the Brixton riots of 1981 and the subsequent Scarman report (1982), which suggested that the police approach to certain sections of the community was oppressive and that this had contributed towards a worsening of police–public relations. The police were identified as little more than agents of the 'authoritarian state' when they used paramilitary tactics during the miners' strike in 1984/5 (Scraton, 1985). Other reasons for concern about the police came about with the doubling of the crime rate between 1981 and 1991 (Home Office, 1993). This rise in crime, along with falling levels of satisfaction with the police, caused considerable worry for the government. Other incidents, including infamous miscarriages of justice in such cases as those of the 'Birmingham Six' and the 'Guildford Four', as well as serious allegations of misconduct and corruption against certain forces such as the West Midlands Serious Crime Squad, produced a picture of an unaccountable and badly managed police service, which had little influence over crime.

A number of Home Office reports (Morris and Heal, 1981; Clarke and Hough, 1984) as well as independent research questioned different aspects of policing, including its role, the nature of the police culture, and the structure of the organization. This Home Office research:

... debunked and demythologized the 'reality' of policing as it was portrayed by the police; it presented a picture of police work which differed considerably from the public image. For example it indicated that contrary to police and media characterization, law enforcement and crime-related work accounted for a relatively small proportion of police time and that most calls were related to the '24-hour social service' side of policing. It questioned whether increased expenditure on the police would have any significant impact on levels of crime and disorder.

(McLaughlin and Murji, 1997, p. 88)

Research completed by the Policy Studies Institute, and originally requested by Metropolitan Commissioner of Police Sir David McNee, examined relations between the public and the police in London (Smith and Gray, 1985). It found that contacts between certain sections of the population, most notably those of West Indian origin, and the police were predominantly of a 'negative kind'. Other findings which emerged from this report emphasized a lack of supervision of the lower ranks, and expressed concern over performance in terms of career advancement and the lack of clearly defined objectives. The report argued that a more positive approach towards management which would include 'the attempt to define tasks and objectives for working groups of police officers or to help them define tasks for themselves; an emphasis on encouraging and rewarding good work for example by promotion or other career opportunities' and 'regular evaluation of the performance of individual officers in the light of policing objectives' (p. 589). While emphasizing the need to improve the management structure, the report was also of the view that the responsibility for actions against crime could not be left entirely to the police: 'it must not be assumed that action to combat crime is the responsibility of the police alone, or that police performance can be assessed purely in terms of the crime rate or the amount of public concern about crime' (p. 572).

Criticism of police management and inefficiency also came from other political quarters. Sir John Wheeler, who was part of a Home Affairs Committee considering policing in Europe, argued that there needed to be an 'overhaul of complex structures and funding systems' in order to resolve the 'glaring deficiencies, incompetent use of resources and blinding incompetence in police management' (*Independent*, 26 July 1990). The Audit Commission, which came to play a key role in promoting managerial reform throughout the public sector, was also critical of the police's management structure and its inefficiency

(Audit Commission, 1990). The aim in this, and subsequent reports written by the Audit Commission (e.g., 1993), was to consider ways of achieving value for money and improving police performance.

The police service itself became increasingly concerned about the constant criticism it received, and began to attempt to alleviate public concerns about its inability to control crime and meet public demand. The three police staff-associations – the Police Federation, the Association of Chief Police Officers (ACPO) and the Superintendents Association – joined together to produce a document that set out standards for policing (Association of Chief Police Officers, 1990). This document aimed to introduce a schema that could measure the quality of service while meeting the needs of the community.

However, the attempts by the police to alleviate criticism by introducing their own policies to improve performance and community relations were undermined by Home Secretary Kenneth Clarke in 1992, when he announced that the police service was ripe for reform. This was followed by a series of reports that attempted to establish firmly performance indicators in the police service. One of the most controversial reports of the time was the result of the Sheehy Inquiry (1993). The terms of reference for the Inquiry were to consider rank structures and conditions of service, to examine whether flexible systems of rewards for performance existed, and to ensure adequate remuneration in order to recruit, retain and motivate officers. The final report presented a number of recommendations, including reducing the ranks structure (by eliminating some ranks, such as Chief Inspectors), dissolving a top-heavy management structure, establishing fixed-term appointments for all ranks, and introducing performance-related pay.

The Sheehy Inquiry was not viewed favourably by the police. Following its publication, criticisms of the recommendations were made from every quarter of the police ranks. At the highest level of the police, the Association of Chief Police Officers and the Police Superintendents Association believed that, if accepted, the proposals would result in adverse consequences for the police service in terms of recruitment, retention and the morale of police officers (Leishman et al., 1996). John Burrows. the president of ACPO at the time, argued that the introduction of contracts and performance-related pay for officers would turn the police 'into just another job, with people coming in and out, rather than giving dedicated service over many years [and] would affect the nature of the police force and the job it does' (Daily Telegraph, 19 July 1993). At the other end of the scale, the Police Federation, which represents those officers below the rank of Superintendent, organized a rally at Wembley to express its anger at the proposals and to air its members' objections. Despite this opposition, Sir Patrick Sheehy continued to defend the report. He argued that 'these and other measures were essential to bring the police into line with other workers and to allow the management flexibility. The police have failed to adopt reform and would now have to face imposed change (*Daily Telegraph*, 22 July 1993). Initially it appeared as if the government would stand by the Sheehy Inquiry and adopt most of its recommendations. However, in October 1993, after months of criticism, Michael Howard, by then Home Secretary, stressed that he no longer accepted large sections of the report.

In the same period, the White Paper on police reform, *Police Reform: A Police Service for the 21st Century* (Home Office, 1993), set out an alternative agenda for the police service. The main proposals were that the Government would set key objectives for the police against which their performance could be measured. These objectives would reflect the government's main belief that the police should be responsible for fighting crime. There were also plans to restructure local police authorities making them smaller and with broader representation. The aim of the authorities would be to ensure that the Constabulary, under their direction, met local objectives. The paper also proposed that Chief Constables should be provided with 'greater freedom to manage the resources at their disposal'. The White Paper also suggested that local commanders should have responsibility for local policing, and recommended the strengthening of HMIC in order to make sure that standards were maintained and that the best quality of services was being provided. The police would also have a duty to consult local communities to ensure that they were setting priorities according to public desires.

Although there was some debate about the White Paper, and a number of amendments were made (see Cope *et al.*, 1997), most of the main proposals mentioned above were drafted into the Police and Magistrates and Court Act 1994 (PMCA). This Act signalled both the simultaneous decentralizing and centralizing of the police. While Chief Constables were given greater say over priorities, they were still bound to meet the key objectives set by the Home Secretary. It has been suggested that these key objectives have been one of the most centralizing influences related to policing in recent years (Loveday, 1995; Leishman *et al.*, 1996; Cope *et al.*, 1997; McLaughlin and Murji, 1997). This feature of police reform demonstrates some of the contradictory effects of restructuring, which have dogged the police in recent years. While the government has attempted to provide local police authorities and Chief Constables with a greater sense of management control, this has also been restricted by the development of a strong performance culture associated with the objective of crime control.

A Performance Culture

Improving the performance of an organization was one of the dominant rationales behind the introduction of NPM (Loveday, 1999). The belief here is that making an organization meet specific targets set within a budget will not only make it more efficient, but will help it focus on the task at hand, making it more effective. It is also believed that defining priorities for the organization means that other tasks, which are not relevant, will and can be 'hived-off' to alternative providers. This was, of course, a key message of the Posen Inquiry (Home Office, 1995b) which attempted to define the core activities of the police service and rid it of ancillary tasks. The key message from this inquiry was that crime control was the fundamental job of the police. Consequently, the Conservative government, under the PMCA, set key objectives for the police, which focused predominantly on crime. Performance would also be measured at a local level. Police authorities in conjunction with their local forces were expected to define local priorities and set annual targets. While supported by the government as the best way to measure value for money in the police service, the performance culture has, in fact, had an adverse effect. Rather than make the police accountable to the public and the government following 'decentralization', it has undermined accountability. There have been repeated reports of the massaging of figures by the police, and some critics have argued that these practices have undermined the development of community policing (Loveday, 1995; Hallam, 2000).

A key measure of police performance throughout the 1980s and 1990s was the use of police-generated crime statistics. Although the police service is generally aware of the limitations of these statistics, and of the reliability of such measures as the 'clear-up' rate, the government, the public and the media tend to rely on these figures as indicators of police efficiency (Loveday, 1999; 2000). Reliance on these figures raises two issues. First, police control over both the collection and presentation of these statistics is always likely to undermine the validity of these figures both within the police service and outside. Second, the measures employed are not reliable or sophisticated enough to measure something as complex as effectiveness.

The massaging of figures is a major problem. Ethnographic research by M. Young (1991), a former police sergeant, identifies how certain tactics are used by different forces to boost their detection rates. One of the most notable practices used to clear up crimes is to encourage already convicted prisoners to admit to other offences (see Young, M., 1991). Other practices have included targeting specific crimes in order to produce positive results. For example, one of the Key Objectives set by the Home Secretary in 1996/97 was to increase the detection of violent crime. In order to secure more detections rank-and-file officers tended to concentrate on offences such as domestic violence. While prioritizing this type of offence may appear to have been a positive step, the way in which these crimes were 'detected' was not. In many of these domestic-violence cases officers recorded the crime and detected it using a downgraded definition of detection (Hallam, 2000). Grading domestic violence as 'detected' no proceedings usually means that an officer does not need to spend too much time on the case and can then add the result to the weekly target. Although it is true to say that the police service in general has improved its approach to domestic violence (see Grace, 1995), the relative ease of detecting domestic violence has assisted in increasing the detection level of this offence.

Both the HMIC and Audit Commission have warned about the dangers of performance indicators, despite the fact that part of their roles has been to ensure that police forces are meeting key objectives. A recent thematic report by the HMIC, *Police Integrity*, stated that:

> The increasingly aggressive and demonstrable performance culture has emerged as a major factor affecting integrity, not least because for some years there has been an apparent tendency for some forces to 'trawl the margins' for detections and generally to use every means to portray their performance in a good light.
>
> (HMIC, 1999, p. 19)

While, on the one hand, the Audit Commission has promoted the need for the police to improve performance and productivity with the resources provided, and has put performance indicators in place for the police since 1992 (Local Government Act 1992), it has, on the other, also emphasized a need for caution when interpreting police statistics. For example, the Audit Commission report *Helping with Inquiries: Tackling Crime Effectively* (1993) highlights a number of deficiencies in crime and detection rates as performance measures. They state that 'the volume of crime is not directly a measure of police performance' and that in terms of detection a charge counts even though a person may not be convicted later at court.

A related issue concerns the lack of discretion that the performance culture allows to both the rank-and-file officers and Chief Constables. Having to meet specific targets means that at times behaviour deemed a minor infraction of the law, rather than being ignored or resulting in an unrecorded warning, is reported in a conscious attempt to inflate the figures. Hallam argues that 'discretion was rarely exercised with a consequence that the results produced in the name of performance have not always been in the interests of justice or reflected a credible service to the public' (Hallam, 1999, p. 92). It could be argued, in line with the zero-tolerance approach to policing, that even minor infractions of the law should not be ignored (Johnston, 2000; Young, J., 1999). However, in order to retain a reasonable level of community support some level of discretion on the part of officers is necessary. Pollard argues that removing police discretion through the adoption of zero-tolerance policies results in a largely counterproductive form of 'short-termism', by placing an 'undue emphasis on the numbers game', and that this 'poses an enormous threat to the future' (Pollard, 1997).

As well as undermining discretion at the lower levels it has been argued that financial changes and the ability of the Home Secretary to set objectives undermines the independence of Chief Constables. Robert Reiner (2000) argues that a recent House of the Lords judgement illustrates this point (*Regina v. Chief Constable of Sussex Ex Parte International Traders Ferry Limited*). The case involves a company called International Traders Ltd, who, from the beginning of 1995, transported livestock to the Continent from Shoreham in Sussex. Because of possible outbreaks of disorder from demonstrators, International Traders Ltd kept the police informed about shipments from Shoreham. In order to reduce disorder it was decided that a police presence would be necessary. However it was decided by the Chief Constable that in the long run the police could only provide a minimal amount of support at specific times, because of other priorities. International Traders Ltd applied to quash the decision of the Chief Constable to restrict policing to particular times. Although the case was not upheld, it was important in two respects: first, the ruling by the House of Lords took into account the Chief Constable's independent role in deciding what should be a priority for his areas, suggesting that under the PMCA real decentralization had occurred. On the other hand, the judgement reasserted the need for the Chief Constable to take into account the national objectives and priorities of the Home Secretary. As Reiner states, this judgement leaves the concept of 'police operational independence' as an 'empty shell' and, as other commentators have suggested, while Chief Constables are allowed to 'row', the direction they are moving in is very much 'steered' by the Home Secretary (Reiner, 2000, p. 197)

The drive to save money and the use of objective criteria to direct the police towards clearing up crime meant that other areas of policing were being neglected. Barry Loveday (1994) argues that despite some realization by senior ranks of the police that their main role was not crime fighting and that they must incorporate community relations and public reassurance as priorities these factors were ignored by the Conservative government. Loveday further states that 'without the support of the community crime fighting cannot take place' (p. 29). This sentiment is shared by a number of other commentators (e.g., Kinsey *et al.*, 1985), who agree that in order to clear up crime it is necessary to have the support of the community. This is not to say that following the Scarman report there was not a valid attempt by the government to encourage forms of community-based policing. The White Paper (1993) as well as suggesting managerial reforms also emphasized that 'the police service alone cannot tackle the problem of crime, they need the active support and involvement of the communities whom they serve' (paragraph 1.3). Initiatives that favoured multi-agency and local approaches to crime problems flourished throughout the 1980s and 1990s. The Home Office set up the Home Office Crime Prevention Unit (1983) to encourage the involvement of all agencies in crime prevention. It also encouraged and supported various initiatives, such as the Safer Cities Initiatives dealing with regeneration in specific localities and the establishment of Crime Concern, which helped to provide advice and support to local projects and worked with other agencies including the police to reduce crime. In the Home Office Circular 44/90 agencies such as the police, fire service, social services and local government were encouraged to work on joint initiatives. Other developments included the increased use of Neighbourhood Watch Schemes and various attempts to introduce specific styles of community policing (see Newburn, 2002). Strategies such as 'problem-orientated policing' (POP), which actively encourages the police to identify and solve underlying problems in communities, have also been adopted (Leigh *et al.*, 1996, 1998; Wright, 2002).

Rather than an integrated approach to local policing, which would encourage better communication between the police service and communities, the approach taken by the Conservatives was patchy. As Tim Newburn (2002) emphasizes, the government failed to implement the recommendations of the Morgan report (1991), which had recommended a partnership and coordinated approach to crime. Newburn states that crime prevention initiatives were pursued merely at a rhetorical level, and although identified as core issues for police they remained a 'fairly narrowly defined specialism' (Newburn, 2002). As suggested by Nigel Fielding (1995), those who carried out a community policing role were often distant from other police officers. It can also be argued that although senior ranks of the police service viewed community relations as important this was not necessarily a shared view. Research on police occupational culture argues that there are different attitudes among those at the top of the organization and those at the lower level (Chan, 1996). It could be suggested that pressure on Chief Constables to achieve certain levels of performance filters down to the rank and file, who then use this pressure to reinforce their role as crime fighters (Reiner, 2000; Loveday, 2000).

The Conservatives' determination to reduce public spending and their preference for the private sector meant that the discourse of performance culture and managerialism became the dominant one in many public services, including the police. While there has been an acceptance that assessing the performance of the police simply by counting police 'outputs', such as response times and the number of detections, is fraught with difficulty, this remained the principle model of evaluation throughout the early 1990s. Furthermore, the criticism of the ability of the police to control crime, and the effect that the performance culture has had on police and community relations, seems to have been ignored. The question then was: would this situation change if a different government were to be elected? Would New Labour's approach to law and order release the police from the continued onslaught of having to meet performance targets and saving money?

New Labour, the 'Third Way' and modernization

A fundamental component of New Labour's 'Third Way' is the emphasis on modernizing government. This is sold as a package of reforms and programmes, which can be used to update government and public services, and which works a means to move beyond the assault on pubic services that occurred under the Conservatives (Newman, 2000). Newman notes that the modernization agenda goes beyond that of the previous managerial paradigm:

> The emerging discourses of Best Value, partnership, public consultation and democratic renewal appear to offer an expanded concept of 'managing for public purpose', going beyond the

narrow confines of efficiency – seeking organizational restructuring, 'downsizing', contracting and quasi-markets. Modernization
also offers a more dynamic image of the process of management
itself.

(Newman, 2000, p. 47)

Labour's pragmatic policy-approach was underlined by three main
shifts (Newman, 2000). The first was from a concern with short-term
efficiency towards longer-term planning and effectiveness. This can be
witnessed in the way that Labour has mapped out financial
arrangements for public services. For instance, one of the first tasks of
the Treasury was to draft the Comprehensive Spending Reviews (Her
Majesty's Treasury, 1998). These reviews identified the level of
spending for all public services over a three-year period. This
financial planning was underpinned by Public Service Agreements for
every department that set out long-term goals over the same period.
The second shift identified by Newman was that rather than focusing
on institutional reform, such as the introduction of quasi-markets,
modernization prioritized the use of certain tools and techniques to
achieve policy outcomes. So, rather than specifying exactly how
policy goals were to be achieved, the Labour government was to
encourage, within a legislative framework, the development of
innovative ways of working. For example, Best Value was implemented as a way to ensure efficiency, effectiveness and quality in public
service, but in the process local authorities, and police and fire
authorities, have been provided with the opportunity to decide on
how they review and deliver services. The third shift from managerialism to modernization has emphasized a collaborative approach,
where government and public agencies work in partnership with each
other, and with other organizations, including those within the
private and voluntary sector.

Modernization is concerned not just with changing the way the
public services are managed, but also with the impact of crime on
society and addressing the underlying causes of crime. The Criminal
Justice Strategy combines the objectives of reducing crime and disorder
and the effects that they have on people's lives, with the need to
dispense justice fairly and objectively, taking into account the requirements of both defendants and victims. In this sense New Labour's
approach attempts to move back to values and priorities traditionally
associated the criminal justice system such as justice, fairness and
equity (Raine and Wilson, 1997). In order to reduce both the fear of
crime and crime itself New Labour has also promoted the need for

individuals and communities to be responsible for crime in their areas. Again, the emphasis is on working in partnerships with professionals and agencies in order to resolve localized problems.

While New Labour has attempted to reposition itself beyond managerialism, there remain continuities within the modernization and managerial agendas. New Labour maintains the need for public services to be more efficient and provide value for money and the requirement for the public sector to retain performance management frameworks in order to measure its achievements. New Labour has tried to distance itself from the performance measures used by the Conservatives by emphasizing objectives and targets based on outcomes rather than the narrow efficiency-output measures employed previously. New Labour has also stressed a need to measure service standards and employ a whole-system approach, with targets being set for the criminal justice system as a whole (Cabinet Office, 1999). Despite these attempts to move beyond managerialism, it will be argued that this has not been a major transition. Although Labour has implemented legislation and policies to put in place its modernizing agenda, the sustained concentration on performance and efficiency has undermined its attempt to readjust the difficulties that organizations such as the police faced under the managerial regime. This point will be illustrated by taking into account pieces of key legislation that have affected the police. It will be argued that despite New Labour's aim to implement a new holistic approach this has been undermined by the persistent requirement for evidence to show that the police perform well. It will also argue that, despite a renewed emphasis on quality within performance measures, the police are still assessed in the narrowest of terms.

The Crime and Disorder Act

The Crime and Disorder Act 1998 embodied a number of core measures that attempted to represent the objectives set out by New Labour. It included measures to tackle youth crime, reduce delays in the criminal justice system and prevent the anti-social behaviour that was seen as contributing to the fear of crime. It also adopted the recommendations of the Morgan report (1991), which placed a statutory duty on Chief Constables and local authorities to work in cooperation with police authorities, the probation service and health authorities in order to formulate and implement a 'strategy for the reduction of crime and disorder in the area' (Crime and Disorder Act 1998, sections 6–8). Of course, while the focus was on joint working, the Crime and Disorder Strategy set out local priorities and included targets and performance measures which had to be met.

Best Value The Crime and Disorder Act 1998

Originally intended for local authorities, the statutory duty of Best Value was introduced into police authorities under the Local Government Act 1999. It is a key mechanism developed by New Labour to improve public service delivery, presented as a 'rigorous system for delivering high quality, responsive services based on locally determined objectives' (Cabinet Office 1999, p. 41). Its aim is to secure continuous improvements in service delivery. Under Best Value police authorities are required to review all services they provide over a five-year period, taking into consideration the four Cs:

Challenge – why and how a service is provided
Compare – performance with other service providers with a view to improving the service
Compete – to ensure that the service they provide is the most efficient
Consult – with local taxpayers, service users and the business community.

The duty of Best Value is not just about reviewing the service provided, but is set within a rigorous performance framework that provides a number of performance standards and indicators that each police authority must meet. Police authorities must also set out a local performance plan, which provides details of their local performance targets for the coming year. This performance plan is to be available to the public. In order to ensure that police authorities and the police force under their control are meeting the requirements set out by Best Value there is an extensive inspection regime, which involves both the Audit Commission and HMIC. Furthermore, each police force must strive to meet the performance of top 25 per cent of performers in police league tables, and the targets they set must reflect the aim to achieve this level over the five-year period. The final, and most challenging, aspect of Best Value is the power of the Secretary of State (in this case, the Home Secretary) to intervene if any constabulary is perceived to be failing to achieve an adequate level of performance (Home Office, 1999).

In addition to Best Value and the Crime and Disorder Act the police service must also take account of the ministerial priorities as set out by the Home Secretary. As part of the Comprehensive Spending Review it must include within the Annual Policing Plan (initially set out by the PMCA and confirmed by the Police Act 1996) an efficiency plan that demonstrates 2 per cent savings, year on year, and how aims and objectives are being delivered in the most cost-effective way. Overarching aims and objectives have been set for the police service, which are to be used to provide a top-down perspective for the whole criminal justice system. The police service also has a duty to meet Audit Commission indicators under the Audit Commission Act 1998. The intention of these indicators is to measure cost, efficiency and effectiveness, and they are used to make comparisons between police forces.

The pieces of legislation discussed above do seem to reveal an attempt to move beyond managerialism. First of all, within the Crime and Disorder Act (1998) there is a realization that no one agency is responsible for crime control, thus moving beyond the premise that crime control is purely the responsibility of the police. As Newburn (2002) illustrates, by accepting key elements of the Morgan report, which emphasized the need for partnership, the government was accepting that the police could not deal with crime and disorder on their own. In addition, the Crime and Disorder Act 1998 relocates responsibility for crime and disorder with the local authorities, who are to work in conjunction with the police. In most areas crime and disorder strategies are the responsibility of chief officers at divisional level, making the focus even more local. Newburn (2002) indicates that the Crime and Disorder Act also attempts to 'reinsert' the community into policing (p. 109). Emphasis is placed on the participation of community groups and organizations, as well as on adopting the interests of women, the elderly and ethnic minorities. Consultation exercises must attempt to coordinate the views of all these groups and target those groups considered hard to reach (see Newburn, 2002). But, despite attempts to restore the community aspect to policing and develop partnership approaches, the dominance of the performance culture undermines the positive aspects of this legislation.

One concern is that of the unresolved issues between locally and centrally driven objectives and between the targets that are prioritized. Butler (2000) argues that it could be difficult for police authorities' annual plans to account for all the competing priorities set within authorities' jurisdictions. Each authority will comprise at least a couple of local crime and disorder audits and have to take account of the key objectives set by the Home Office. The desire of Chief Constables to retain a certain level of performance within national league tables means that the possibility of central objectives undermining local priorities is still present. Although 'it would be wrong to "name and shame" a police force for failing to deliver when at district level the crime and disorder plans were achieving their targets' (Butler, 2000, p. 311), research has demonstrated that local crime and disorder strategies have tended to adhere to central objectives. A review of the first round of crime and disorder strategies found that a high priority was given to burglary, vehicle crime and violent crime, which were clear priorities for the government (Phillips *et al.*, 2000). This review also argues that while there is a realization that different crime and disorder partnerships may have different priorities, because of local crime patterns, there remains an emphasis on partnerships attempting to define six core issues to tackle. This advice may mean that government priorities continue to dominate local agendas.

The need for organizations to meet individual targets also affects the partnership approach. Some commentators have suggested that when organizations are assessed on distinct performance measures (recorded crime, for the police) this creates discord for inter-agency relationships as intra-organizational priorities dominate (Newburn, 2002; Crawford, 2001). Furthermore, as emphasized in a recent Audit Commission report, 'the requirements to fulfil national top-down requirements may thus inadvertently weaken the link between community safety and the concerns of local communities' (Audit Commission, 1999, p. 30). This report further points out that police forces were still assessed in relation to detection rates because of the reliance on national performance indicators (Audit Commission 1999, p. 37). It is true to say that the key Best Value Performance Indicators (BVPIs) and other crime reduction targets set by the government lean heavily on recorded and detected crime as measures of success. One of the core service-delivery outcomes noted within the BVPIs is the total percentage for recorded crime per 1,000 population detected. In support of these indicators the Home Office Strategic Plan argues that 'the top priority is ensuring that police performance indicators are developed to capture whether police action is achieving objectives – such as lower crime or increased confidence' (Home Office, 1999b). Other reports, including the HMIC thematic report 'Winning the Race' (1999) and the recent 'Policing London' (2002) report, which replicated much of the previous 1980s' research by the PSI, both highlighted the negative effect of the performance culture on community relations with the police, particularly in relation to ethnic minorities.

Best Value was not just aimed at improving the efficiency and effectiveness of public service but also included service quality as a major element of the reform. Rather than just have performance indicators focusing on efficiency, there has been an attempt to consolidate performance indicators that measure quality and corporate health using indicators such as sickness levels, medical retirements, and percentage of staff from ethnic minorities (DETR, 1999). In general, performance indicators 'endeavour to reflect the resources devoted to the service, the efficiency with which they are used, the quality of service and the service users' expectations'. Despite this attempt to gain a more rounded approach through Best Value, the reality is that efficiency and outcomes that focus on the police's ability to clear up crime continue to dominate how the police are assessed.

Recent media coverage reinforces this view and in turn reinforces the belief of the public that low levels of detection mean that their local forces are failing to provide an adequate service. Headlines such as 'Revealed: the Country's Worst Police' (*Observer*, 2 December 2001) and 'Blunkett Says Police Fail Public' (*Guardian*, 3 December 2001) depict the inability to meet performance targets as indications of a 'failing' service. The levels of performance discussed in such examples are connected to outcomes such as detected crime and response times. These measures do not necessarily tell us anything about police efficiency or quality of service but continue to be presented as measures of both. (For example, a response time may be quick but the operator may not have managed to gather all the relevant information from the caller before sending out the patrol. Consequently, officers may arrive at the scene unprepared and misinformed.)

In terms of efficiency it is claimed that Best Value provides 'continuous improvement' in service delivery. This 'continuous improvement' appears to be heavily influenced by a police force's ability to achieve the 2 per cent efficiency gains set out by the Comprehensive Spending Review. The HMIC states that one of emerging themes from the Best Value inspections has been the inability of forces to adequately cost services and identify where cost savings could be made, and how this has fed into the process of improving efficiency (Todd, 2002). Recent research by the present author, which included observations of the Best Value Inspections conducted by the HMIC, demonstrated that a key area of concern was whether savings made as a result of Best Value were fed into the overall process of efficiency planning. The danger here is the extent to which 'costing of services' plays into the 'continuous improvement' element of Best Value. If making cost savings continues to be a key factor of success in measuring individual performance then a number of difficulties can arise. As Butler (2000) stresses, some police forces that have already successively made efficiency gains in recent years and may no longer be able to do so may be punished under this regime. Butler (2000) also emphasizes the difficulties in costing police activities, plus the difficulties in comparing cost between different forces because of different cost-sampling methods.

These continued priorities of achieving value for money and assessing police forces via performance indicators might invoke other sections of the Best Value legislation. As in other areas of the public sector the Secretary of State has power to intervene where services appear to have failed. While this may seem like an extreme measure, intervention has occurred in 20 local education authority areas that were not seen as meeting standards (Audit Commission, 2002). Not only does this threaten constabulary independence it also threatens local policing, as the possible amalgamation of forces means that local priorities might be overtaken not only by central objectives but also by regional ones. While, at present, the regionalization of the police service may seem a distant possibility, the hiving-off of police functions seems certain to continue. Again, how this will develop is still difficult to assess, but with increasing focus on failing police forces that fail to meet targets the prospect that private firms could take over the policing of certain areas is feasible. The main issues here concern the effect that alternative providers of policing services have on accountability and forms of regulation. There are also questions over how alternative policing bodies engage with communities and what kind of services they can provide.

Policing for the twenty-first century

The Home Secretary David Blunkett's apparent disgust at police performance and media speculation about violence on the streets spiralling out of control have re-emphasized the crime control aspects of policing. The tendency for crime control imperatives and the need to assess police performance have continued to dominate recent reforms. The National Policing Plan (Home Office, 2002b), introduced as one of the provisions of the recent Police Reform Act 2002, sets out national priorities for the whole police service. The central message is the need for the police to drive up performance and to set clear priorities. Police authorities will have to take account of these national objectives and performance targets when drawing up their own annual plans. These key priorities centre mainly on crime and its detection, and include: tackling anti-social behaviour and disorder; reducing the volume of street, drug-related and violent crime; increasing the efforts against serious and organized crime; and increasing the number of offences brought to justice (Home Office, 2002b, p. 3). As in most of New Labour law-and-order policies, cooperation with other agencies, both police and non-related, is seen as essential in achieving these aims. The need to ensure public reassurance, public safety and public satisfaction is also apparent. Other developments with regard to police reform include the setting up of the Police Standards Unit, the aim of which is to improve police operational performance, raise standards and reduce the variability between police performance. Recently, police performance monitors have also been published (Home Office, 2003). These are believed to cover a wider range of policing activity than previous performance regimes. The intention of the monitors is to allow comparisons between comparable police forces in terms of reducing crime, crime investigation, promoting public safety, the effective use of resources and citizen focus. The police monitors that are being developed to form the new Police Performance Assessment Framework will expand over the next couple of years. The aim of this framework is not just to assess performance but also to incorporate the cost of police activity across police forces.

Conclusion

New Labour came into power promising to modernize the public services in order to provide services that were not only efficient but which also provided quality services that met user expectations. Despite attempts to reinstate relationships between the police and the community by introducing legislation such as the Crime and Disorder Act, the continued motivation to demonstrate that police forces are clearing up crime undermines the more positive aspects of New Labour law-and-order policies. Although David Blunkett has rejected the view that his reform agenda and national policing priorities will not centralize the police further (Home Office, 2002a), the fact that police authorities will feel obliged to give precedence to the key objectives decided by the Home Secretary may mean that local priorities set as a result of the Crime and Disorder Act are ignored. Furthermore, the emphasis on continuous improvement and on meeting efficiency and savings targets means that police will have to consider what tasks take priority as they will not be able to fulfil all demands placed on them with the resources provided. The police service may feel further alienated at the further development of the league-table mentality, which pits police force against police force. The introduction of yet another set of performance standards does not make comparison between present and past particularly easy. The new proposed framework, while arguably measuring issues such as promoting public safety, centres on people's concerns about three main areas of crime, namely burglary, vehicle crime and violent crime. Public safety will be measured by how much the public worry about being subject to one of the above offences. People may be unduly concerned about these issues, though that does not necessarily mean that the police service in their area is not dealing with these crimes or that a member of the public is likely to be subject to such an offence. Persistent attempts to measure police success via the use of performance measures that concentrate on crime will not improve police–community relations nor do they accept that the police can only have a minimal impact on crime. There are other underlying issues that must be addressed before crime can truly be reduced.

References

Association of Chief Police Officers [ACPO] (1990) *Setting Standards for Policing*, London: ACPO.

Audit Commission (1990) *Effective Policing: Performance Review in the Police*, London: HMSO.

Audit Commission (1993) *Helping with Enquiries: Tackling Crime Effectively*, London: HMSO.

Audit Commission (1999) *Safety in Numbers: Promoting Community Safety*, London: Audit Commission.

Audit Commission (2002) *A Force for Change: Central Government Intervention in Failing Government Services*, London: Audit Commission.

Butler, T. (2000) 'Managing the Future: A Chief Constable's View', in F. Leishman, B. Loveday and S. Savage (eds) *Core Issues in Policing*, 2nd edition, Harlow: Longman.

Cabinet Office (1999) *Modernising Government*, Cmnd 4310, London: HMSO.

Chan, J. (1996) 'Changing Police Culture', *British Journal of Criminology*, 36(1), 109–34.

Clarke, R. and Hough, M. (1984) *Crime and Police Effectiveness*, London: HMSO.

Committee of Inquiry into the Police (1978) *Report on Negotiations Machinery and Pay* (I and II), Cmnd 7283, London: HMSO.

Conservative Party (1979), *Conservative Manifesto*, London: Conservative General Office.

Cope, S., Leishman, F. and Starie, P. (1997) 'Globalization, New Public Management and the Enabling State', *International Journal of Public Sector Management*, 10(6), 444–59.

Crawford, A. (2001) 'Joined-Up But Fragmented: Contradiction, Ambiguity and Ambivalence at the Heart of New Labour's "Third Way"' in R.

Matthews and J. Pitts (eds) *Crime, Disorder and Community Safety*, London: Routledge.

DETR [Department of the Environment, Transport and the Regions] (1999) *Achieving Best Value through Performance Review*, London: DETR.

Dunleavy, P. and Hood, C. (1994) 'From Old Public Administration to New Public Management', *Public Money and Management*, 14(3), 9–16.

Fielding, N. (1995) *Community Policing*, Oxford: Oxford University Press.

Fitzgerald, M., Hough, M., Joseph, I. and Qureshi, T. (2002) *Policing for London*, Cullompton, Devon: Willan.

Grace, S. (1995) *Policing Domestic Violence in the 1990s*, London: HMSO.

Hallam, S. (2000) 'Effective and Efficient Policing: Some Problems with the Culture of Performance', in A. Marlow and B. Loveday (eds) *After Macpherson: Policing after the Stephen Lawrence Inquiry*, Lyme Regis: Russell House.

Her Majesty's Treasury (1998) *Modern Public Services for Britain: Investing in Reform*, Cmnd 4011, London: HMSO.

HMIC (1999) *Police Integrity: Securing and Maintaining Public Confidence*, London: Home Office.

HMIC (1999b) *Winning the Race: Policing Plural Communities Revisited*, London: Home Office.

Home Office (1983) *Manpower, Efficiency and Effectiveness in the Police Service*, Circular 114/83, London: Home Office.

Home Office (1991) *Safer Communities: The Local Delivery of Crime Prevention through the Partnership Approach*, London: HMSO (the Morgan report).

Home Office (1993) *Police Reform: A Police Service for the 21st Century*, Cmnd 2281, London: HMSO.

Home Office (1995) *Digest 3:Information on the Criminal Justice System in England and Wales*, London: Home Office.

Home Office (1995b) *Review of Core and Ancillary Tasks, Final Report*, London: HMSO.

Home Office (1999) *Ministerial Priorities, Key Performance Indicators and Efficiency Planning for 1999/2000*, London: Home Office.

Home Office (2001) *Policing a New Century: A Blueprint for Reform*, Cmnd 5326, London: HMSO.

Home Office (2002a) 'Partnership Way Forward to Drive Up Police Standards', Home Office press release (13th May).

Home Office (2002b) *The National Policing Plan*, London: Home Office.

Home Office (2003) *Police Performance Monitors: Improving Performance, Tackling Crime*, Home Office press release (19 February), London: Home Office.

Hood, C. (1991) 'A Public Management for All Seasons', *Public Administration*, 69(1), 3–19.

Johnston (2000) *Policing Britain: Risk, Security and Governance*, Harlow: Longman.

Kinsey, R., Lea, J. and Young, J. (1985) *Losing the Fight against Crime*, Oxford: Blackwell.

Leigh, A., Read, T. and Tilley, N. (1996) *Problem-orientated Policing: Britpop*, Police Research Group Paper 75, London: Home Office.

Leigh, A., Read, T. and Tilley, N. (1998) *Britpop II: Problem-orientated Policing in Practice*, Police Research Group Paper 93, London: Home Office.

Leishman, F., Cope, S. and Starie, P. (1996) 'Reinventing and Restructuring: Towards a "New Policing Order"', in F. Leishman, B. Loveday and S. Savage (eds) *Core Issues in Policing*, Harlow: Longman.

Loveday, B. (1994) 'Ducking and Diving: Formulating a Policy for Police and Criminal Justice in the 1990s, *Public Money and Management*, July–September, 25–30.

Loveday, B. (1995) 'Reforming the Police: From Local Service to State Police?', *Political Quarterly*, 66(2), 141–56.

Loveday, B. (1999) 'The Impact of Performance Culture of Criminal Justice Agencies: The Case of the Police and Crown Prosecution Service', Occasional Paper 9, Portsmouth: Institute of Criminal Justice Studies, University of Portsmouth.

Loveday, B. (2000) 'Managing Crime: Police Use of Crime Data as an Indicator of Effectiveness', *International Journal of the Sociology of Law*, 28, 215–37.

McLaughlin, E. and Murji, K. (1997), 'The Future Lasts a Long Time: Public Police Work and the Managerialist Paradox', in P. Francis, P. Davies and V. Jupp (eds) *Policing Futures: The Police, Law Enforcement and the Twenty-First Century*, Basingstoke: Macmillan.

Morris, P. and Heal, K. (1981) *Crime Control & the Police*, London: HMSO.

Newburn, T. (2002) 'Community Safety and Policing: Some Implications of the Crime and Disorder Act 1998', in G. Hughes, E. McLaughlin and J. Munice (eds) *Crime Prevention and Community Safety: New Directions*, London: Sage.

Newman, J. (2000) 'Beyond the New Public Management? Modernizing Public Services', in J. Clarke, S. Gewirtz and E. McLaughlin, *New Managerialism, New Welfare*, London: Sage.

Phillips, C., Jacobson, J, Considine, M. and Lewis, R. (2000) *A Review of Audits and Strategies Produced by Crime and Disorder Partnerships in 1999*, Home Office Briefing Note, London: Home Office.

Pollard, C. (1997), 'Zero-Tolerance: Short-term Fix, Long-term Liability?', in N. Dennis (ed.) *Zero Tolerance: Policing a Free Society*, London: IEA Health and Welfare Unit.

Raine, J.W. and Willson, M.J. (1997) 'Beyond Managerialism in Criminal Justice', *Howard Journal*, 36(1), 80–95.

Reiner, R. (2000) *The Politics of the Police*, 3rd edition, Oxford: Oxford University Press.

Savage, S.P. (1990) 'A War on Crime? Law and Order Policies in the 1980s', in L. Robins and S.P. Savage (eds) *Public Policy under Thatcher*, Basingstoke: Macmillan.

Scarman, Lord (1982) *The Scarman Report: The Brixton Disorders*, London: HMSO.

Scraton, P. (1985) *The State of the Police*, London: Pluto.

Sheehy, P. (1993) *Inquiry into Police Responsibilities and Rewards*, Cmnd 2280, London: HMSO.

Smith, D.J. and Gray, J. (1985) *Police and People in London*, Aldershot: Gower.

Wright, A. (2002) *Policing: An Introduction to Concepts and Practice*, Cullompton, Devon: Willan.

Young, J. (1999) *The Exclusive Society*, London: Sage.

Young, M. (1991) *An Inside Job*, Oxford: Oxford University Press.

Chapter 9

Of crowds, crimes and carnivals

Patrick Slaughter

Introduction

The Northumberland Police were expecting trouble. The National Criminal Intelligence Service (NCIS) had passed on intelligence indicating that all the big 'firms' were intent on being in Sunderland for the European Championship qualifier between England and Turkey (Wednesday 2 April 2003). All leave was cancelled, more than one thousand officers were deployed to police the match. Before and after the game the police clashed with fans. One hundred and five people were arrested. Writing in the immediate aftermath of the violence Paul Kelso (*Guardian*, Friday 4 April 2003) concluded that; '. . . the scale of the exercise required to police England fans at a home game should leave no one in any doubt that the benign behaviour of supporters at the World Cup was a rare bright spot on a deeply tarnished record.' Such sentiments are echoed in recent declarations of NCIS who warn that after a lull in football violence in England throughout much of the 1990s the problem has resurfaced. From a criminological perspective that most stubbornly resistant and persistent strain of folk devil, the football hooligan, is back on the agenda once more.

Kelso's contention that the 2002 World Cup, hosted by Japan and South Korea, was out of the ordinary is, from the perspective of English football, correct at a number of different levels. Many people predicted that the England football squad would not qualify from their opening group matches in the so-called 'group of death'. But they defeated Argentina, many people's pre-tournament favourites, and easily disposed of Denmark. Their defeat in the quarter-finals by Brazil by the odd goal (a particularly odd goal in this instance) was regarded as a valiant battle by plucky heroes.

It was perhaps not only the members of the English Football Association who felt the need for self-congratulation; surely New Labour, the Home Office, and the National Criminal Intelligence Squad had a good tournament too? Months of meticulous planning to prevent, or at least minimize, the scenes of crowd disorder which persistently accompany the England team's foreign jaunts appeared to have paid dividends in quite spectacular fashion. Not only were there no violent incidents involving the followers of the national team, but England fans were showered with praise by Japanese police officials for their impeccable behaviour throughout the tournament. England played well and peace broke out on the terraces in the 2002 World Cup: all very unexpected.

This hardly means that New Labour's notion of, and campaign against, football hooliganism was vindicated. It is only in the appropriate historical context that the particular initiatives taken by New Labour – the Football (Disorder) Act 1999, the Football (Disorder) Act 2000, and the establishment of a new England Members Club (as proposed in the final report and recommendations of the Working Group on Football Disorder 2001) – can be evaluated and compared with previous initiatives and legislation. It is suggested in what follows that a fully social understanding of the football crowd is unlikely to be achieved if we do not broaden out our focus of analysis and consider not just why the football crowd becomes increasingly problematized, but why crowds in general have tended to demonstrate a capacity for confrontation with authority over the last 30 years.

The policies on football crowd behaviour that have evolved over the past two or three decades are part of a transition, in which society moves away from a model of inclusion and rather seeks to *essentialize* and *exclude* (Young, 1999). From the 1970s onwards, first the police, then football clubs and the football authorities, then the courts and then the government have confronted and acted against the 'hooligan problem'. The 'hooligan problem' is, on the one hand, very real (thousands of youth engaged in public displays of gratuitous violence), and on the other, a product of a distorting media coverage (Hall, 1978) and an increased tendency on the part of the public and authorities alike to demonize problematic *others* (Young, 1999). The hooligan problem presents peculiar difficulties to those charged with its containment. Not only must the hooligan be seen to be defeated, but the idea of the hooligan, so firmly etched in the public consciousness, so eagerly reproduced in the media, must also be managed (not necessarily laid to rest – the idea of the hooligan can be played upon to good effect). The efforts of one political administration after another to deal with the problem are fundamentally flawed, in that they are underpinned by a failure to pose the question of why the football crowd begins to have the capacity to present difficulties for authority at a specific time in history.

The following pages will not be concerned with the fine detail of New Labour's response to 'hooliganism', but with trying to 'place' historically the crowd in general and the football crowd in particular. In this I take a great deal from John Lea's conceptual framework for the rescuing of 'social crime' (Lea, 1999), in which he brilliantly captures the way in which the loosening social relations of crime control thrust upon us forms of criminalized behaviour that are not of the crudely parasitic nature experienced in what Jock Young characterizes as a more 'inclusionary' earlier period (Young, 1999), but tend more and more to be motivated by social protest. What Lea demonstrates is that this increase in 'social crime' is reminiscent of an earlier period of transition, that from feudalism to emergent forms of mercantile capitalism.

How the crowd has changed

Crowds are present throughout history, coming together to celebrate, protest, spectate or mourn. There are certain defining characteristics of the crowd, which are present across time independent of the historical context. At times the crowd is spontaneous and chaotic, and at others it is meticulously organized and marshalled. The cause or focus of the crowd may be a semi-permanent feature of a particular society (e.g., the scaffold in medieval England) or something episodic and short-lived (Thatcher's 'poll tax'). The crowd is sometimes *for*, and sometimes *against*, sometimes seemingly revolutionary and sometimes apparently conservative. A leader might call up the crowd; or alternatively it may simply gather. The profiles of those individuals that constitute the crowd do vary, sometimes more male, sometimes more Black, sometimes less affluent. In short, crowds can be very different from one another. Even any particular crowd, in our own example the 'football crowd', will behave differently depending on time, place and situation. The temptation can be to dismiss the crowd in general as a serious focus of rigorous academic study, the nature of the beast being regarded as too slippery, ephemeral, unfathomable. Alternatively, the crowd is packaged into discrete types: the political crowd, the football crowd, the riotous mob, the festive revellers and so on. The crowd, in its entirety and in all of its manifestations, is a social fact. As with any social fact, changes in its structure, purpose, profile, and organization cannot be explained without reference to wider social-historical processes; and at the same time, again, changes in 'the crowd' will in turn affect those wider social processes and our understanding of them. Even the report of the Working Group on Football Disorder (Home Office, 2001) glimpsed this:

> English football disorder cannot be removed from its social context. In many ways it is a manifestation of a wider social problem of alienated young males demonstrating their frustration in an anti-social and violent way. It occurs in high streets and up and down the country every weekend. Mediterranean holiday resorts are equally at risk. Football is not immune and football cannot be expected to eliminate its disorder problems until the wider social problems have been tackled.

From the 1970s onwards the crowd undergoes a 'master change' in the way that it manifests and organizes itself, and this provokes changes in the way in which the crowd is regarded and responded to. It becomes less concerned with the future, and more concerned with the present and with tinted visions of the past. The crowd starts to become more volatile and less receptive to 'reason'. Its various manifestos are informed more by conservatism than radicalism. The crowd's participants relate to the creed of short-term hedonism rather than the rules of deferred gratification. Leadership of the crowd becomes less democratic and more difficult to discern. The mood of the crowd becomes more difficult to understand; where there is protest there is also celebration; the intolerant crowd is also inclusive in character. The tradition of ritual becomes less significant as the crowd strives toward innovative forms of expression.

Two crowds either side of the 'master change'

June 1966: London

In the dying moments of the 1966 World Cup final between Germany and England the British commentator Kenneth Wolstenholme was finding it difficult to disguise his own feelings of excitement and slightly premature jubilation. England was leading by the narrowest of margins (3–2), and the nation willed the final whistle. Wolstenholme's attention was caught by action away from the game itself: 'some people are on the pitch; they think it's all over'. And in that split second his eyes came back to the game as Geoff Hurst scored England's fourth goal, and put the game beyond the Germans: *'It is now!'*. The crowd inside Wembley Stadium roared and danced its delight. The collective celebration spoke of much more than the winning of a football tournament. The scene became part of the collage of a moment: *never ever having had it so good; liberation through education; the 'swinging sixties'; meritocracy; mini-dresses; the Beatles; Harold Wilson's pipe*; and a myriad other images to make everyone happy.

June 1968: Paris

The crowd is mainly made up of earnest young men and women, mainly students and trade unionists, all of them intent on destabilizing the political status quo. They confront the police in battle. Although in many ways this is a ragtag army – no uniform, their most elaborate weapon the Molotov cocktail, and with little clear sense of fighting strategy – there is a clear sense of optimism and expectation. The forces of the state are shaken, and viewed by many to be on the verge of surrender.

There is, of course, a seemingly clear and obvious contrast between the patriotic crowd of Wembley (all whoops and flat caps thrown in the air) and the revolutionary crowd of Paris. The crowd in each instance has constituted itself for very different reasons. However, these crowds are intrinsically connected. The crowd in this period identifies itself with change. The 'something extra' that fuelled the delirium of the Wembley crowd was the feeling of being there when the world got better, with England winning the World Cup as just another indication (albeit slightly more magical and abstract, perhaps, than say free milk for schoolchildren) that everything is moving on, improving. Paradoxically, the ugly scenes of confrontation in France are born of a similar spirit. The French government's attempts to reform university matriculation requirements along more elitist lines are regarded as being out of kilter with the progressive period, and are resisted. To reiterate the point, the crowd comes together in this period to express and symbolize the public's support for the seemingly 'progressive' dynamic of the times. It can do so in a number of different ways: in celebration of an event that symbolizes advancement; in symbolic demonstrations of the united will for further advancements; in confrontation with the forces of reaction.

And now we move on to a different time.

June 1998: Marseilles

Another football match, the same tournament, and a very different crowd. England's opening game in the 1998 World Cup sees them cruise to a comfortable 2–0 victory over Tunisia. The media, politicians, and the public in general are, however, more preoccupied with the images of mass crowd disturbances than with the result. Marseilles has become lost in a fog of tear-gas as England fans, local youths (mainly second-generation North African immigrants) and the crack French CRS riot squad wade into one another in a 48-hour orgy of violence (see Varley, 1998). In the worst incident a young England fan had his throat cut. No fans enter the field of play before the final whistle. If they had, they would not have been looked upon as innocent bad timekeepers, eager to celebrate their team's victory: things have changed since 1966.

June 1999: London

A carnival against capitalism. The crowd gathers because it under-stands that everything is going wrong, and it wants to celebrate the fact that it knows that everything is going wrong. Gathering quite purposefully in the hub of the capitalist machine which it blames for this turn for the worse, the City of London, it made its various points in various ways. The group known as the Biotic Bakers aimed custard pies at the richest bankers. Those who raged against the pressures to reform did not; instead they paraded naked. McDonalds was targeted for all sorts of reasons, but probably mostly because the crowd understood that it had come together to celebrate its understanding of what was going wrong, and that this could be characterized as the 'McDonaldization' of society. As the day progresses, confrontation between the crowd and the police increases. At the end of this carnival over 40 people require hospital attention for injuries sustained in the clashes, and damage estimated at £40 million has been caused (*Sunday Times*, 29 June 1999).

When looking at these two crowds we are, again, initially tempted to discern contrast. We are seduced into stereotypical assumptions about the fighting football crowd – its xenophobia, gratuitous machismo (see Campbell and Dawson, 2001) and propensity to commit indiscriminate violence. Somehow this is different from our less clearly defined image of the carnival-against-capitalism crowd. Disruptive and destructive they may be, but at least they have a cause. Their at times bizarre behaviour, their music and dancing and their unconventional dress give them a bohemian edge, which seems radically distant from the union-jacked, ugly yob mob. But when we dig below the surface and begin to extract the spirit that drives these two crowds to come together we are struck by their similarity to each other, and by the differences from those earlier crowds of the 1960s.

The central unifying feature of the two crowds is that they seek to resist the pressure of change. Both crowds identify recent changes in social relations as constituting threats. In a world which no longer seems to set any great store by displays of muscular strength and outward signs of machismo, the young male descendants of the industrial working classes lash out in displays that over-emphasize, exaggerate and ultimately distort the legacy of their forebears. In making sense of the new world, one which readily accepts the difference of others but reacts against the difficulty posed by macho man (see Young, 1999), they seek out others of their ilk in the crowd of yesterday and celebrate an imagined time when they and their friends would have been better appreciated and understood. In very similar ways the protester against global capitalism is disenchanted with the present. The subject of the protest is the way in which global capitalism has broken free from the constraints that in a previous time, had managed to moderate and avoid the worst excesses of the 'free market'. Under the banner of 'Reclaim the Streets' the exact nature of what would constitute a victory for this crowd is unclear; we are left only with the notion that they wish to reclaim 'something' (this something is obviously much more than 'streets' in a purely literal sense). Again, the crowd reacts against the present and seeks to reclaim something from the past.

The two examples of the crowd on this side of the master change are, it is argued, representative of the crowd during the recent period. The trade-unionists caught up in the picket-line violence of the 1970s and 1980s increasingly become a crowd protesting about anti-union legislation and practices: the crowd ultimately struggles to reassert the legitimate strength of the union. By the 1990s, and in the formative years of the new millennium, the discrete trade union crowd becomes increasingly diluted in the new anti-globalization crowd. The *discrete* customs of the trade-union crowd (the pageantry of the march, the ritual of the picket-line) are less frequently played out, but nevertheless individuals seeking out others who share their misgivings about weakening of the unions still find a crowd (indeed, a bigger crowd, one that is growing) within which they can hoist their banners. The inner-city rioters of the 1980s can be seen as openly rebelling against the overt and covert racism that has determined the fate of young West Indians in terms of employment, housing, education, etc. That the scope and impact of discrimination and exclusion is incremental on this side of the master change is borne out by the riots that took place in 2001 in Oldham, Bradford and Burnley (see Ouseley, 2001; Cantle, 2001), where young Asians fought the police in scenes strikingly reminiscent of what went before in places such as Toxteth, Handsworth and Brixton. For the rioter, things cannot go on as they are; the implicit promise of equality once made to their parents in more optimistic times needs to be restated, and fulfilled. The illegal raver of the late 1980s and early 1990s (see Collins, 1998), in manic displays of short-term hedonism, defies the claim that 'there is no such thing as society' and, all 'loved-up', euphorically joins with the crowd in a re-enactment of a Summer of love – when things were happier.

The crowd on this side of the master change is different from the crowd of the previous period. It comes together to unite against what it sees as the threatening and destructive character of the present. Unlike the previous crowd, which seemed to have a fairly clearly defined vision of its objective and its role in the unfolding social project, the modern crowd, in its different manifestations, seems somewhat confused as to its long-term purpose, and is more concerned with the immediate symbolic gesture. In this period the crowd comes together in: protest against the immediate content and threat of now; symbolic demonstrations of the united will for a return to a less threatening past; reaction and confrontation with the forces of 'advancement'.

In developing the argument so far it may seem that we have done little more than throw together some random examples of the crowd and attempted to extrapolate some defining characteristics, which, even if they do truly apply, do not go very far at all in explaining wider social processes. It is now necessary to revisit an established body of work emanating from a group of social historians in the 1970s, relating to 'social crime' and the crowd in 18th-century Britain. By doing so it becomes possible to see the true significance of the changes already touched upon. It is in this context that the particular initiatives undertaken by New Labour – the Football (Disorder) Act 1999, the Football (Disorder) Act 2000, and the establishment of a new England Members Club (as proposed in the final report and recommendations of the Working Group on Football Disorder 2001) – must be evaluated and compared with previous initiatives and legislation.

Social crime and the crowd

The concept of social crime as applied by historians in their evaluation of unrest and criminal activity in the eighteenth century proves to be a useful conceptual tool in understanding (among other things) the phenomenon of 'crowd disorder' in the late twentieth century. We follow in its main lines the argument of Meszaros that since the onset of the 1970s we find ourselves in a period which can in its essence be characterized as one of the 'destructive self-reproduction' of the social-metabolic order ruled by capital (Meszaros, 1995). During this period whole swathes of society feel the pressure to 'readjust' to the new economic reality, a reality which is very much about uncertainty, personal insecurity and instability (see also, Bauman, 2000; Beck, 1992; Giddens, 1990; Young, 1999), as capital enters a new phase where its productive limits have been reached and we see the onset of a new period where the metabolism of capital – essentially uncontrollable – necessarily negates the possibility of progressive social development.

The focus of this chapter is the football crowd in particular, as well as the 'disorderly' crowd more generally. That is to say, we are concerned with individuals joined together with a seemingly common purpose whose assembly is deemed as constituting a threat to 'order' and 'legitimate authority'. It is argued that although the crowd has always been viewed as potentially problematic by the authorities (even the patriotic celebration of a nation needs to be policed for the anarchic minority), nevertheless there are particular characteristics of the contemporary crowd and the way that it is understood by authority that bear comparison with the crowd of the eighteenth century. The suggestion is that the crowd can, to a certain extent, be understood as being motivated by a desire to reject pressures to readjust to the new world order, and that the crowd constitutes itself in order to defend old practices and, indeed, seek rights to new ones.

It is conceded that at first sight it may seem slightly absurd to attempt any comparison of today's football hooligan, raver, inner-city rioter, hunt-saboteur, with the pleb whose very existence was threatened by the transition to capitalist social relations . However, by appropriating the concept of social crime as it was used by those social historiographers with whom it has come to be associated, and applying it to an understanding of today's crowd, a crowd whose individual constituents live in an historical epoch where the limits of the productive forces of capital are beginning to be met and we enter a period of destructive self-reproduction, it is possible to discern the unravelling of a social process, the consequences of which will have a major impact on the way that we properly understand the issue of 'crime' and its control.

The focus in historical studies of social crime has been eighteenth-century (mainly) rural England. The two key characteristics of social crime are that: there is a violation of law as a more or less explicit form of protest; and there exists a degree of community support for the activities of the criminal. E.P. Thompson and his collaborators and successors (Hay, Rule, Linebaugh) develop their argument to suggest two further characteristics: the criminalization of custom, and the blurred boundaries of social crime. Do contemporary crowds and social crime have these characteristics?

Social crime as protest

Crime, in nearly all of its manifestations, can, especially through the lens of the radical or Marxist criminologist, be perceived as protest. To infringe the rules of an unfair system, a system that promotes inequality, can be seen in a simplistic way as a challenge to that very system. The temptation, then, can be to lapse into an idealist stupor in which all rule-breakers are seen as proto-revolutionaries, defenders of 'the cause'. Hobsbawm's analysis of social crime as protest suggests that a narrower and more sophisticated analysis is required. For him, social crime constitutes:

> . . . a conscious, almost a political, challenge to the prevailing social and political order and its values . . . [which] . . . occurs when there is a conflict of laws, e.g. between an official and an unofficial system, or when acts of law-breaking have a distinct element of social protest in them, or when they are closely linked with the development of social and political unrest.
>
> (Hobsbawm, 1972, p. 5)

How does such a tightening of the definition of crime as protest help us establish a better understanding of the contemporary crowd? In the case of the football crowd, certain congruences become apparent. As we have already seen the football crowd on the earlier side of the master change is regarded as being largely unproblematic (although, interestingly, the work of Dunning et al., *The Roots of Football Hooliganism*, establishes that football matches in this country have throughout the history of the game consistently excited violence and unruly behaviour). It is from the 1970s onwards that the football hooligan establishes himself in the public consciousness as an enduring folk-devil. The development of social and political unrest during this period manifests itself in a plethora of different ways, but key to our analysis are: the growing marginalization of the industrial working class; rising unemployment; high immigration levels and increasing racial tensions; and the attack on traditional masculinity. The conflict between those laws governing the official and the unofficial systems can, in this context, be seen as one between 'the law of the working-class jungle' (hard, proud, macho, territorial) and the increasingly less tolerant law of the state (which sees the football crowd as presenting increasing levels of difficulty and reacts in an increasingly punitive manner; see Armstrong and Hobbs, 1994). The increasing levels of violence, an escalation in other forms of fan disorder (pitch invasions, throwing of missiles, violent and racist chanting) and the mass participation of thousands of (mainly) young men in these activities, can be seen as a conscious, almost a political, challenge to the political and social order and its values.

When many of the 'hooligans' drape themselves in the Union Jack, this means something very different for them than for members of the political elite. In many ways the flag is a historical artifact which represents a better place and a better time. It speaks of the days of empire, dominance, power, of a time when the industrial working classes were recognized as playing a central role in the success of the nation. On the recent side of the master change the fighting football fan who unfurls the colours of his country at the side of the pitch while he engages in the kind of behaviour talked of as the 'British disease' (see Williams *et al.*, 1984) seems to do so more in the spirit of protest, challenging the new political and social orthodoxy which he perceives as threatening.

Community support for social crime

The young man who kicks out in anger against a system he perceives as unfair is, of course, not necessarily engaging in social crime. A consistent theme in work on social crime is that to a certain extent the criminalized activity must be regarded by others as being legitimate. Indeed, for Thompson and his collaborators it is the degree of legitimacy afforded to the criminalized activity by either the partici-pants themselves or the immediate community around them that is of central importance in distinguishing social crime from other forms of criminal activity, and to this extent the 'protest' element of the crime is secondary. John Rule makes the point nicely when he urges us to differentiate between:

> crimes which draw their collective legitimation from their explicit protest nature, and actions which although against the law were not regarded as criminal by the large numbers who participated in them whether their purpose was to make protest or not. ... The most important characteristic of 'social crimes' lies in positive popular sanction, not in the often present element of protest.
>
> (Rule, 1979, pp. 51–2)

The degree of support necessary to constitute social crime fluctuates between absolute support (for example, the solidarity of a whole community in defence of the poacher, as described in the work of Douglas Hay and his colleagues (Hay *et al.*, 1975)) and simply the willed refusal of a community to accept as criminal activities that they regard as normal and non-harmful. It is our contention that on the recent side of the master change the crowd engaged in criminal activities enjoys a (fluctuating) level of support similar to that enjoyed by the crowd of eighteenth-century England. At times the spur for that support may be aroused primarily (at least seemingly primarily) by the protest component of the crowd's actions – for example, during the J18 Carnival against Capitalism when the radical community at large might have sympathized with and applauded the actions of the Biotic Bakers and their assorted friends because of its own strongly held misgivings about the destructive influence of global capitalism.

Where the social-protest components of the crowd's action are less easy to discern we still detect support for the activity, both from the participants themselves as well as the various 'communities' on the immediate fringes of the 'action'. Football hooliganism serves as a useful, if somewhat oblique, example here. As indicated above, it is possible to regard the seemingly anti-social behaviour of the hooligan as an articulation of disapproval and protest; but more significant is that the activities of the hooligan are not met with universal condemnation, and that some sections of society endorse their actions.

The fact that there has occurred such a sharp increase in the incidence of hooliganism (to the extent that virtually every League club had an associated fighting 'firm' by the 1980s) would seem to be indicative of the fact that for the many thousands who have participated in football violence this kind of behaviour is somehow 'normal' (rather than pathological, criminal). Beyond this, research would seem to suggest that the larger community from which the majority of hooligans are drawn accepts, and in terms of lifestyle implicitly supports, these violent activities. Williams *et al.* (1984) relate that the majority of hooligans in their study came from the 'rougher' sections of lower working-class communities – those that placed much greater emphasis on machismo, territoriality and loyalty. Within such communities the ability to handle and engage in violence is not only expected and tolerated, but comes to constitute a vital component of the cultural capital required to survive and prosper in such an environment. As Williams *et al.* put it:

> A useful way of expressing it would be to say that such sections of lower working-class communities are characterised by a 'positive feedback cycle' which tends to encourage the resort to aggression in many areas of social life, especially on the part of males. The best fighters are apportioned great respect, and there is a tendency for males from these kinds of areas to see fighting as an important source of meaning and gratification in life. That is, there are males in communities of this sort who tend to be excessively macho, to follow the norms of what one might call a 'violent masculine style'. In fact along with gambling, street 'smartness', an exploitative form of sex, and heavy drinking ... fighting is one of the few sources of excitement, meaning and status available to males from this section of society and accorded a degree of social toleration.
>
> (Williams *et al.*, 1989, p. 142)

To the extent that Williams, Dunning and Murphy recognize and identify the fact that part of the legitimacy relied upon by hooligans to justify their own particular actions derives from a wider cultural base, we agree. However, their wider thesis is, we believe, flawed. For these authors football hooliganism as a social issue is best explained by the application of Norbert Elias' concept of the 'civilizing process' (Elias, 1982). In particular they account for the moral panic on hooliganism as being a direct consequence of the greater incorporation of the middle and respectable working classes into the mores and standards of the elite. What transpires is a gap between the sensibilities shared by these sections of society and the 'rough' working classes. The readiness to resort to violence which is characteristic of the 'roughs' comes increasingly to jar against the moral beliefs and values of those who stand above them. The hooligan, for Williams and his colleagues, is in many ways a historical hangover – violence at football matches has always existed but it becomes increasingly problematic and less tolerated as the dynamics of the civilizing process increasingly sensitizes large sections of the population as to the destructive consequences of violence. What supposedly occurs is an internal pacification of western societies (see Elias and Dunning, 1969).

In analysing the crowd in general, and not just the football crowd in particular, we come to regard the wider social processes which impact upon the mood and behaviour of the crowd as being much more about exclusion than incorporation (see Young, 1999). Paradoxically this trend towards greater exclusion, differentiation, and marginalization of groups has at the same time allowed for far greater mobility between distinct groups. That is, the individual can pass from one group to another with much greater ease than was previously possible. The main reason for this is the fracturing of traditional communities into a plethora of what we might wish to describe as in-groups and out-groups. In Young's work on social exclusion and crime he charts the growth of 'bulimic' tendencies in contemporary societies, whereby the increasing numbers who are regarded as deviant are spewed out in the wasteland of social exclusion. At the same time Young insists that membership of a subculture is not the exclusive preserve of the deviant gang, but rather that we all necessarily belong to subcultures by virtue of our incorporation into distinct groups who have particular ways of making sense of the world.

What can be detected here is the creation of countless numbers of interlocking communities or enclaves – communities not in the traditional sociological meaning of the word, but rather the 'peg-communities' that Bauman (2001) writes about. Within this tendency it is unlikely that the individual social agent belongs exclusively to one community or another; he or she is more likely to cross from one community to another in the course of navigating the complexities of contemporary existence. So, for example, the individual may, at a particular stage in life, belong to the following 'communities': the male community; the white community; the respectable working-class community; the building-worker community; the thirty-something community; the married community; the parent community. These groups may not in themselves appear problematic – the individual belongs to a number of 'in-groups'. However, it may well be the case that joint membership of communities also includes the recreational ecstasy-using community and/or the macho violent community. In which case this individual is not only a member of in-groups but also of out-groups (those which society increasingly seeks to pathologize and expel). Each of these communities, or subcultures as Young would have it, consumes, digests, understands, explains news of deviancy in different ways:

Subcultures, therefore, relate to the wider values and structures of society, and to the local problems and predicaments of particular groups. In a highly interrelated society, they cannot be hermetically separate – even if their members try – and far from consisting of 'essences' – cultural dispositions which merely unfold – they change constantly, as the problems of each group change over time.

(Young, 1999, p. 90)

The individual will respond to the hooligan differently depending on what time of the day it is and what community he inhabits at that time. At midday on Wednesday in the environs of the macho building-worker community he may give ribald congratulation to the local fighting 'firm' that is in the news for attacking a group of rivals. On Thursday night, sitting as part of both the married community and the parent community, he may explain to his little boy (at his wife's behest) the mindlessness of thuggery. The values of each particular community are internalized and the correct responses to particular issues are rehearsed and learned. It is not simply the case that the in-group will always condemn the antics of a particular out-group, or that one out-group will regard as legitimate the activities of another out-group. Our notional (male) individual, all 'luvved up' on a Saturday night and surrounded by the recreational ecstasy-using community, may well express his non-comprehension and rejection of hooliganism.

The hooligan crowd, the rave crowd, the environmental-protestor crowd, the carnival-against-capitalism crowd, etc. – all of these are examples of the new communities that proliferate and complicate modern living. The football hooligan who has belonged to West Ham United's Inter-City Firm for the last 15 years believes that his fellow gang-members provide a community that legitimizes and structures his actions on a Saturday afternoon. In a society that collapses into smaller and smaller communities, and where the tendency is increasingly to identify and expel outer groups, it is likely that the attempt to demonize and exclude one community will excite fluctuating levels of sympathy and support from other communities – especially those communities that share joint membership. In many ways this is what distinguishes social crime from other forms of criminality. The murderer does not belong to a murdering community – the communities which he does belong to do not sanction murder, and his crime is not interpreted as being representative of their mores and values.

Certainly, all of this seems very different from the clear-cut and distinct communities of eighteenth-century Britain, and indeed it is;

but what we believe is similar to that period is that the collective conscience of the fractured communities of today can lend support and legitimation to the criminal activities of the crowd in much the same way that the collective conscience of the 'absolute' community did. This does not, of course, mean that everyone has access to every community; access will still be determined largely by the community into which one is born. The crucial axes determining membership of alternative communities will be gender, race, and class.

The criminalization of custom and social crime

John Lea insists that today, in contrast to eighteenth-century England, 'there are no pre-capitalist economic relations to be defended; mean- while the existence of a large entrepreneurial organized crime sector means that any activity which extends beyond the operations of a few amateurs is likely to become absorbed by more organized enterprise' (Lea, 1999, p. 320). What is suggested here is that the contemporary crowd not only seeks to establish alternative forms of economic distribution to the prevailing ones, but also alternative economies of leisure, status, gratification and meaning. They do so, of course, not in defence of pre-capitalist economic relations, but rather in defence of economic and social relations on the earlier side of the master change (or at least in defence of a set of relations thought to exist at that time). That the social conditions of the previous period (whether that be feudalism or industrial capitalism) were less than ideal is not the point.

The Saturday football fan serves us as a good example here. The unruly football crowd is anything but a new phenomenon. However, the identification of the football hooligan as a social problem from the early 1970s onwards results in increased policing of the football crowd. The intensification of the problem since that time is, for the purposes of this argument, indicative of a section of the football-fan community attempting to reassert what is seen as the right to a 'good old punch-up'. But football violence on the recent side of the master change is different from any fan disorder on the other side of the change. Characteristic of the new football violence are: the active identification of the football fan with a particular gang (or 'firm'); the degree to which it is pre-planned and organized; the level and intensity of its use; and the antipathy of its perpetrators to new prevailing mainstream ideologies. The violent football fan is not drawn to the scene of the action by random coincidence but does so by virtue of his active membership of the violent football-fan community.

That individuals would bother to seek out and commit to such a seemingly misanthropic mission is explicable through a wider understanding of social change. As has already been suggested, much of the content of the present is perceived as threatening by the descendants of the industrial working classes. In terms of social fulfilment the football 'firm' can offer a source of status and meaning in a period when many other sources have dried up, and it neatly articulates (albeit in a not very articulate manner) his resentment and antipathy towards these unwelcome changes. The vast majority of what the violent football fan does is unrewarding in any material sense, but in a generally hostile world the community of the violent football fan represents an alternative economy of leisure, meaning, status and gratification. Interestingly, as the number of outer groups increases, and because of the increasing fluidity of movement between groups (inner to inner, outer to outer, inner to outer and back again), the non-instrumental activities and organization of the hooligan increasingly lend themselves to new alternative economies of distribution. This is best exemplified in the crossover between the rave crowd and the football crowd. Members of the football firms quickly discovered that the skills they had been refining in the two decades before the onset of the rave scene were easily modified for the purposes of crowds seeking out nights of hedonistic ecstasy. The hooligans' old skill of bypassing the police to confront the enemy was put to effective use in the planning of illegal parties. Members of the firms quickly established themselves as the main providers of security for the events (see, for example, the memoirs of self-confessed Inter-City Firm leader, Cas Pennant (Pennant, 2000)). Contacts established between rival firm members (usually for the purposes of pre-planning confrontations, but also the outcome of friendships formed on England away trips where domestic allegiances were temporarily forgotten) were also key in the development of new national drug-distribution networks springing up to meet the enormous increase in the demand for recreational drugs, which fuelled the rave crowds. Indeed, the rave scene is the most compelling example of crowd's being able to effect an alternative economy of distribution.

Blurred boundaries

For those who seek a fully social understanding of why it is that more and more individuals flock to immerse themselves in certain periods in increasingly troublesome crowds the moral disposition of the actor or the particulars of the action is secondary (Maffesoli 1996). More important (indeed, crucial) is that to properly understand the significance of the crowd and the actions of its members, we must first understand the crowd's impetus. The sociologist, historian, criminologist, anthropologist, who seeks absolution or blame in his subject is unworthy. Lea's insistence on Thompson's assertion (Thompson, 1972) that we are unlikely to find ' "nice" social crime here and "nasty" anti-social there' immediately lifts the false burden of being on the right or the wrong side.

Much 'social crime' of the kind described here has undoubtedly nasty consequences. Its impetus is decidedly non-virtuous from the perspective of the self-styled progressive. Let us be clear about that; let us remember that we are dealing with the dynamics of social disintegration and the appropriateness of social concepts, as opposed to the moral appropriation of a disintegrating social concept. From that standpoint let us revisit the political parameters that this investigation set itself. Meszaros writes that: 'in our own historical epoch ... productive self-expansion is no longer a readily available way out of the accumulating difficulties and contradictions' (Meszaros, 1995, p. 808). No, it is not.

To be clear, our own historical epoch is one that sees the individual members of the crowd slip-sliding, crushing, and bruising, in a desperate and ignorant manner, toward a future that scares and unsettles them. Within this process many of them join together and react in ways that provoke essentialist typologies and damnation from a section of their peers and their supposed betters. The crowd *coming out* of a period where industrial capitalism is in its ascendancy will inevitably be informed by a popular culture and moral base sharply distinct from the culture of a crowd *entering* such a period. History gifts to its readers the powerfully seductive assertion of judgement: 'this was a fair thing to do in the face of terrible oppression', or alternatively, 'how could they?', etc. However correct politically, theoretically and/or historically such judgements in respect of 'old' social crime might be, 'new' social crime is conditioned by capitalism's inability to allow meaningful social development. Martyrs are less obvious than self-servers and seeming parasites. Unsurprisingly, social crime on the recent side of the master change is read by nearly all of its immediate consumers as antisocial and nasty – and to a very large extent it is.

The extent to which such things as organized crime, intra-class crime, hate-crime (inspired by racist, misogynist or homophobic ideologies) come out of, or are inseparable from, modern forms of social crime is indicative that Meszaros is correct. Social crime in its incipient form had many blurred boundaries, but its modern incarnation has seemingly been lost in the haze. What needs to be remembered is that just because the social element of protest is regarded as being banal, vindictive or whatever, it is a social element nonetheless.

Conclusion

In criminology and associated disciplines, there are new social and cultural processes that demand our attention. Behind the recently developed concepts of exclusive/inclusive society (Young), risk society (Beck), the golden age (Hobsbawm) and its ending, lies this fundamental question, of whether a whole historical mode of production and a social system are now encountering their structural limits. If people are now indeed confronted with a qualitatively changed framework of existence, with new problems (among the most important, a structural unemployment that goes beyond the cyclical unemployment and 'reserve army of labour' of past times), in which everyone is, in one way or another, aware of a disintegration of recently accepted authority and values, what is to become of 'law and order', 'social control', let alone the mythical 'stakeholder society'? How will it be possible to go beyond organizing for defence of living standards and democratic rights and instead discover and devise ways of countering a now 'destructive self reproduction' (of capital), which threatens humanity's 'very existence'?

References

Armstrong, G. (1994) 'False Leeds', in R. Giulianotti and G. Williams (eds) *Game without Frontiers*, Aldershot: Arena.

Armstrong, G. (1998) *Football Hooligans: Knowing the Score*, Oxford: Berg.

Bauman, Z. (1995) *Life in Fragments: Essays in Postmodern Morality*, Oxford: Blackwell.

Bauman, Z. (2000) *Liquid Modernity*, Cambridge: Polity Press.

Bauman, Z. (2001) *Community: Seeking Safety in an Insecure World*, Cambridge: Polity Press.

Beck, U. (1992) *Risk Society: Towards a New Modernity*, London: Sage.

Campbell, B. and Dawson, A. (2001) 'Indecent Exposures: Men, Masculinity and Violence', in M. Perryman (ed.) *Hooligan Wars*, Edinburgh: Mainstream.

Cantle, T. (2001) *Report of the Community Cohesion Review Team*, London: Home Office.

Clarke, J. (1976) 'The Skinheads and the Magical Recovery of Community', in S. Hall and T. Jefferson, *Resistance through Rituals*, London: Hutchinson.

Cohen, S. (1985) *Visions of Social Control*, Cambridge: Polity Press.

Cohen, S. (1973) *Folk Devils and Moral Panics*, St Albans: Paladin.

Collins, M. (1998) *Altered State: The Story of Ecstasy Culture and Acid House*, London: Serpent's Tail.

Crumney, D. (ed.) (1986) *Banditry, Rebellion and Social Protest in Africa*, London: James Currey.

Dunning, E., Murphy, P. and Williams, J.(1988) *The Roots of Football Hooliganism*, London: Routledge.

Elias, N. and Dunning, E. (1969) *The Quest for Excitement: Sport and Leisure in the Civilising Process*, Oxford: Blackwell.

Foucault, M. (1977) *Discipline and Punish; the Birth of the Prison*, London: Allen Lane.

Garland, D. (1996) 'The Limits of the Sovereign State', *British Journal of Criminology*, 36(4), 445–71.

Garland, D. (1997) 'Governmentality and the Problem of Crime', *Theoretical Criminology*, 1(2), 17–27.

Giddens, A. (1990) *The Consequences of Modernity*, Cambridge: Polity Press.

Gilman, M. (1994) 'Football and Drugs: Two Cultures Clash', *International Journal of Drugs Policy*, 5(1), 40–8.

Hall, S. (1978) 'Images of Football Hooliganism in the Press', in R. Ingham (ed.) *Football Hooliganism*, London: Inter-Action.

Hay, D., Thompson, E.P. and Linebaugh, P. (eds) (1975) *Albion's Fatal Tree: Crime and Society in Eighteenth Century England*, London: Allen Lane.

Hobbs, D. and Armstrong, G. (1994) 'Tackled from Behind', in R. Giulianotti *et al.* (eds) *Football Violence and Social Identity*, London: Routledge.

Hobsbawm, E. (1959) *Primitive Rebels: Studies in Archaic Forms of Social Movement During the Nineteenth and Twentieth Centuries*, Manchester: Manchester University Press.

Hobsbawm, E. (1969) *Bandits*, London: Penguin.

Hobsbawm, E .(1972) 'Social Criminality: Distinctions between Socio-political and Other Forms of Crime', *Bulletin of the Society for the Study of Labour History*, 25, 5–6.

Home Office (2001) *Working Group on Football Disorder: Report and Recommendations*, London: Home Office.

Lea, J. (1999) 'Social Crime Revisited', *Theoretical Criminology*, London: Sage.

Linebaugh, P. (1991) *The London Hanged*, London: Allen Lane.

Maffesoli, M. (1996) *The Time of the Tribes*, London: Sage.

Meszaros, I. (1995) *Beyond Capital*, London: Merlin Press.

Murphy, P., Dunning, E. and Williams, J. (1990) *Football on Trial*, London: Routledge.

O'Malley, P. (1979a) 'Social Bandits, Modern Capitalism and the Traditional Peasantry: A Critique of Hobsbawm', *Journal of Peasant Studies*, (6)4, 489–501.

O'Malley, P. (1979b) 'Class Conflict, Land and Social Banditry: Bush-ranging in Nineteenth-Century Australia', *Social Problems*, 26(3), 271–83.

Ouseley, H. (2001) *Community Pride Not Prejudice – Making Diversity Work in Bradford*, Bradford: Bradford Race Review.

Pennant, C. (2000) *Cass*, London: John Blake.

Rule, J. (1979) 'Social Crime in the Rural South in the Eighteenth and Early Nineteenth Century', *Southern History*, 1, 35–53.

Rule, J. (ed.) (1982) *Outside the Law: Studies in Crime and Order 1650–1850*, Exeter: University of Exeter, Department of Economic History.

Sunday Times (1999) (29 June), 29.

Thompson, E.P. (1967) 'The Moral Economy Eighteenth Century', *Past and Present* 50, 76–136.

Thompson, E.P. (1972) 'Conference Report', *Bulletin of the Society for the Study of Labour History*, 25, 2–5.

Thompson, E.P. (1977) *Whigs and Hunters: The Origins of the Black Act*, London: Penguin.

Thompson, E.P. (1977) *The Making of the English Working Class*, London: Penguin.

Thompson, E.P. (1991) *Customs in Common*, London: Merlin Press.

Varley, N. (1998) *Parklife: A Search for the Heart of Football*, London: Michael Joseph.

Williams, J., Dunning, E. and Murphy, P. (1989) *Hooligans Abroad*, London: Routledge.

Young, J. (1999) *The Exclusive Society*, London: Sage.

Chapter 10

Probation into the millennium: the punishing service?

Anthony Goodman

The origins of probation

Since its inception in 1907, the nature, role and status of probation has changed considerably. For much of the period the probation service has been caught in the middle of a debate on treatment versus punishment, but in recent years it has begun to move beyond these conceptual confines. The probation service is the only criminal justice agency with the mandate to punish offenders, although whether it is perceived as 'real' punishment is open to debate. As with other community-based responses to offending it has long been subject to the criticism that it is a soft option and not proper punishment.

The early stages of probation were not concerned with considerations of punishment or public protection; redemption or salvation was the key issue. The present author's communication with Guy Clutton-Brock, who in 1936 was made the first Chief Officer of the London Probation Service, indicated that many probation officers did not see their probationers, after giving them 'five bob' and a Bible. He saw his role as one of integrating 'casework'-trained probation officers from university social-studies courses with former missionaries who had been taken over by the Home Office, in 1938, from the Church of England Temperance Society (CETS).

From the pessimism of 'nothing works' to 'what works'

Martinson (1974) was famous for his assertion that 'nothing works' and that, in consequence, probation work with offenders was a waste of time and money. His commissioned research was originally suppressed and he had to go to court to get it published. Hence its impact became even more powerful, as was his language. He wrote:

> ... even if we can't 'treat' offenders so as to make them do better, a great many of the programs designed to rehabilitate them at least did not make them do *worse* ... *the implication is clear: that if we can't do more for (and to) offenders, at least we can safely do less.*
> (Martinson, 1974, p. 48; emphasis in original)

Martinson recanted this pessimistic conclusion five years later:

> On the basis of the evidence in our current study, I withdraw this conclusion. I have often said that treatment added to the networks of criminal justice is 'impotent', and I withdraw this characterization as well. I protested at the slogan used by the media to sum up what I said – 'nothing works.' The press has no time for scientific quibbling and got to the heart of the matter better than I did.
> (Martinson, 1979, p. 254)

Despite this retraction, the 'nothing works' label became very powerful and led to a crisis in confidence in the 'treatment' casework model in working with offenders. Harris commented that Martinson was a convenient tool for those out of sympathy for the treatment ideal to use to denigrate contemporary practice: 'it offered *post hoc* support for ideas moving into prominence for rather different reasons' (Harris, 1996, p. 124).

The professional identity of probation officers

In the same year as Martinson's retraction, an article appeared in the *British Journal of Social Work* that was enthusiastically picked up by Chief Probation Officers (CPOs). Bottoms and McWilliams (1979) restated in their article the four aims for the probation service, which can be summed up as:

1. The provision of appropriate help for offenders

2. The statutory supervision of offenders

3. The diversion of appropriate offenders from custodial sentences

4. The reduction of crime.

They did not assume empirically that the successful pursuit of the first three aims would lead to the fourth being achieved. The publication of their non-treatment paradigm sent shock waves through the probation service, as it questioned the 'treatment' model substituting a 'help' model instead. The work of the probation service at this time should not be seen in isolation, but in the wider context of social work in general. In the late 1960s and 1970s as social work became an important part of the 'welfarist project', so, in Britain, this approach began to experience strains 'in both its political rationality and technological utility' (Parton, 2000, p. 458). Parton concluded that social work was associated with all that was deemed wrong with welfarism. With the demise of welfarism, social work became marginalized in influence, and this was true of the probation service within the criminal justice system.

The first set of National Standards, implemented in 1992, forced services to take reporting much more seriously and devolve 5 per cent of their budget to the private (voluntary) sector to carry out core probation tasks. This was the start of changing probation officers from caseworkers to case managers. This could be interpreted as a move to hive off tasks to leave the probation service as a 'correctional agency', enforcing statutory orders. By then, a new Home Secretary, Michael Howard, who publicly espoused a 'prison works' philosophy, was in post, and a further Criminal Justice and Public Order Act (1994) sharply reduced individual civil liberties (in the areas of right to silence, take intimate body samples, trespass, raves, rights to be a traveller, secure provision for children, etc.) (see Goodman, 1995).

Control over probation; the role of Her Majesty's Inspectorate of Probation – themed inspections

The HM Inspectorate of Probation (HMIP) was started in 1992, with a dual role of conducting thematic reviews and inspecting individual probation services. However, it also instigated work on producing effective practice initiatives, under the theme of 'what works'. The first annual report by the Chief of HMIP, and its initial overview, resembled a mission statement. It started with an acknowledgement that it was 'a difficult time to write a report' (paragraph 1.1) as the probation service 'must win and maintain the community's support and respect ... ineffectively supervised community penalties will increase crime costs and prison numbers' (paragraph 1.2). If this generated a suspicion that the report was addressed more to the government than to the service and the public, this was confirmed in the very next paragraph: 'it is essential that this Inspectorate, and probation services generally, listen closely to what *users* of their services want from them' (paragraph 1.3, my emphasis). It would be a very naive person who assumed that the service-user referred to was the offender. Rather, it was the courts, as the National Audit Office (NAO) had suggested back in 1989, that made use of probation and were therefore its primary customers. And the government decided to make compulsory prison after-care standard on automatic conditional release for sentences of 12 months and longer (see later thematic inspection report). The report, as well as mapping out the way that HMIP would operate, made two very important other points. First, the probation service should certainly not be regarded as an aspect of social work: 'I have already made use of the phrase *community corrections* to include probation services and all other agencies and organisations who receive public money and operate in the field of offering rehabilitation in the criminal justice system' (paragraph 1.6, my emphasis). Second, 'this inspectorate has a role with the *voluntary and private sectors* which are expected in the future to play a greater part in the delivery of community based penalties' (paragraph 1.6, my emphasis). Thus, 'creeping' privatization was on the cards. Privatization has been threatened within probation, for example in the area of hostels, but has not taken place other than using the voluntary and private sector to provide direct specialist services to offenders. Most recently, the National Probation Directorate has shown that it is firmly committed to privatizing about 400 cooks, cleaners and other staff in hostels and probation offices (*NAPO News*, February 2002).

The growth of managerialism

McWilliams has criticized the managerialist position, arguing that 'procedural codes and handbooks' only offer a minimum standard, they relocate professional discretion up the hierarchy, and they remove the spotlight from individuals (McWilliams, 1992). If probationers were happy with the service they were receiving from their supervisors, the managerialist position ignored the question of whether this was because of probation management or despite it. The danger that management could become stifling and overbearing had been recognized for a considerable time. A major problem was the growth in management, which did not have responsibility for carrying out the work, and which could create a split with those who did (Coker, 1988).

Wade, a senior probation manager, looked at the impact of managerialist culture on the probation service with its 'management by objectives', 'key performance indicators', 'supporting management information needs', and 'better quality services', and inspections based on 'efficiency and effectiveness', 'quality and effectiveness', and now 'performance inspection programmes'. She expressed concern that management was becoming efficient at carrying out tasks on behalf of others, and that debates would become focused on 'how' rather than 'why' probation was working in a particular way. T. May commented that probation officers criticized their managers for the loss of social work in policy initiatives, which he attributed to 'Home Office directives . . . and the use of Home Office Inspectors' (May, 1995, p. 34). This was not surprising, as the report by the HM Inspectorate of Probation in 1993 conveyed the stark message that 'deliberate failure by probation staff to comply [with National Standards] would lead to disciplinary action' (HM Inspectorate of Probation, 1993, p. 10 iii).

The change of Government from Conservative to Labour in 1997, which included a change in Home Secretary from the right-wing Michael Howard, who espoused a 'prison works' philosophy, to Labour's Jack Straw, did not lessen the pressure on the probation service to demonstrate a 'toughness' towards offenders, utilizing the language of punishment. Lord Williams, Minister of State in the Home Office with responsibility for both prisons and probation, spoke at a debate at the annual general meeting of the National Association of Probation Officers in October 1998. While trumpeting a change in funding by the Labour Government, intended to give the probation service an extra £18 million for the financial year 1999–2000 (when the Conservatives had intended to cut the service by £6 million), he indicated that the government supported the view of a recent Home Affairs Committee report:

> In the main the Committee's concerns are our concerns, and the report majors on ensuring the effectiveness of community punishment. . . . The Home Affairs Committee commented that National Standards are a minimum basic set of requirements, and said that they were 'alarmed' to discover that how frequently National Standards are not adhered to. They went on to observe – quite rightly – that strict enforcement of community sentences is vital if they are to represent a credible alternative to prison.
>
> (Home Afffairs Committee, 1998, p. 4)

The probation response was voiced in the comments of the new Deputy Chief Probation Officer of the Inner London Probation Service (the largest), David Sleightholm, who provided the continuity of ethos and purpose with the previous political regime. The probation service could be the social-control agency to provide half of the Labour Party mantra 'tough on crime', if not the second half of the mantra, 'tough on the causes of crime': 'The public see us too much delivering services to offenders, and not enough as delivering effective punishment, control and surveillance' (Sleightholm, 1998, p. 12)

From casework to corrections

In recent years there has been a growing debate about social work values and the probation service (e.g., Nellis, 1995; Spencer, 1995; James, 1995; Williams, 1995). Other probation academics have been determined to discuss the need to practise in an anti-discriminatory manner (Denny, 1992). Nellis did not believe that there should be a link between social work, seen as too generic, and probation training. Instead, he favoured 'anti-custody', 'restorative justice', and 'community safety' as appropriate values. James, while acknowledging that these three concepts, derived from criminological theory, may provide useful elements for criminal justice policy, argued that they did not help with notions of what to do with the offender. Spencer was critical, arguing that what were held up as values were really aims, and by following this approach he accused Nellis of wanting to turn the probation service into a correctional agency, which would not be equipped to work directly with individuals to change their behaviour.

Roberts, writing in 1996 for the new Oxford University Probation Studies Unit, commented that 'it is still the case that there has been remarkably little research into the supervisory work of probation officers' (Roberts *et al.*, 1996, p. vii). The research described by Roberts, Burnett, Kirby and Hamill was a pilot study for evaluating practitioner practice. However, it stated that of the 90 offenders studied, a random survey of new cases started in the test area over a timed period, *only* 16 were women and only seven were from ethnic-minority groups. Thus, the research was evaluating predominantly interventions with white males.

Probation, which traditionally had been the caring side of the criminal justice system, was under pressure to demonstrate that it was effective, but what this actually meant was confused (Mair, 1997). McGuire (1995) recommended neither being punishing towards offenders nor indulgent; what was needed was constructive action, typically drawing on the cognitive-behavioural approach. The Home Office, in

What Works: Reducing Re-offending Evidence-Based Practice (1999), gave the principles used to evaluate the pathfinder projects that would become the model throughout England and Wales for delivering all (evidence-based practice) programmes. This is set to become central to the way that offenders will be worked with. In many ways the proposition that practice should be 'evidence-based' is hard to argue with, but it is the context that is important, rather than the decontextualized statistical power (Smith, 2000b). Smith was concerned that 'a great deal of evaluative research is not very good' (Smith, 2000b, p. 4). He despaired that many papers submitted to him, while he was the editor of the *British Journal of Social Work*, 'showed a preoccupation with statistical testing combined with very little understanding of what statistical tests are for and in what circumstances they are useful' (ibid., p. 4). His article reads as a strong warning to be careful in naively believing the scientific promise of this approach, in which offenders are atomised into their criminogenic and non-criminogenic elements, with the criminogenic seen as the parts to be worked on. This approach ignores social factors, despite the research of the Home Office highlighting the influence of these. The message of young people, in custody (contained in Lyon *et al.* (2000) enjoys a foreword by Paul Boateng, then a Home Office Minister, which urged the reader to listen to what the young people had to say, and the message spelt out in the Executive summary from the young people was that 'many had had to struggle to survive in difficult and disrupted circumstances. They talked about "rough, nasty areas" where violence, crime, drug use, unemployment and poverty were just part of everyday life' (Lyon *et al.*, 2000, p. viii). A further edited Home Office paper, Reducing Offending (Goldblatt and Lewis, 1998), made the non-surprising discovery that risk factors for later criminal behaviour included:

> poverty and poor housing; poor parenting . . . association with delinquent peers, siblings and partners; low measures of intelligence, poor school performance and persistent truancy; high levels of impulsiveness and hyperactivity; and being brought up by a criminal parent or parents.
>
> (Goldblatt and Lewis, p. 123)

The limit in the usefulness of this (rather obvious) shopping-list-of-problems approach is exposed as the narrative continues:

> Although we *cannot predict accurately which individual will become an offender on the basis of the risks to which they are exposed,* we do know

that children exposed to multiple risks and those who engage in anti-social or criminal behaviour at an early age are more likely to end up as serious or persistent offenders.

(ibid., p. 124, my emphasis)

The offender is damned by her/his personal circumstances, the more unfortunate, the more they are labelled as being at risk. The more they will be targeted by the programme, the higher the level of intervention as they have a more criminogenic level of risk. The danger with a centrally orchestrated and tightly managed system, even allowing for Smith's concerns that it is difficult to research the effectiveness of programmes, is that the needs of the individual are assumed to be those dealt with by the programme. The problems are located within the offender, rather within the wider society, and are therefore ignored if they require structural challenge and change. Probation research has shown that offenders find it difficult to maintain a decision to abandon crime, and need guidance from probation officers, whom they see as being concerned with their well-being (Rex, 1999). It remains to be seen whether implementing pathfinder programmes, at a time when individual offenders are receiving less time with probation officers (POs) each month, and when community orders are backed up with more punitive sanctions, will allow this concern for offenders by POs to be demonstrated. Will there still be scope for individual treatment by POs?

Probation since the change to a Labour government

The Labour election campaign was unprecedented in the degree to which it sought to establish Labour as the party to be tough on law and order and this aim was carried out in its subsequent practice (Brownlee, 1998). The incoming Labour government, elected on 1 May 1997, inherited a rapidly rising prison population and the new Criminal Justice Act, the Crime (Sentences) Act 1997, which abolished automatic release from prison and parole, and substituted a 'discount' system for good behaviour and cooperation. It also imposed mandatory life sentences for second convictions of serious sexual or violent offences and a minimum sentence on third-time Class A drug offenders and domestic burglars. It allowed fine defaulters to be given community-service orders and/or be electronically tagged. Thus, the penal climate continued in its more punitive trajectory; indeed, the Labour government implemented the automatic three-year sentences for third cases of burglary.

Jack Straw, who became the Home Secretary in this first Labour Party administration in 18 years, continued a seamless theme with his Conservative predecessors, placing responsibility for offending firmly with offenders and having no time for 'strain theory' explanations for offending. Speaking on how to make 'prisons work', he commented that the first priority was that 'we should be directly challenging the underlying attitudes and behaviours that propel inmates back into crime. Most offenders lack respect for themselves and others' (Straw, 1999, p. 11). This approach avoided the need to consider issues of discrimination and unfairness in the criminal justice system. If the United Kingdom were to follow the example of the United States, the racial and ethnic imbalance within prisons, already demonstrated in the United Kingdom, could be further skewed. Traditional probation training, with its emphasis on 'anti-discriminatory practice', would not fit comfortably into a system which discriminated to this extent (Pitts, 1992; Vanstone, 2000).

The Labour government placed on record its intention to increase the use of electronic monitoring, and in 1999 there were four pilot projects, with the purpose of evaluating the use of tagging to ensure compliance with curfew conditions as laid down in the Criminal Justice Act 1991 but not implemented. Paul Boateng, when Minister of State at the Home Office, confirmed this in his keynote speech to Chief Probation Officers and Chairs of Probation Committees in October 1999 (Boateng, 1999). He commented that the 'Home Detention Curfew scheme' had started in January 1999, whereby prisoners were released on discretionary controlled release (parole). He saw this as 'an effective means of easing the transition from custody back into the community'. A more cynical response would be that tagging represented a cheap way of ensuring home confinement and a way of reassuring the public that the prisons were not being emptied in a 'soft' manner. He continued by stating that 'it provides an element of stability, which can help to disrupt offending patterns', and hinted that this would be useful for prisoners serving sentences of less than one year, who were not subject to compulsory probation post-release supervision. Thus, Stan Cohen's warning of the blurring of the boundary between prison and the community becomes more apparent. Boateng considered the use of what he described as 'reverse tagging' whereby people could be excluded from certain areas. He linked this to a 'comprehensive response to domestic violence', but it was clear that this was not the sole possibility, as he added: 'our work is at an early stage but this is an exciting and growing area'.

The above propositions would constitute the ultimate break with probation's social-work past, with a sole concentration on reporting for its own sake. Combining police and probation resources makes 24-hour supervision a 'highly accountable reality' (Harding, 2000b). Boateng made this explicit: '[the] Probation Service is a law enforcement agency. It is what we are: it is what we do' (Boateng, 1999).

The cognitive approach to dealing with offenders is a valid method of helping them to change, by working on the 'here and now', rather than focusing on what had happened to offenders in their past, the traditional psycho-dynamic approach. However, the overriding focus and preoccupation with reporting, and the use of, and mechanical dependence on, actuarial risk-assessment scales in assessing individuals, decontextualizes offending, its causation, notions of fairness, oppression, indeed all the traditions of society, leaving the individual as simply an entity to be reprogrammed, or at least to be trained solely in methods designed to stop their offending. In an interview (with Celia May), the Permanent Under-secretary at the Home Office, David Omand (since January 1998), a career Civil Servant (previously Director of GCHQ, and with mostly experience in the Ministry of Defence), put across his opinion of how the probation service had to change:

> In his view, the crucial element of the [prison/probation] review centres on convincing the public that the Probation Service has a 'hard edge' to its work and that a community sentence is not shorthand for 'getting off scot free'.
>
> (May, p. 7)

Probation and the punitive tendency

The Home Affairs Committee's third report in July 1998 carried the title *Alternatives to Prison Sentences*. It is worth quoting from the report in detail:

> Strict enforcement of community sentences is vital if they are to represent a credible alternative to prison and retain the confidence of sentencers and the public. If community sentences are to be credible they must be enforced stringently. It is therefore entirely unacceptable that local probation services are, on average, taking breach action in accordance with the National Standards relating to probation orders in barely a quarter of cases. The Home Office should set a minimum target for all local probation services to comply with these standards, ensure that the Inspectorate assesses

each local service on this every year and that it requires publication of the results, and take action against those which fail to meet
the target. Consideration should be given to reworking the
funding formula for local services to provide an incentive for
services to meet this target.

(Home Affairs Committee, 1998, paragraph 87, p. xxvi)

The early ethos of 'advise, assist and befriend' has been put to rest and
in its place are the central tasks of assessing and managing risk. In June
1999 the Home Office published the regulations for the new Diploma
in Probation Studies, and in the first section, entitled 'Regulatory
Framework and Guidance Notes', the role of the newly qualified
probation officer is articulated. This new course took on its first intake
in September 1998, and the first staff qualified in July 2000. The
responsibilities of probation officer in this context are described as
follows:

- Working effectively within a framework of statutory duties and
  powers and alongside other organizations, particularly those in the
  criminal justice and community justice systems, the probation officer
  seeks to protect the public, promote community safety and prevent
  crime by

- evaluating information in order to make assessments and providing
  reports, in respect of risk and other matters of concern, to those
  organizations using the service in both criminal and civil jurisdictions

- managing and enforcing both orders of the court and licences

- working directly with offenders in order to bring about changes in
  behaviour which reduce the impact on victims and the risk of harm
  to members of the community

- managing and co-ordinating the contribution of other services.
  (Probation Officer Recruitment and Training Implementation, p. 1)

The new job description, from this list, can be articulated along the
lines of: assess risk, manage and enforce legal sanctions, change/
challenge offending behaviour, be a case manager. In order to assess
risk, the Home Office has utilized several different assessment programmes, including the Offender Group Reconviction Score (OGRS),
the Assessment Case Management amd Evaluation (ACE) and Level of
Service Inventory – Revised (LSI–R). Her Majesty's Inspectorate of

Probation produced a report in 1998 entitled 'Strategies for Effective Offender Supervision', by Andrew Underdown, as part of the HMIP What Works Project. Underdown reported on a number of projects operating around the country and proposed a model whereby the probation officer as case manager would oversee, at the highest level of involvement, cognitive skills/social skills training. This might include behaviour therapy for self-control and self-understanding. The next layer would include providing victim awareness, input on substance abuse and other issues, for example, driver re-education, citizenship and health. The next layer down would concern resolving problems/meeting needs in the family and the community, for example, support within the family, accommodation, financial advice, access to employment, education, health provision. This model has been breached, however, by the announcement of Paul Boateng that probation officers must engage with homelessness, the bottom rung of the model, typically worked with in partnerships. The discovery, from the rough sleepers Initiative, that many of the homeless are offenders has brought a new spin to priorities. The problem with this is that one cannot atomize the offender and deal with discrete aspects in descending order. There is a danger that new style workers will not have the holistic knowledge and skills of their predecessors, and practice will not prove to be effective after all.

It can be seen, therefore, that one likely future scenario is that offenders will be given an assessment of their criminogenic potential and risk to the public. This could then be used to decide on what type of offending-behaviour group they should attend, indeed what services they should receive. The programmes, to ensure quality and consistency, would then be delivered, without variation, and ongoing further assessments would be carried out to check on possible changes to criminogenic potential. With programmes delivered to script, it is unclear whether qualified probation officers would be needed – probably not. Thus, the probation role becomes one of case manager and overseer of compliance to court orders, in line with National Standards.

Feeley and Simon (1994) described the institutionalizing process of actuarial justice:

> Supervision consisted of monitoring levels of risk as determined by several indicators, most prominently drug testing. Moreover, with large portions of the non-incarcerated population in some of the poorest and most crime victimized communities in the country, probation, parole or some other form of community

supervision are becoming a lower end cost alternative to traditional justice.

(Feeley and Simon, 1994, p. 180)

The permanently excluded segment of society has been labelled an underclass. In the United States this group was regarded as being largely comprised of the black and Hispanic population living in the centre of the cities, in poverty. Others might be poor and unemployed, but the underclass were permanently dysfunctional, not integrable, and in a violent culture, 'actuarial justice invites it to be treated as a high-risk group that must be managed for the protection of the larger society' (Feeley and Simon, 1994, p. 192). Finer, at the end of her co-edited book *Crime and Social Exclusion*, examines the consequences of Britain becoming a 'stakeholder' society, which she describes as a situation where the state resembles a 'joint stock undertaking' and society is organized on behalf of its ' "paying" or "paid up members" ' (Finer, 1998, p. 155). She warns that 'Stakeholders want bargains not presents. ... Those without stakes or *sufficient* stakes in a world where stakes are everything will not simply go away' (ibid., pp. 169–70, emphasis in original). Smith and Stewart provide convincing evidence that probation offenders (clients) are indeed 'socially excluded' in terms of 'deprivation, poverty, stress and personal difficulties' (Smith and Stewart, 1998, pp. 97–8) The new penology is not concerned with theories of crime, or moral or clinical descriptions of offenders. Instead it resorts to the actuarial language of probability: the new objectives are neither to punish nor rehabilitate, but to identify and manage the unruly (Feeley and Simon, 1992).

Kemshall, in her book *Risk in Probation Practice*, describes the assessment of risk as the core business of the probation service, 'supplanting ideologies of need, welfare or indeed rehabilitation' (Kemshall, 1998, p. 1) This carries the implication that these factors could somehow be separate to, unrelated or irrelevant to the risk of reoffending. In fact Kemshall, while acknowledging the shortcomings of basing assessments of risk purely on clinical judgement, also comments that the 'psychometric tradition of risk assessment has been criticized for failing to incorporate a social dimension into its approach' (ibid., p. 31). Despite her balanced approach, which places value on both aspects, the clinical approach has fallen out of favour with policy makers. The new assessment tool, the Offender Assessment System (OASys), developed by the Home Office will define level of risk, and ensuing 'treatment programme' from a repertoire of pathfinder agreed programmes which cannot be deviated from for the sake of programme integrity. This is linked to electronic tagging in some instances and multi-agency co-operation and surveillance for heavy-end offenders.

According to Williams, 'there is a widespread understanding among those who work in the system that punishment alone will not change offenders' behaviour' (Williams, 1996, p. 34). This advances the possibility of a schism between probation managers and frontline staff as well as undermines the potential for preventing reoffending. This is a pity, as the STOP programme, evaluated by Raynor *et al.* (1994), appeared to show good potential for a cognitive approach, which allowed probation staff to work with offenders on issues like how they managed their anger and frustration.

The Labour government therefore, it can be argued, is clear about how it views the future of the probation service, which is largely as a service working to tight guidelines, where professional discretion is limited. The Home Affairs Committee report, published in 1998, is very critical of the failure of probation officers to take offenders back to court, and wants this National Standard adhered to much more closely. Yet this is one of the few areas where there might be a professional decision taken that an offender might be trying to change and reorganize her/his life. If the offender has demanding dependents, has a substance misuse problem, is homeless or destitute, has mental health problems, etc., it may be beyond her/his ability to manage the rigours of weekly reporting or attendance on a programme.

There is a gap between what effective practice needs for a sufficient 'dose' of probation-officer time to work effectively (Chapman and Hough, 1998) and what is actually offered, and this has been blamed on the structure of probation supervision (Smith, 2000a). McClelland (2000) calculated that in 1998 offenders were being seen for about 16 minutes per week, less than half the time available in 1992. The third version of National Standards (April 2000) became operational on the first day of that month, and in them the relationship between probation officer and offender has even less scope for discretion. Hedderman and Hough, who carried out two national audits of probation compliance to the 1995 National Standards for the Association of Chief Officers of Probation, the first in early 1999 and the second six months later, found increasing compliance, which they thought should increase public confidence in the probation service. Despite this, the recent Criminal Justice and Court Services Act (2000), and in particular Clause 46, gives courts less discretion when dealing with breaches of community sentences, as the expectation contained in the Bill is that breaches will be dealt with by a term of imprisonment. Their article, 'Tightening up Probation: A Step Too Far', warned:

> The gains made by offenders prior to breach proceedings will be sacrificed on the altar of tough-mindedness; probation officers will no longer be able to use the breach process as a sharp reminder to recalcitrant offenders of the need to comply with supervision. There will be more breach proceedings, at a time when demands on the police and on the courts are already injecting unacceptable delays in serving warrants and listing cases; some probation officers will simply avoid using formal warnings in cases where a prison sentence would be disproportionate; sentencers will be denied a constructive role in monitoring the progress of probationers; some sentencers are likely to pass nugatory sentences in cases where a prison sentence would be disproportionate, signalling a lack of confidence in the legislation.
>
> (Hedderman and Hough, 2000, p. 5)

Tony Leach (2000), in an article in the probation managers' journal *Vista*, came closest to criticizing the current drive to standardize programmes for all offenders, attacking it on a number of fronts. Although initially articulating his ambivalence to writing at all, for fear of being misinterpreted (by fellow senior managers or the Home Office?), he started by questioning what was meant by effective practice, and then turned to the courts, where orders are still being made on 'welfare grounds'. First, he argued that, as the courts (to quote an old Audit Commission report) were the legitimate customers of the probation service, it was their right to do this. Second, he stated that knowledge of 'what works' was still in its early stages, and the jettisoning of earlier practices was akin to putting all the eggs in one basket. Third, the complexities of and differences among offenders could be open to being underestimated, and 'offenders will be made to fit willy nilly, even if it means stretching them a bit or lopping off bits here and there' (Leach, 2000, p. 145). Fourth, he felt that social factors of individuals were being ignored, especially when group programmes were seen as addressing offenders' dysfunctional behaviour. Finally, there was a danger of 'applying the effective practice approach in a very rigid, simplistic, centralized and monolithic fashion which would shut off other legitimate goals of supervision' (ibid., p. 148).

Joining up the prison and probation services

In 1998 the Home Office published *Joining Forces to Protect the Public: Prisons–Probation*, a review of the relationship between the prison and probation services. The report acknowledged that as prison governors became responsible for their budgets so the number of prison probation officers declined. In financial terms the decline represented a fall in budget from £16.7 million in 1996–97, to £15.6 million in 1997–98. Numbers of prison probation officers fell from 659 at the end of 1995 to 561 by the end of 1996. The report envisaged a 'harmonisation of training' for both services and a 'harmonisation of the competence framework', and 'Joint commissioning of competence-based training involving the identification of common priorities for both services. . . . A target for joint training – provisionally 5 per cent in the first place. . . . Senior management exchanges and cross-postings' (Home Office, 1998, paragraph 4.12).

It is worth restating the remit of the prison service, which is: 'Her Majesty's Prison Service serves the public by keeping in custody those committed by the courts. Our duty is to look after them with humanity and to help them lead law-abiding lives in custody and after release.' This does imply fertile ground for sharing. However, as the prison-service corporate plan of 1995–98 made clear in the strategic priorities, 'security is our top and overriding priority' (paragraph 4.2). Thus, the harmonization of the two services is more likely to involve issues of risk management, security and control, rather than rehabilitation. There is a danger that the training base of probation officers could be downgraded to match the much shorter training of prison officers. The report looked at the name of the probation service, and this part is worth quoting in full:

> It is important that the names, language and terminology used by the services should give accurate and accessible messages about the nature and aims of their work. Where there are mismatches, changes could be useful in marking a new start, and could have indirect benefit by influence culture and behaviour. The focus here is on probation work rather than the work of the Prison Service because there is no perceived problem in the terminology used about prisons. On the probation side some of the terms used have been criticized, for example because: they are associated with tolerance of crime (e.g. 'probation' which can be seen as a conditional reprieve and inconsistent with 'just deserts' or even a rigorous programme aimed at correcting offending behaviour) or

they can be misunderstood (e.g. 'community service' which sounds like voluntary activity), or they are too esoteric to be understood outside the two services (e.g. 'through care' which sounds more associated with the 'caring' services.

(ibid., paragraph 4.14)

The review then produced 17 potential names (not, incidently, the later proposed 'Community Punishment and Rehabilitation Service' or even 'Community Rehabilitation and Punishment Service') that sounded sufficiently 'macho', with connotations of corrections, control, risk management, etc. A letter sent to the present author at Christmas 1999 from a former probation colleague referred to the self-deprecation whereby probation officers referred to themselves as the 'Crappies service': the name change was having an effect on morale. The confirmation on spin was confirmed with the statement that court orders should also have their name changed, followed by the recommendation 'that the public consultation process be used to test attitudes to these options' (ibid., paragraph 4.19, in bold type in original). As Ryan comments, there has been an emergence of 'powerful media monopolies', and politicians use focus groups to gather opinion, rather than listen to those who suffer most disadvantage (Ryan, 1999, pp. 11–12). After protests the probation service retained its name, but the Criminal Justice and Court Services Act 2000, which established a National Probation Service with coterminous boundaries with police, Crown Prosecution and the court areas, renamed probation orders as 'community rehabilitation orders' and community service as 'community punishment' orders. However, Community Probation and Community Service in the form of a combination order are not called community rehabilitation and punishment orders (CRAPOs) but Community Punishment and Rehabilitation Orders. The probation service will inevitably change name in the future, now that it is disconnected by name from the orders officers supervise.

Practice under National Standards is likely to lead to a levelling down of prisoner contact, linked to pre-discharge risk assessments for parole (discretionary conditional release) and sentence planning. Indeed, Maguire *et al.* (2000) document how probation contact with ex-prisoners has decreased. The Housing Act 1996, like the previous Homeless Persons Act 1977, defines 'priority need' in a way to exclude predominantly the single homeless (Arden and Hunter, 1997). Ironically the Rough Sleepers Unit in its strategy paper recognized the importance of forming relationships with the vulnerable, including people leaving prison (Rough Sleepers Unit, 1999, p. 17). This is an unimpressive example of 'joined up thinking' between government departments, as this client group is seen as a low probation priority compared to 'heavy-end' offenders.

The *Prisons–Probation* review was not concerned with the petty persistent offender. Harding, the retiring Chief Probation Officer of the old Inner London Probation Service, accepted the rationale of the review, which wanted a 'co-terminosity of the boundaries of probation and prison services and the acceptance of cognitive programmes under the effective practice initiatives'. He then turned to the ethos of the services:

> . . . the thrust of 'Joining Forces' is unbalanced displaying a *flawed understanding* of probation's *traditions, values and strengths* as a series of *locally based services at the hub of criminal justice* with its point of reference focusing outwards towards a complex web of connections with local communities, local authorities and the independent sector. . . . The probation service is more at ease in understanding the community context in which crime takes place, of playing a central part in the community safety planning arrangements which are enshrined in the Crime and Disorder Act 1998. . . . We are, as Paul Boateng suggests, 'a law enforcement agency' but one whose conceptual roots lie in community justice.
>
> (Harding, 2000a, p. 28)

For Harding, probation strengths were in local multi-agency approaches, including crime prevention, working on troubled estates, working with vulnerable offenders, in partnership with police (something absent from the *Prisons–Probation* review). He regarded prison 'as a place of exile' and clearly his major focus for alliance was not in this sphere. The danger from the review was clear: it represented a major realignment of the probation service, whatever it was going to be called, away from a sense of community towards being a punishment-oriented, correctional, control agency.

Probation approaching the millenium

The *Guardian* newspaper, in an editorial entitled 'Postcode Sentencing – Computers Cannot Deliver Justice' (21 August 2000) quoted from the Chief Inspector of Probation, Sir Graham Smith: 'we have relied too much on nous, instinct and feel. In the past nous has been important, but people have used it in different ways.' The editorial stated that courts, as well as having a pre-sentence report written by a probation officer, would also have a computer generated risk prediction. According to the *Guardian* this would be based on 'criminal record, education, training, employability, lifestyle and associates; alcohol and drug use; emotional stability, relationships, attitudes to crime, general social behaviour and *postcode* (the *Guardian*, my emphasis). The *Guardian* recoiled at this innovation for a number of reasons: Sir Graham needed to be more honest at the system's limitations, the prediction could only place a person in a risk category, a 70 per cent chance of reoffending meant that 30 per cent would not be reconvicted, the civil rights of the 'false positives' needed to be protected, how good was each predictor and why should postcode be included? The newpaper was concerned, like the Law Society, that this represented a 'serious shift in sentencing – from what an offender has done to what he or she might do'. Their conclusion was that computers could aid, but not be a substitute for, human discretion. They located this in the delivery of justice. This should include the way that offenders are dealt with by the probation service and not just the courts. Humanity, and a personal knowledge of the offender, with proper controls, allows for a fairer criminal-justice system than could be operated by an inflexible computer system.

This inflexibility, coupled with the increasing level of breaches of community orders, could explode the prison population. However, there is a relief valve on the pressure cooker, as the arrest warrants are being incompetently dealt with. The *NAPO News* of February 2002 reports that it is estimated that there were at least 14,000 outstanding warrants at the end of December 2000. There was no database in existence and insufficient officers of the court to execute them. Practice has been to withdraw warrants after one year so the injunction to breach orders in National Standards then leaves them floating in the ether. A more efficient system could greatly increase the prison population, an area the United Kingdom already excels in.

In July 2001 the Home Office published the Halliday report, entitled *Making Punishments Work*, which recommends more 'support for crime reduction and reparation while meeting the needs of punishment' (Home Office, 2001, p. ii). It also recommends modifying the just deserts principle, whereby previous offending history, including persistence, should add to the sentence, reviving the old notion of preventative detention which was abolished many years ago. Bizarrely, it also harks back to the origins of the probation service, as it states: 'the probation service should consider ways in which religious and other groups could be involved more directly in work with offenders' (ibid., p. vii). There should be 'a new generic community punishment order' with a set of 'ingredients best suited to meeting the needs of crime reduction, and exploiting opportunities for reparation, within the appropriately punitive "envelope"' (ibid., p. vi).

At the time of writing, the *Guardian* newspaper contains an article where the current Home Secretary, David Blunkett, is reported as saying that he has told prison governors to expand the home-detention curfew by more than 60 per cent in order to release 1,000 further inmates. This is to cope with the sudden rise in prison numbers (68,181), even with 1,636 released early with electronic tags (*Guardian*, 15 November 2001, p. 12). The prison population rose by more than 2,000 in the first five months of Mr Blunkett's tenure at the Home Office, and the number of women prisoners broke through the 4,000 barrier for the first time. And numbers continue to rise. There is an element of being hoist with one's own petard of 'toughness', as there is the supreme irony that while the failure rate is low at 5 per cent, the rigorous enforcement for breach of curfew has resulted in 1,800 being recalled to prison. It would surely help the Home Secretary in his quest to reduce numbers in prison and to protect the public if the probation service was allowed to work with offenders in such a way that instead of only using programmes probation officers were allowed to 'assist, advise and befriend' a little, as a vehicle for actually getting to know their offenders and to learn why they might not be attending, so that breach is no longer a first resort. Otherwise the approach represents not toughness but narrowness.

The vehicle for the National Probation Service to change its way of working with offenders was published in August 2001, and is called *A New Choreography*. It was described as an integrated strategy, and was the strategic framework for 2001–2014. The aims are not modest:

- by 2004 to establish itself as a world leader in designing and implementing offender assessment and supervision programmes that effectively reduce re-offending and improve public safety; and
- By 2006 be recognized as a top performing public service as benchmarked by the European Excellence Model.

(National Probation Services, 2001, p. 1)

There are nine 'stretch objectives' where the service must change if it is to deliver over the next three years what it is charged to do. These are: more accurate and effective assessment and management of risk and dangerousness; more contact and involvement with the victims of serious sexual and other violent crime; the production and delivery of offender programmes that have a proven track record in reducing re-offending; intervening early to take young people away from crime; enforcement; providing courts with good information and pre-trial services; valuing and achieving diversity in the National Probation Service and the services it provides; building an excellent organization that is fit for its purpose; building an effective performance-management framework. The government targets are for reconviction rates for those under supervision to be reduced by 5 per cent and for those who misuse drugs by 25 per cent.

The jury is therefore out. The new-style probation service, tightly managed and regulated, bears little resemblance to the probation service of even a few years ago. There has been a huge purge of Chief Officers, following the move to a National Service, by way of early retirements and other packages. Main-grade staff have little ability to decide how they would like to work with offenders because of the use of actuarial scales and accredited programmes. The key question now is will it all work or will we rediscover that offenders are individuals who do not fit neatly into pre-packaged programmes? Are we moving to a system of home confinement and surveillance, with probation officers acting as 'soft cops'?

References

Arden, A. and Hunter, C. (1997) *Manual of Housing Law*, 6th edition, London: Sweet and Maxwell.

Audit Commission (1989) *The Probation Service: Promoting Value for Money*, London: HMSO.

Barnes, M. and Warren, L. (1999) *Paths to Empowerment*, Bristol: Policy Press.

Boateng, P. (1999) *Speech to Chief Probation Officers and Chiefs of Probation Committees*, London: HMSO.

Bochel, B. (1976) *Probation and After-Care: Its Development in England and Wales*, Edinburgh: Scottish Academic Press.

Bottoms, A. and McWilliams, W. (1979) 'A Non-Treatment Paradigm for Probation Practice', *British Journal of Social Work*, 9(2), 159–202.

Brownlee, L. (1998) 'New Labour – New Penology? Punitive Rhetoric and the Limits of Managerialism in Criminal Justice Policy', *Journal of Law and Society*, 25(3), 313–35.

Chapman, T. and Hough, M. (1998) *Evidence Based Practice: A Guide to Effective Practice*, London: HM Inspectorate of Probation.

Coker, J. (1988) *Probation Objectives: A Management View*, Social Work Monographs, Norwich: University of East Anglia.

Faulkner, D. (1995) 'The Criminal Justice Act 1991: Policy, Legislation and Practice', in D. Ward and M. Lacey (eds), *Probation: Working for Justice*, London: Whiting and Birch.

Feeley, M. and Simon, J. (1992) 'The New Penology: Notes on the Emerging Strategy of Corrections and Its Implications', *Criminology*, 30(4), 449–74.

Feeley, M. and Simon, J. (1994) 'Actuarial Justice: The Emerging New Criminal Law', in D. Nelken, (ed.) *The Futures of Criminology*, London: Sage.

Finer, C.J. (1998) 'The New Social Policy in Britain', in C.J. Finer and M. Nellis (eds) *Crime and Social Exclusion*, Oxford: Blackwell.

Garland, D. (2000) 'The Culture of High Crime Societies: Some Preconditions of Recent "Law and Order" Policies', *British Journal of Criminology*, 40(3), 347–75.

Goldblatt, P. and Lewis, C. (1998) *Reducing Offending: An Assessment of Research Evidence on Ways of Dealing with Offending Behaviour*, Home Office Research Study 187, London: Home Office.

Goodman, A. (1995) 'The Criminal Justice and Public Order Act 1994', *Capital and Class*, 56 (Summer), 9–13.

Harding, J. (2000a) The Probation Service in the 21st Century, *Criminal Justice Matters*, 38, 27–8.

Harding, J. (2000b) 'A Community Justice Dimension to Effective Probation Practice', *Howard Journal of Criminal Justice*, 39(2), 132–49.

Harris, R. (1996) 'Telling Tales: Probation in the Contemporary Formation', in N. Parton (ed.) *Social Theory, Social Change and Social Work*, London: Routledge.

Hedderman, C. and Hough, M. (2000) 'Tightening up Probation: A Step Too Far?', *Criminal Justice Matters*, 39(5).

Haxby, D. (1978) *Probation: A Changing Service*, London: Constable.

HM Inspectorate of Probation (1993) *Annual Report: 1992–93*, London: Home Office.

Home Affairs Committee (28 July 1998) *Alternatives to Prison Sentences*, Third Report, vols I–II, London: Stationery Office.

Home Office (1984) *Probation Service in England and Wales: Statement of National Objectives and Priorities*, London: HMSO.

Home Office (February 1990) *Crime, Justice and Protecting the Public. The Government's Proposals for Legislation*, Cm 965, London: HMSO.

Home Office (February 1990) *Supervision and Punishment in the Community: A Framework for Action*, Cm 966, London: HMSO.

Home Office (April 1990) *Partnership in Dealing with Offenders in the Community: A Discussion Paper Issued by the Home Office to Complement the White Paper 'Crime, Justice and Protecting the Public' (Cm 965) and the Green Paper 'Supervision and Punishment in the Community: A Framework for Action' (Cm 966)*, London: Home Office.

Home Office (undated [1991]) *Organising Supervision and Punishment in the Community: A Decision Document*, London: Home Office.

Home Office (August 1998) *Joining Forces to Protect the Public: Prisons–Probation: A Consultation Document*, London: Home Office.

Home Office (1999) *What Works: Reducing Re-Offending Evidence-Based Practice.* London: HMSO.

Home Office (July 2001) *Making Punishments Work: Report of a Review of the Sentencing Framework for England and Wales*, London: Home Office.

James, A. (1995) 'Probation Values for the 1990s – and Beyond?' *Howard Journal of Criminal Justice*, 34(4), 326–43.

Kemshall, H. (1998) *Risk In Probation Practice*, Aldershot: Ashgate.

Leach, T. (2000) 'Effective Practice: Some Possible Pitfalls', *Vista*, 5(2), 141–9.

Lloyd, C. (1986) *Response to SNOP*, Cambridge: University of Cambridge Institute of Criminology.

Lyon, J., Dennison, C. and Wilson, A. (2000) *Tell Them So They Listen: Messages from Young People in Custody*, Home Office Research Study 201, London: HMSO.

McClelland, M. (2000) 'Who Knows Where the Time Goes?' *NAPO News*, 122 (August), 4.

McGuire, J. (ed.) (1995) *What Works: Reducing Reoffending*, Chichester: John Wiley.

McLaren, V. and Spencer, J. (1992) 'Rehabilitation and CJA 1991: A World Still to Win', *Probation Journal*, 39(2), 70–3.

McWilliams, B. (1992) 'The Rise and Development of Management Thought in the English Probation System', in R. Statham and P. Whitehead (eds) *Managing the Probation Service: Issues for the 1990s*, Harlow: Longman.

Maguire, M., Raynor, P., Vanstone, M. and Kynch, J. (2000) 'Voluntary After-Care and the Probation Service: A Case of Diminishing Responsibilities', *Howard Journal of Criminal Justice*, 39(3), 234–48.

Mair, G. (ed.) (1997) *Evaluating the Effectiveness of Community Penalties*, Aldershot: Avebury.

Martinson, R. (1974) 'What Works? Questions and Answers about Prison Reform', *The Public Interest*, 35, 22–54.

Martinson, R. (1979) 'New Findings, New Views: A Note of Caution Regarding Sentencing Reform', *Hofstra Law Review*, (7)2, 243–58.

May, C. (1998) 'Interview with Sir David Osmand', *Probation*, 24 (October), 7.

May, T. (1995) 'Probation and Community Sanctions', in M. Maguire, R. Morgan and R. Reiner (eds) *The Oxford Handbook in Criminology*, Oxford: Clarendon Press.

NAPO (1992) *CJA 1991 and National Standards: Limiting the Damage*, London: NAPO.

National Audit Office (17 May 1989) *Home Office: Control and Management of Probation Services in England and Wales*, report by the Comptroller and Auditor General, London: HMSO.

National Probation Service (August 2001) *A New Choreography*, London: Home Office.

Nellis, M. (1995) 'Probation Values for the 1990's', *Howard Journal of Criminal Justice*, 34(1), 19–44.

Parton, N. (2000) 'Some Thoughts on the Relationship between Theory and Practice in and for Social Work', *British Journal of Social Work*, 30(4), 449–64.

Pitts, J. (1992) 'The End of an Era', *Howard Journal of Criminal Justice*, 31, 133–49.

Probation Officer Recruitment and Training Implementation Group (April 1999) *Diploma in Probation Studies*, London: Home Office.

Raine, J. and Willson, M. (1993) *Managing Criminal Justice*, London: Harvester Wheatsheaf.

Raynor, P., Smith, D. and Vanstone, M. (1994) *Effective Probation Practice*, London: Macmillan.

Rex, S. (1999) 'Desistence from Offending: Experiences of Probation', *Howard Journal of Criminal Justice*, 38(4), 366–83.

Roberts, C., Burnett, R., Kirby, A. and Hamill, H. (1996) *A System for Evaluating Probation Practice*, PSU Report 1, Oxford: University of Oxford Probation Studies Unit, Centre for Criminological Research.

Rough Sleepers Unit (December 1999) *Coming in from the Cold: The Government's Strategy on Rough Sleeping*, London: RSU Department of the Environment, Transport and the Regions.

Rutherford, A. (1993) *Criminal Justice and the Pursuit of Decency*, Oxford: Oxford University Press.

Ryan, M. (1999) 'Criminology Re-engages the Public Voice', *Criminal Justice Matters*, 34, 11–12.

Ryan, M. and Sim, J. (1998) 'Power, Punishment and Prisons in England and Wales 1975–1996', in R. Weiss and N. South (eds) *Comparing Prison Systems*, Amsterdam: Gordon and Brench.

Sleightholm, D. (1998) 'Optimistic View of the Future by New Deputy Chief' *Probation*, London: ILPS, 12.

Smith, D. (2000a) 'The Logic of Practice in the Probation Service Today', *Vista*, 5(3), 210–18.

Smith, D. (2000b) *What Works as Evidence for Practice? The Methodological Repertoire in an Applied Discipline*, www.nisw.org.uk/tswr/smith.html.

Smith, D. and Stewart, J. (1998) 'Probation and Social Exclusion', in C.J. Finer and M. Nellis (eds) *Crime and Social Exclusion*, Oxford: Blackwell.

Spencer, J. (1995) 'A Response to Mike Nellis: Probation Values for the 1990s', *Howard Journal of Criminal Justice*, 34(4), 344–9.

Straw, J. (May 1999) 'Speech to Chief Probation Officer', *NAPO News*, London: NAPO.

Underdown, A. (1998) *Report of the HMIP What Works Project: Strategies for Effective Offender Supervision*, London: Home Office.

Vanstone, M. (2000) 'Cognitive-Behavioural Work with Offenders in the UK: A History of Influential Endeavour', *Howard Journal of Criminal Justice*, 39(2), 171–83.

Wade, S. (2000) 'The Probation Service and Managerialism', *Criminal Justice Matters*, 15–16.

Williams, B. (ed.) (1995) *Probation Values*, Birmingham: Venture Press.

Williams, B. (1996) *Counselling in Criminal Justice*, Buckingham: Open University Press.

Chapter 11

Rethinking penal policy: towards a systems approach

Roger Matthews

Introduction

Much attention in recent years has understandably focused on the rapid increase in the prison population on both sides of the Atlantic. The fact that the population imprisoned in the United States now exceeds 2 million has been widely referred to, while the prison population in England and Wales increased by 50 per cent between 1993 and 2000. There is also a growing sense among criminologists that the penal system is undergoing a significant transformation. Various explanations have been presented in the past to account for these developments, but few have been found to be convincing (see Matthews, 1999, chapter 6). In the recent period, however, an additional set of explanations have been put forward to explain these changes, and these accounts are gaining considerable ground as plausible explanations.

One main reasons given for the remarkable rise in the prison population is the perceived growth in punitiveness among politicians and the general public (Garland, 2001; Simon, 2001). Much of this punitiveness, it has been argued, has been disproportionately directed towards certain racial groups (Mauer, 1999; Wacquant, 2001). A further, but not unrelated, explanation is that the penal system is becoming more polarized and has developed into a dual track or 'bifurcated' system, with the introduction of more austere 'super max' prisons on one hand and the proliferation of community-based sanctions on the other (Cavadino and Dignan, 1992; Rose, 1999). It has also been suggested that the emergence of the 'new penology', with its focus on the control of aggregate populations – predominantly the underclass – through the use of different forms of risk assessment has widened the focus of penal intervention and stimulated the expansion of the penal system (Feeley and Simon, 1992, 1994). Finally, it has been argued that the development of a 'prison-industrial complex' has increased the scale of imprisonment, as investors and local communities have come to view prisons as sources of income and profit, and have a vested interest in maintaining prisons as a site of investment and economic activity (Lapido, 2001; Parenti, 1999).

In the course of this paper it will be argued that while most of these accounts have a rational core, they do not individually or collectively provide a convincing explanation of recent developments in penal policy or fully account for the rise in the prison population. In some cases they provide partial or 'ideological' accounts, which confuse rhetoric with reality, contingent and generative causes, or appearances with underlying processes. In contrast, it is suggested that there are other important, but largely neglected processes at work, which have been less conscious and less deliberate (and consequently more difficult to counter) than many of these accounts suggest.

The punitive turn?

Are we becoming a more punitive society? The answer on both sides of the Atlantic is generally affirmative. The adoption of mass incarceration and the widespread use of the death penalty across the United States, the reintroduction of boot camps, the adoption of 'three-strikes' legislation along with determinate, mandatory and so called 'honest' sentencing are all seen as indicative of a widespread surge in the level of punitiveness. Similarly, in the United Kingdom the rapid growth of the prison population since 1993, the increase in the average length of prison sentences, the 'naming and shaming' of paedophiles, and the spread of vigilantism are all seen as examples of increased punitiveness both within and outside of the criminal justice process. For many who accept that we are experiencing a rising tide of punitiveness the main issue is whether it is a function of changing public tolerance and sensibilities or is orchestrated by manipulative politicians and the media (Simon, 2001; Mauer, 2001).

The increase in punitiveness, however, is only one part of the story, and the exclusive focus on the introduction of tougher measures is in danger of losing sight of the greater diversity of penal sanctions that have emerged in recent years. In contrast, for example, to the increased severity in the sentences meted out to certain offenders there has been, in England and Wales at least, a decrease in the number (and by implication the proportion) of those sent to prison for offences such as burglary and theft. In contrast to the reintroduction of boot camps (which never really took off in the United Kingdom) there is a growing interest in the development of the more seemingly benign responses such as restorative justice (Daly, 2001). In contrast to the introduction of determinate and mandatory sentencing strategies we have seen the growth of mentoring and 'buddy' schemes designed to assist and befriend offenders, as well as witnessing the expansion of pre-court diversion schemes. Just as the penalties for violent crime have increased, so penalties against some 'non-victim' crimes have decreased. Alongside the use of capital punishment and incarceration in the United States we see the massive growth in the number of community-based programmes organized around the monitoring, supervision and surveillance of offenders.

These changes, however, do not represent simply a shift along a continuum of punitiveness, moving from severity at one end to leniency at the other. Rather, there seems to have been a discernible shift in the character and purpose of official sanctions. This includes the development of what John Pratt (2001) has referred to as 'emotive and ostentatious' punishments, which involve new forms of humiliation and degradation as well as public displays of remorse. Examples of such punishments include the introduction of chain gangs in America as well as other measures that involve the performance of menial labour and the wearing of stigmatic clothing in public. The pre-capitalist nature of some of these sanctions has been referred to by some as 'the neo-feudalization of punishment' (Shearing, 2001).

Other commentators, such as Pat O'Malley (1999), suggest that contemporary penal policy and practice is characterized by an unusual degree of incoherence and volatility, which is a consequence of the formation of new political configurations rather than an expression of the limits of the sovereign state. Examples of these volatile tendencies in the United Kingdom include the demand at one moment for a crackdown on drugs and at another the virtual decriminalization of certain illegal drugs, while others still are recategorized in order to attract lower penalties. A few years ago there were calls for an expansion of the prison system, but more recently political leaders have called for its reduction. Other examples of rapid changes in the penal climate could be given, but the significant point is that these opposing and contradictory policy developments are often expressed by the same social and political groups over a relatively short period of time.

Despite the development of this increasingly complex mosaic of sanctions there are signs of a change in objectives, with a slowing down in the growth of the American prison population as a result of a levelling-off in prison admissions (Blumstein and Beck, 1999). There is also evidence from different US states of a reduction in the use of mandatory minimum sentences and a greater use of non-custodial options for drug-related and other offences in an attempt to cut the prison population. Similarly, in England and Wales there has been a change of mood over the last year or two with a number of official pronouncements expressing a desire to limit the use of prison (Butterfield, 2001; Home Office, 2001). It is often the case that politicians who talk tough adopt rather different policies when they examine the financial implications of planned interventions. It is salient to note that under the administration of the 'Iron Lady', Margaret Thatcher, that there were not only fewer people being sent to prison annually over the course of her administration, but she also oversaw two virtual amnesties, in which thousands of prisoners in England and Wales were released early.

The disproportionate focus on the rise of the prison population has diverted attention away from the equally rapid increase in community-based sanctions. Just as the prison population in the United States has increased threefold over the 1980s and 1990s, so community-based sanctions have also increased by the same amount over the same period, with the consequence that there are, at the time of writing, 3.8 million people on probation and 725,000 on parole (Bureau of Justice, 2001). The simultaneous expansion of both incarceration and community-based sanctions, it has been argued, has led to an increasingly bifurcated system, with the development of more intensive forms of custody on one side and expansion of a growing array of 'softer' non-custodial options on the other.

Beyond bifurcation

The term 'bifurcation' has come into common usage since its original formulation in the 1970s (Bottoms, 1979). Although the term has been used in a number of different ways since then, it has come to denote a 'twin-track' policy, which differentiates between minor or 'ordinary' offenders, who can be dealt with in inclusive, welfare-orientated or community-based facilities, and the serious or 'exceptional' offenders, who are the subjects of tougher measures, usually in the form of exclusionary forms of confinement. There has been a consensus for some time that this 'twin-track' approach is an entrenched feature of penal policy, in Britain at least, and that the gap between these two tracks is widening (Cavadino and Dignan, 1992; Rose, 1999; Sparks, 1996). Whatever viability these distinctions may have had in the 1970s, the depiction of the contemporary penal process as an essentially bifurcated system is both misleading and ideological, since it captures inaccurately the relations between the available penal responses, while perpetuating outmoded conceptions of the distribution of penal populations.

To some extent the promotion of the notion of bifurcation has been sustained through the examination of the distribution of offenders at one point in time, or at a series of specific points in time. The presentation of official statistics as a series of snapshots tends to reinforce the conception of the penal system as being highly differentiated and segmented. Viewed in this way, custodial and community-based responses are seen as 'alternatives', catering to different populations. However, if we examine the movement of offenders over a period of time we discover that there is a continual flow of individuals between these different sites such that a significant percentage who are currently in prison will be subject to community-based sanctions in the future, and vice versa. The belief in the reality of bifurcation inadvertently reinforces the official ideology that prisons are reserved for the serious and exceptional offenders, while community-based sanctions cater for minor offenders.

It is also the case that the divisions associated with the concept 'bifurcation' are based on an explicit or implicit assumption that custodial and exclusionary forms of punishment are concerned with the containment and disciplining of the body; while community-based sanctions are more concerned with the mind of the deviant, seen to be capable of reform. This ideological demarcation between different types of offenders, located in different facilities has also been sustained by a division between different professional groups; that is, between those who focus on the containment and control of the body and those who specialize in training, education and personal development (Cohen, 1985). These divisions, which may have some basis in the past, are not only being eroded, as rehabilitation programmes aimed at the mind and body proliferate in British prisons; while any aspirations to provide education, training or rehabilitation in community-based facilities are steadily diminishing. At the same time there has been a gradual blurring of the boundaries between custodial and community-based sanctions, as the latter have become more 'intensive' in order to gain credibility and secure 'clients'.

In many jurisdictions custodial and community-based sanctions are no longer seen as 'alternatives' but as complementary and mutually reinforcing options. Supervision, curfews, monitoring and the like are increasingly presented as a necessary *complement* to incarceration. This mixing of different forms of punishments has been developing for some time, and recent Home Office discussions on the introduction of so-called 'seamless sentencing' signifies a conscious attempt to combine a number of different types of exclusionary and inclusionary sentences into a single package (Home Office, 2000).

The notion that community-based facilities are reserved predominently for minor offenders has been undermined by the evidence of a doubling in the proportion of individuals on probation who have been convicted of a violent offence between 1990 and 2000; while those who were given a sentence of probation for burglary decreased by half between 1998 and 2000, dropping from 12 per cent to 6 per cent. (Home Office, 2002). As in the United States, the number of people given probation is increasing steadily, while the case-loads of probation officers, who are predominently involved with low-key monitoring and surveillance practices, is rapidly rising.

In the United States the connections between different types of sanctions has become more apparent in recent years, particularly in relation to the use of parole as an early release strategy. This strategy was originally designed to return prisoners to the community under supervision, and thereby reduce prison overcrowding, while giving inmates an incentive to conform. However, recent research has found that approximately one third of those currently incarcerated in the United States are imprisoned for parole violations. In some states, such as California, the proportion of people incarcerated for parole violations reached an alarming 60 per cent in the 1990s (Petersilia, 1999). Of those admitted to prison as a consequence of parole violation some 40 per cent in 1997 were for violations of the technical conditions of parole, rather than for new crimes.

It appears to be the case that breaches and violations, which have been a frequent but an often neglected feature of certain community-based programmes, are becoming less tolerated by officials (Worrall, 1997). As a result of better methods of detection, new styles of management, such as New Public Managerialism with its insistence on measurable outcomes, breaches are seen as less acceptable than previously was the case.

It is also important to note that one of the implications of the New Public Managerialism is that the pursuit of greater efficiency and the strict adherence to specified targets necessarily involves the development and enforcement of stricter sanctions. That is, the pursuit of greater cost-efficiency generates its own inherent punitiveness, such that managers, whose aim may understandably be to improve performance, become less tolerant of 'failure'. Thus, part of the shift towards greater punitiveness in the penal system, and elsewhere, is a consequence not so much of an inherent desire to 'get tough' but a product of attempts to develop and enforce more stringent procedures.

Similar evidence of the ineffectiveness of current supervision and monitoring practices in England and Wales is also available. In a recent 'in house' review of the effectiveness of the transformed probation service, HM Inspectorate of Probation found that of 210 programmes being delivered most were 'poorly designed, variable in length, intensity and methods used, are applied indiscriminately and are misunderstood by the courts' (HM Inspectorate of Probation, 1998). Only 12 programmes were found to make any impact on reconviction, and only four were found to work in any effective way. The programmes that demonstrated any real effectiveness were those that spent a considerable amount of time with low-risk offenders, while the main factor which appeared to reduce re-offending was having a job to go to on release. Significantly, intensive probation was seen to have only a minimal effect on reducing the likelihood of re-offending.

Thus, rather than talk about bifurcation it is probably more appropriate to see these developments as examples of 'transcarceration'. That is, the high level of recidivism, which has become associated with these different sanctions, involves the circulation of individuals through different agencies and institutions over time. Also, in an increasing proportion of cases, individuals are not being returned directly to the 'community' but are instead being placed in the hands of different agencies or institutions (Lowman et al., 1987). This may involve the movement of individuals through a series of criminal justice as well as treatment agencies, some of which may be operated by the state while others are privately run. The cumulative long-term effect of moving among these different sites is rarely explored, and the combined personal, social and economic costs of this recycling process tend not to appear in the formal calculations of cost-effectiveness (Arrigo, 2001). What is therefore required is not a snapshot of the distribution of offenders, but rather the tracing of the movement of individuals through these regulatory agencies. In this way we are less likely to see custodial and community-based sanctions as two divergent courses. Rather, we may be better able to appreciate the collaborative and mutually reinforcing nature of these sanctions.

It is indeed arguable that one of the major trends in recent years has been the repeated attempt to reduce the prison population by diverting offenders into the growing network of non-custodial alternatives. We

229

have seen a proliferation of measures, whose introduction has often been justified in terms of their promise to take pressure off the prison system. Over the past decade a number of so called 'intermediate' or 'smart' sentences have been developed, and their introduction has been rationalized precisely in these terms. These developments involve mainly the introduction of 'third level', sanctions which are neither inclusive nor exclusive, but which involve predominantly surveillance, monitoring and supervision. The growth of these 'third level' sanctions in itself would suggest that the penal system has become 'trifurcated' rather than 'bifurcated'.

Intermediate sentences

The 1990s have been described, with some justification, as the decade of intermediate sanctions (Clear and Byrne, 1992). The widespread adoption of different sentencing options, including intensive probation, house arrest, community service and shock incarceration, both in the United States and Britain, has significantly increased the number and range of sentencing options available. The growth of these options, however, has not been dependent on the production of research evidence demonstrating that they work, but has been largely a result of a belief among policy makers and practitioners that there is a need for a new set of sanctions to be located 'between prison and probation' (Morris and Tonry, 1990). That is, many policy makers have been receptive to the arguments that there are a considerable number of people who are sent to prison each year who do not need to be there, while existing forms of probation and other community-based sanctions have become increasingly seen as 'soft' options, which do not serve as credible alternatives to prison. In a period of steadily growing prison populations, mounting costs and widespread overcrowding, the possibility of dealing with offenders through ostensibly cheaper non-custodial options appears attractive.

Shortly after the introduction of intensive supervision programmes, preliminary studies claimed that they were more cost-effective, that they served to reduce the pressure on the prison population, and that they provided an effective crime-control mechanism through close supervision, while helping to reduce crime by reducing the level of recidivism. Despite these early claims of success it became increasingly evident over the decade that the majority of these claims were unfounded, and were based on erroneous assumptions and often a misunderstanding of the relation between prison, existing 'alternatives' to custody and intermediate sanctions. For the most part, comparisons made between the cost-effectiveness of prison and intermediate sanctions were unrealistic, since the majority of those given intermediate sentences would not have been sent to prison, but would have been more likely to have been given probation or some other existing community-based option. Research measuring recidivism rates for different intermediate sanctions showed very little difference from existing sanctions. In one extremely frank and honest review, involving one of the original advocates of intermediate sanctions, it was admitted that:

> Few such programs have diverted large numbers of offenders from prison, saved public monies or prison beds, or reduced recidivism rates. These findings recur in evaluations of community service, intensive supervision, house arrest, day reporting centers, and boot camps. The principal problems have been high rates of revocation and subsequent incarceration (often 40–50 per cent) and the assignment of less serious offenders than program developers contemplated.
>
> (Tonry and Lynch, 1996, p. 99)

Thus, it would seem that rather than provide a series of options that reduce the pressure on the prison system, by virtue of more appropriate and cost-effective sanctions, the impact of these intermediate sentencing options has been to contribute inadvertently to the expansion of the prison system. Critics of intermediate sanctions have pointed to the net-widening effects that often accompany the introduction of new 'alternatives' to custody; but a more serious problem is the way in which the proliferation of sentencing options creates a larger self-referential or autopoietic system, which recycles individuals through a more closely linked network of agencies (Brans and Rossbach, 1997; Luhmann, 1995). It is also the case that the introduction of intermediate sanctions has increased the sites of decision-making. Thus, when Michael Tonry and Mary Lynch (1996) and others claim that the way to salvage intermediate sanctions is to structure judicial decision-making they forget that many of the decisions concerning the use of sanctions, such as probation and parole, are made by prison authorities and other non-judicial bodies. In fact, the major difficulty of introducing these various sentencing options is that it is extremely difficult to control for whom, and to what purpose, they are used .

At the same time, each sentencing option tends to be justified not so much in terms of its merits but rather in terms of the 'failure' of other options. That is, rather than acting simply as alternatives to incarceration they act as alternatives to each other. These problems became apparent in the 'decarceration debate' in the 1970s and 1980s, but it would appear that the lessons have not been learned (Cohen, 1985; Matthews, 1989). As a result we have experienced an expanding network of sanctions with ever finer gradations, making the transition from one to another ever easier. It is also the case that the response to the perceived failure of the existing array of sanctions is not to rationalize the number available but rather to develop additional sentencing options, which, it is hoped, will resolve the problem.[1]

It should be noted, however, that the suggestion that so called intermediate sanctions sit 'between' prison and probation is inaccurate. While some measures, such as boot camps, represent an intensification, and arguably a distortion, of existing forms of incarceration, other intermediate sanctions are of a different order, and are neither properly inclusive nor exclusive, neither welfare-orientated nor strictly punitive. Instead, they are concerned with monitoring, surveillance and the regulation of behaviour. They involve what Stanley Cohen (1983) once referred to as the 'new behaviorism', concerned with monitoring offenders without either trying to reform, correct or rehabilitate them. These are essentially managerialist techniques, designed to restrict the freedom of movement of individuals. The failure of these monitoring and surveillance strategies to address the causes of crime or make an attempt to reform offenders has resulted in a growing scepticism about the value of intermediate sentences. One of the leading commentaries on the subject, for example, concludes:

> Although most intermediate sanction programs have been 'sold' to legislators and the public at large based on their surveillance and control components, it now appears that it is the *treatment* component of these programs that results in changes in the subsequent criminal behavior of offenders. Unless policy makers and program developers recognise this fact by providing resources for *both* offender control and treatment intermediate sanction programs will *not* be viewed as examples of 'smart' sentencing; they will be viewed as simply further evidence that 'nothing works'.
>
> (Petersilia, Lurigio and Byrne, 1992, p. xiv)

The recognition of the limitations, and indeed the failure, of intermediate sanctions, however, does not always provide a disincentive to policy makers. Even among those who claim to operate within a pragmatic 'What Works?' perspective, the repeated failure, for example, of electronic monitoring programmes in England and Wales did not deter policy makers. Indeed, it seemed to make them try harder to 'demonstrate' the viability of this sentencing option. One of the most recent publications on electronic monitoring produced by the Home Office is aptly entitled 'Making the Tag Fit' (Mortimer et al., 1999). But the aim, it would seem, is not so much to adopt the tag because it fits the offender or the offence, but because it fits with current policy interests and priorities.

The problem, however, is no longer the costs and benefits of specific sentencing options but how they fit within the widening network of disposals, which now includes a complex mix of inclusive and exclusive monitoring and surveillance strategies, each pursuing different and competing objectives. Within this increasingly diverse penal system there is a growing tendency for individuals to be recycled through different types of programmes in the course of their life. A surprising proportion of those who will at some point spend some time behind bars will also be subject to other penal sanctions at other times. There has been a significant 'blurring of the boundaries' between prison and community-based sanctions, probably most evident in the fusing of the prison and probation services in England and Wales (Home Office, 1998). This fusing of agencies and institutions is seen to have been stimulated by the emergence of a 'new penology', involving new forms of discourse, policies and practices.

The new penology

It is claimed by Malcolm Feeley and Jonathan Simon (1992), in their much quoted article on the 'new penology', that the development of a growing network of sanctions and the expansion of the prison sector are, in part, functions of the emergence of actuarial justice. The authors claim that the 'old penology', with its emphasis on the rehabilitation of individual offenders, is being superseded by forms of risk assessment aimed at the control of aggregate populations – particularly the underclass – which have ushered in a wide range of responses in order to more effectively distribute offenders according to risk (Feeley and Simon, 1994).

Although there can be little doubt that different forms of risk analysis are becoming a central feature of contemporary penal systems in different countries, the degree to which this development accounts for the proliferation and shaping of the current range of punishments is questionable. The two examples offered to support their argument are the shift towards incapacitation as the leading rationale for incarceration, by which prisons come to take on 'waste management function', and the spread of surveillance and monitoring techniques. The problem with the first example is that while the emphasis on incapacitation may have increased in the United States, penal policy in the United Kingdom has taken a different direction. Second, while there is no doubt a close 'fit' between surveillance and monitoring operations on the one hand and risk analysis on the other there is a question of aetiology and causality, since the drift towards surveillance has been encouraged not so much by a preoccupation with risk analysis but rather is a product of wider social and economic developments associated with the emergence of what has been referred to as 'surveillance sociey' or 'control society' (Boyne, 2000; Deleuze, 1995).

Whereas it may be the case that prison use in the United States is increasingly rationalized in terms of incapacitation there has been a very noticeable reaffirmation of both the principle and practice of rehabilitation in the United Kingdom in recent years. In England and Wales there has been a considerable expansion and regeneration of rehabilitative programmes, particularly in the form of drug treatment and testing, literacy programmes, violence-reduction courses, sex-offender and cognitive-skills programmes, not to mention different training schemes and job-creation programmes. What is significant about many of these programmes is that they are new, that they are often directed at the most difficult and 'dangerous' offenders, and that they are, in penal terms at least, relatively well funded. These programmes may receive a mixed bag of responses, based on different conceptions of rehabilitation and may be the object of dubious forms of evaluation (Matthews and Pitts, 1999). But it is important to note that rehabilitation in prisons is not being 'displaced', as Feeley and Simon suggest, neither are the programmes invariably tied to conceptions of risk. Educational and training programmes, health and drug pro-grammes are now widely available, as are a series of aftercare programmes designed to help ex-offenders back into work. At the same time the role and meaning of 'rehabilitation' itself is being redefined within the prison setting, and currently combines a number of individual and social objectives (Cullen and Gilbert, 1982; Palmer, 1992; Rotman, 1990).

Central to these objectives remains the notion of recidivism. Al-though an unreliable and ambiguous measure, recidivism remains the main yardstick by which penal interventions, both those linked to rehabilitation and to risk analysis, are measured (Maltz, 1984). At the same time there appears to be a widening gap between a growing body of penal 'experts' – particularly prison psychologists, who have no doubt greatly improved their professional standing through the promotion of risk analysis – and others, both inside and outside of the penal system, who continue to talk the language of individual treatment, needs, reform and adjustment (Miller, 2001; Simon and Feeley, 1995).

It is not too difficult to determine the basis for the resurgence of rehabilitation in its different guises. Despite its apparent 'failure', rehabilitation continues to draw support from the general public, who do not want offenders returning to their neighbourhoods any more of a burden or a threat than they were before entering prison. These neighbourhoods characteristically have more than their fair share of problems. Second, the principle of rehabilitation is gaining increasing support from politicians, who want to reassure the public. Third, many prisoners and their families have an interest in rehabilitation inasmuch as it helps them to deal with their own personal, social and economic problems.

Thus, what we are seeing is the expansion of both rehabilitative programmes and risk analysis, which are combining in new and unexpected forms (Robinson, 2002). The term 'risk' has been concep-tualized in a number of different and contradictory ways. Consequent-ly, these different conceptions of risk have been used to justify competing and conflicting penal strategies (Brown, 2000). This has resulted in the creation a new set of tensions in the penal system as objectives and interventionist strategies are becoming more unstable and contradictory. In many cases rehabilitation programmes are assessed in terms of need, while those selected for treatment or training programmes are selected on the basis of risk assessments. Consequent-ly, at one moment interventions are couched in the language of individual justice, treatment and rehabilitation, and at another in terms of risk and probability.

In relation to surveillance and monitoring strategies, Feeley and Simon (1992) are unclear about the causal connection between these two developments. However, a review of the emergence of surveil-lance and monitoring strategies in the United Kingdom indicates that they were well established a decade or so before risk analysis became incorporated into penal discourse. The reduction of 'face-to-face' work with offenders and the growth of monitoring strategies tied to administrative and managerialist approaches – particularly for young offenders – began to take shape in the late 1970s and early 1980s (Lilly,

1992; Pratt, 1989). There may be an 'elective affinity' between surveillance and risk analysis, but it is perfectly possible to develop surveillance and monitoring strategies that do not have an explicit actuarial component. Moreover, it cannot be assumed that it is the emergence of actuarial justice that has stimulated the proliferation of non-custodial sanctions. Again, the beginnings of the expanding network of community-based sanctions was already well underway in the 1970s, resulting in the overall extension of the welfare–punishment continuum (Cohen, 1985; Austin and Krisberg, 1981).

The impression given in the 'new penology' thesis that risk analysis is coming to dominate penal discourses and practices, while rehabilitative strategies are disappearing does not therefore square with the evidence. As rehabilitation has been reaffirmed and redefined, critiques of risk analysis have begun to emerge, particularly in relation to its presumed objectivity and utility. Thus, rather than becoming a permanent and unassailable feature of contemporary penal systems it would appear that actuarial justice is increasingly becoming an object of criticism.

Within the criminal justice system there are competing ways of conducting risk analysis, and it has been suggested that the selection of variables, the choice of modelling techniques and the methods of calculation employed to identify and reduce risk are often unreliable. This unreliability is compounded by the inclusion of different forms of bias. As Peter Jones (1996) notes in his review of the risk-prediction literature:

> Almost all criminological prediction studies use some form of official record of offending as the criterion variable, usually arrest, conviction or incarceration. This has significant theoretical implications, as one can never disentangle the extent to which official measures confound actual criminal behavior with the labeling of criminality in the criminal justice system. Thus, if arrest is the criterion measure and police agencies are biased or selective in their arrest procedures – by race or social status, for example – then the study will likely identify those factors associated with police selection procedures as 'predictors' of criminality.
>
> (Jones, 1996, p. 45)

Thus, official measures may confuse the behaviour of the individual with the activities and interests of agencies, such that a circular and self-fulfilling logic comes into operation as a result of inadvertently introducing structural bias into predictions. In addition, and equally worrying, is that under a system of actuarial analysis, in which the aim is to determine the potential risk of an individual, as part of a particular group, an individual might be deemed to be a risk despite the fact that s/he has never committed a criminal act (Silver and Miller, 2002). In this way the group-based nature of prediction methods may conflict with popular notions of justice, while promoting the continued marginalization of populations already on the fringe of the economic and political mainstream (Hudson, 2001).

A growing concern among penologists is the obfuscation of the moral, social and political criteria involved in actuarial justice. The apparent neutrality and objectivity of risk analysis has been questioned, and 'risk' has been shown to be a highly malleable, gendered and racialized category (Hannah-Moffat, 1999). The application, or in some cases the non-application, of risk predictors in women's prisons is significant. According to the logic of actuarial analysis, women, who are not generally seen as dangerous, might be expected to be dispersed into community-based facilities rather than being imprisoned. However, in the United States the number of women in prison has increased threefold over the last decade, while in England and Wales it has doubled over the same period.

At the same time actuarial methods of prediction do not address the causes of criminal behaviour, and are therefore unlikely to be able to effectively change the conditions which encourage offending. Thus, practically and politically, they are a poor tool for reducing crime or protecting the public. Not surprisingly, there are growing concerns in official circles about the perceived ineffectiveness of risk-based analysis. For example, as the recent Joint Thematic Review by HM Inspectorates of Prison and Probation (2001) put it, 'unless something is done to tackle the *causes* of offending behaviour, and the social and economic exclusion from which it springs, and to which it contributes, prisons will continue to have revolving doors, and the public in the long term will not be protected'. The same report pointed out that probation staff lacked confidence in the ability of the prison staff to undertake risk assessment and that despite the rhetoric many cases were not, in fact, prioritized according to risk and needs assessment at all. In fact, intervention was found to be conditioned mainly by the length of sentence which had been imposed. It is also the case that, as risk analysis combines with rehabilitative measures, the unreliability of risk analysis may compound the 'failure' of rehabilitative efforts.

Thus, if actuarial justice is contributing to the expansion of the penal system it appears that it might be by default. That is, it is associated with promotion of unreliable techniques, which do not address the causes of offending. Neither does it offer consistent and reliable

237

measures to determine when offenders might be released from prison, and involves a tendency to err on the side of caution by keeping some prisoners incarcerated for longer than might be considered necessary. It is also the case, as suggested above, that the new forms of managerialism that have been introduced in recent years have encouraged more stringent enforcement of rules and procedures, such that breaches and 'violations', both inside and outside the prison, are more stringently enforced, thus extending the period of detention.

Thus, although it is difficult to find the evidence to support the contention that the expansion of the penal system has been 'dictated' by the logic of actuarial analysis, it can be argued that risk analysis has contributed indirectly to the rise of the prison population in other ways. Consequently, there is a real danger of giving too much credit to risk analysis and seeing it as a prime motor of change rather than as one factor within a wider set of determinants.

An alternative explanation offered for the growth of incarceration has been the development of the 'prison–industrial complex', which involves the growth of investment in the prison industry, the provision of employment associated with the building of new prisons and the growing emphasis on the use of prison labour.

The prison–industrial complex

Prisons have become a multi-billion dollar business in the United States. The annual expenditure in 1997 was in the region of $32 billion (Hagan and Dinovitzer, 1999). As the industry has grown, a whole new body of financiers and contractors have moved into this potentially very lucrative business with the aim of making substantial profits. Many new prisons are being built in depressed areas where local industries have gone into decline and they provide a much needed source of employment. Local residents, who a decade or so ago were objecting to correctional facilities being built in their localities, are now vigorously lobbying for prisons to be built in their areas, since they are seen to offer an economic lifeline to local communities short of work. Areas in which prisons have been introduced have been regenerated, with a range of new jobs following in the wake of prison construction. In some rural areas the prison has become the main local employer, while the emergence of employment opportunities has tended to push up land values (Parenti, 1999; Wray, 2000).

Within the prison itself there has been a growing emphasis on employment, and a range of firms now hire out prison labour to make a number of different products, ranging from denim jeans to stretch limousines. The productivity, however, is significantly lower than labour in the commercial sector, and therefore it is not generally profitable (see Matthews, 1999). Even with the low profit-levels involved, the prison departments endorse this work because it makes the prison look industrious, teaches some useful skills, and helps to keep prisoners occupied and under control.

Private companies are becoming more centrally involved in the design, construction and running of prisons. Half the private prisons in the United States are run by the Correctional Corporation of America, while the Wackenhut Corporation controls a quarter of the private market. Although there is no indication that these private prisons actually save taxpayers any money (Park, 2000), the drive towards the privatization of prisons is motivated by the belief that the market mechanism is the most effective and efficient way to allocate and prioritize resources. Privatization is also seen as a way of injecting 'modern' management practices into an ailing prison system and a strategy for breaking down traditional working practices. Ironically, in the United States prison workers have developed an active and well-organized union, and one of their main objectives is to limit the spread of privately run prisons.

At one level it does not really make a great deal of difference whether prisons are managed by private or public personnel. There are enough stories of the failings of both. But what is important about the gradual privatization of prisons is that it generally involves a shift toward a more impersonal and automated system of control, in which staff levels are reduced to a minimum, in order to maximize profits. There is little intrinsic interest among these commercial organizations in providing constructive and beneficial programmes for inmates. Neither do private contractors have much interest in reducing recidivism. On the contrary, they are more likely to benefit from the recycling of prisoners.

Christian Parenti (1999), in his discussion of the prison–industrial complex, argues that its emergence cannot be reduced to 'interest group' politics, which reduces this development to the interests of a number of avaricious entrepreneurs. Rather, he claims that it is a function of the American class structure and the need to find suitable 'scapegoats' in order to absorb the surplus population. Capitalism, we are told, needs to manage the poor through forms of segregation, repression or containment. It is not clear from Parenti's analysis, however, why the capitalist class has resorted increasingly to incarceration to control the poor in recent years, and what exactly has changed to make this necessary. Parenti's account, in essence, is too 'top-down' and does not explain why so many of the poor and working class endorse, indeed demand, effective 'law and order' policies, unless one is to assume that they are extremely gullible and are duped into agreement by manipulative politicians. Nor does Parenti address the question posed by Rusche and Kirchheimer (1968) and Michel Foucault (1980) as to why there continues to be a need for such a disciplinary mechanism in an advanced capitalist 'surveillance' society (Bottoms, 1983; Jancovic, 1977).

In a series of articles on the development of imprisonment in the United States, Loic Wacquant (2001, 2002) has argued that the drive towards mass incarceration is not propelled by the emergence of a prison–industrial complex so much as the development of a *carceral continuum*, which ensnares predominantly young Black men who are rejected by the deregulated labour market. The increasing proportion of young African Americans in prison is a consequence, he argues, of the growing obsolescence of the ghetto as a device for controlling this economically marginalized population, with the result that young Black men move continually between the ghetto and the prison. There is therefore, he suggests, a 'functional equivalence, a structural homology and a cultural fusion' between the prison and the ghetto, such that the prison is becoming more like the ghetto while the ghetto is coming to increasingly resemble the prison. As welfare provision has decreased so the caste system in the United States is shored up by means of a new form of governmentality, which relies increasingly on the prison to secure control:

> The emerging *government of poverty* wedding the 'invisible hand' of the deregulated labor market to the 'iron fist' of the intrusive and omnipresent punitive apparatus is anchored not by a 'prison–industrial complex' as the political opponents of the policy of mass incarceration maintain, but by a *carceral-assistential complex* which carries out its mission to surveille, train and neutralize the populations recalcitrant or superfluous to the new economic and racial regime according to a gendered division of labor, the men being handled by its penal wing while (their) women and children are managed by a revamped welfare–workfare system designed to buttress casual employment.
>
> (Wacquant, 2001, p. 97)

For Wacquant it is not primarily a question of class but one of race, and although he mentions Hispanics in passing, it is young Black males that form the focus of his argument. His suggestion that the ghetto is coming to resemble the prison is based on the observation that ghetto areas have high levels of surveillance and police intervention, and are subject to severe spatial segregation. While all these examples are no doubt accurate, the types of controls he refers to are to be found in most high-crime areas, and the spread of surveillance and spatial control is now city-wide (Davis, 1998). In fact, the residential areas which are coming more to resemble the prison are the gated communities of the wealthy. With their high wire fences, barred windows and bolted doors, extensive surveillance and security guards patrolling the perimeter, carefully scrutinizing everybody who goes in and out, they have produced new forms of segregation and confinement. The question that arises is why does the (White) establishment want to spend the time, money and effort processing and recycling so many young Black males through the criminal justice system? From a neo-liberal vantage point it would presumably be cheaper and easier to reduce intervention to a minimum, and to leave ghetto residents to deal with their own problems, while spending their money protecting themselves.

Much is made about the numbers of African Americans who have been incarcerated for drug-related offences. Much less attention is paid to the increasing imprisonment of young Blacks for crimes of violence. In both cases, however, the victims (both direct and indirect) are predominantly Black, and there is a significant demand in many Black communities to deal with the problem of drugs, particularly crack-cocaine, and to reduce the level of victimization. Wacquant, like Parenti, makes no reference to the concerns about crime in Black neighbourhoods, and consequently provides an overly conspiratorial and functionalist account. In cases where the race of the offender is known, approximately three out of four violent crimes are intraracial, while the fact that rates of Black victimization decreased by approximately 60 per cent between 1993 and 1998 might lead some critics to conclude that the extraordinary rate of Black incarceration might have had some impact on the crime rate in some inner-city areas, albeit at a price (Rennison, 2001). It is also not surprising that the prison culture has increasingly come to resemble the inner-city ghetto, as the proportion of Blacks and Hispanics going to prison continues to increase. Although the vast majority of the literature on race and imprisonment, from both ends of the political spectrum, focuses overwhelmingly on the plight of African Americans, it is interesting to note that while the number of Black inmates in the United States increased by 261 per cent between 1980 and 1996, the number of

Hispanic inmates increased by a staggering 554 per cent over the same period.[2]

In England and Wales the level of racial disproportionality is roughly similar to the United States with African Caribbeans making up approximately 13 per cent of the prison population and just under 2 per cent of the general population (Home Office, 1999). While there has been a series of anti-drug campaigns in the United Kingdom their scale and impact have not been anything like the 'War against Drugs' in the United States. Neither do African Caribbeans in the United Kingdom live in the type of ghettos found in the United States – although they do tend to live in poorer inner-city areas. Other European countries are also experiencing a disproportionate number of ethnic minorities in their prisons (Tomasevski, 1994), but this development could not be explained in the terms suggested by Waquant. This indicates that there may be other processes which would need to be included in a comprehensive and convincing account of the growing racial disproportionality in prisons in different countries (Sampson and Lauritsen, 1997).

Overall, however, the major problem with both Waquant and Parenti's analyses is that they present a largely unmediated account of the relation between the community and the prison, which they see as an essentially two-way process of incarceration/decarceration and prison/community. It has been suggested above that it might be more illuminating to study the movement of different social classes and ethnic groups through the penal system over time, and to identify if there are any significant class or race differences that might help to explain the changing penal population. That is, we might ask whether the routes through the penal system are significantly different for different social groups, such that differentials at the point of arrest are exacerbated and compounded once offenders enter the system.

On reflection, it would seem that the development of the prison as a site of investment, employment and manufacture has not been the primary driving force for the expansion of prisons or the penal system. Rather, these influences have served to consolidate an already expanded penal system. Once consolidated in this way, however, it becomes much more difficult to dismantle the penal apparatus and to counter these established interests. It is also the case that, as the balance in the penal system tilts towards different forms of privatization, there is little intrinsic interest in addressing the needs and problems of offenders or reducing the level of re-offending.

Conclusion

This review of recent developments in penal policy makes no claims to be comprehensive. Instead, it offers a series of observations and critical reflections on some selected themes. The aim has been to question some of the taken-for-granted assumptions about the changing nature of penal policy in contemporary society. Evidence from both the United Kingdom and the United States has been considered in an attempt to identify trends and recurring issues. There is always a danger, however, in pursuing a comparative analysis that focuses on similarities but ignores differences (Young, 2003). In many respects, of course, the United States and United Kingdom are worlds apart in terms of crime and crime control, but where similar trends and issues are discernable, some commentary would seem to be in order.

The picture that emerges from this cursory investigation is at odds with a number of current accounts of developments in penal policy, and this is partly because a number of widely shared assumptions, on which much of the literature on the sociology of punishment is based, has been found to be in need of some qualification and revision. The picture presented here, although incomplete, indicates a general shift in the nature of penal policy towards a more diverse, volatile and conflicting set of strategies, which, while being uncertain in their effects, have resulted in the construction of a more elaborate and integrated system. Some old strategies are losing credibility while others are being reaffirmed and redefined. There is, in this period of transition, a lack of clear direction and coherence, but a multiplicity of agencies and institutions now involved in the penal system are producing a self-sustaining network of sanctions, through which a growing number of offenders will be recycled over a period of time.

It has been argued that there is a need to examine in detail the movement of individuals and groups through the various agencies and institutions which make up the penal system. In some cases the analysis also needs to be extended to other regulatory sites, both public and private, outside of the criminal justice system. An examination of the flow of offenders through the system provides a very different picture of their distribution, and the operation of the penal process, than is gleaned from headcounts or from a series of snapshots. The more integrated network of sanctions that now operates on both sides of the Atlantic increasingly involves forms of risk analysis, which target groups rather than individuals, include different forms of rehabilitation, a growing range of intermediate sanctions, as well as an expanded prison system. Much of this development has not been consciously achieved. It is not part of a grand plan or the product of a conspiracy. Rather, it is largely the outcome of unintended consequences of conflicting actions, many of which, paradoxically, were designed to reduce the intensity and scale of the penal system.

Through an examination of these changes it has been argued that the notion that the penal system is becoming increasingly bifurcated or polarized is untenable. This is not so much because intermediate sentences have created a new set of sanctions, which sit 'between prison and probation', since many of these sanctions operate on a different plane, but because of the development of more 'seamless' forms of sentencing on one hand, and the continual flow of offenders through custodial and non-custodial agencies and institutions on the other.

At the same time there are a number of issues which cause concern and need to be addressed. Most prominent among these is the increased reliance on forms of risk analysis in the penal sphere. Despite its claims to objectivity, risk analysis is an unreliable tool and provides an inconsistent and largely ineffective way of identifying, filtering and judging offenders. Its thinly disguised subjectivism serves neither to address the reasons for offending, nor does it make much contribution to protecting the public. Not surprisingly, there has been a reaffirmation of rehabilitative strategies in recent years, but since the deployment and evaluation of rehabilitative strategies are often conducted in terms of risk, there is considerable uncertainty about their effectiveness. It is clear, however, that risk analysis is not displacing individualized notions of justice and reform among prison staff, policy makers and the general public, and that, instead, a new hybrid discourse is currently in circulation producing an uneasy mix of policies and objectives.

The recycling of offenders through different agencies and institutions over time has become a feature of what is now described as the prison–industrial complex, as has been observed, whereby prisons have become big business, attracting private investors, while serving as major local employers. Many of these private investors and contractors are not particularly interested in individual reform or developing rehabilitation programmes. On the contrary, their drive for expansion and for greater profits is largely dependent on developing low-cost, 'no frills' prisons, which rely on increasingly automated and impersonal systems of control.

Breaking the circle requires a form of systems-analysis that can examine the flow of offenders through the penal system, and which can identify the ways that the existing network of sanctions facilitates the process of transcarceration, while deconstructing what has become an increasingly self-referential or autopoietic penal system.[3]

Notes

1 In a recent Home Office publication *Making Punishment Work* (2001) the authors, for example recommend the introduction of 'intermittent custody', which would allow the offender to spend some time out of prison, and 'suspended sentence plus', which would combine a suspended sentence of imprisonment with a community sentence, so that the suspended sentence could be activated if the offender failed to comply with the conditions of the non-custodial sentence. These sentencing policies might conceivably be justifiable in themselves, but there is little consideration in the document of how they might fit into the existing array of sanctions.

2 American criminologists have problems in classifying Hispanics, since it seems that Hispanics are an 'ethnic group' (defined by country of origin and language) while Blacks are a 'race' (defined by skin colour). Also, even liberal and radical criminologists tend to work with crude Black/White distinctions, such that rather than deconstruct the notion of race and show it to be a socially constructed and ideological category, they, for the most part, equate race with skin colour, thereby racializing the analysis (see Matthews, 1999 pp. 208–35).

3 Feeley and Simon (1992) suggest that there is an affinity between risk analysis and systems theory. However, the type of systems approach advocated here draws on the work of writers like Luhmann (1995) rather than the crude forms of managerialism that see the world in terms of inputs and outputs.

References

Arrigo, B. (2001) 'Transcarceration: A Constitutive Ethnography of Mentally Ill Offenders', *Prison Journal*, 81(2), 162–86.

Austin, J. and Krisberg, B. (1981) 'Wider, Stronger and Different Nets: The Dialectics of Criminal Justice Reform'. *Journal of Research in Crime and Delinquency*, 18, 132–96.

Blumstein, A. and Beck, A. (1999) 'Population Growth in US Prisons 1980–96', in M. Tonry and J. Petersilia (eds) *Prisons*, Chicago: Chicago University Press.

Bottoms, A. (1977) 'Reflections on the Renaissance of Dangerousness', *Howard Journal of Criminal Justice*, 16(2), 70–96.

Bottoms, A. (1983) 'Neglected Features of Contemporary Control Systems', in D. Garland and P. Young (eds) *The Power to Punish*, London: Heinemann.

Boyne, R. (2000) 'Post-Panopticism', *Economy and Society*, 29(2), 285–307.

Brans, M. and Rossbach, S.(1997) 'The Autopoiesis of Administrative Systems: Niklass Luhmann on Public Administration and Public Policy', *Public Administration*, 75 Autumn, 417–39.

Bureau of Justice (2001) 'National Correctional Population Reaches New High', press release 26 August.

Brown, M., (2000) 'Calculations of Risk in Contemporary Penal Practice', in M. Brown and J. Pratt (eds) *Dangerous Offenders: Punishment and Social Order*, London: Routledge.

Butterfield, F. (2001) 'States Easing Stringent Laws on Prison Time', *New York Times*, 2 September.

Caplow, T. and Simon, J. (1999) 'Understanding Prison Policy and Population Trends', in M. Tonry and J. Petersilia (eds) *Prisons*, Chicago: University of Chicago Press.

Cavadino, M. and Dignan, J. (1992) *The Penal System: An Introduction*, London: Sage.

Clear, T. and Byrne, J. (1992) 'The Future of Intermediate Sanctions: Questions to Consider', in J. Byrne, A. Lurigio and J. Petersilia (eds) *Smart Sentencing: The Emergence of Intermediate Sanctions*, Newbury Park, California: Sage.

Cohen, S. (1983) 'Social Control Talk: Telling Stories about Correctional Change', in D. Garland and P. Young (eds) *The Power To Punish*, London: Heinemann.

Cohen, S. (1985) *Visions of Social Control*, Cambridge: Polity Press.

Cullen, F. and Gilbert, K. (1982) *Reaffirming Rehabilitation*, Cincinnati: Anderson.

Daly, K. (2001) 'Restorative Justice: The Real Story', *Punishment and Society*, 4(1), 55–79.

Davis, M. (1998) *Ecology of Fear*, New York: Metropolitan Books.

Deleuze, G. (1995) *Negotiations*, New York: Columbia University Press.

Feeley, M. and Simon, J (1992) 'The New Penology: Notes on the Emerging Strategy of Corrections and Its Implications', *Criminology*, 30(4), 449–74.

Feeley, M. and Simon, J. (1994) 'Actuarial Justice: The Emerging New Criminal Law', in D. Nelken (ed.) *The Futures of Criminology*, London: Sage.

Foucault, M. (1980) 'The Eye of Power', in *Power/Knowledge*, London: Harvester Wheatsheaf.

Garland, D. (2001) *The Culture of Control: Crime and Social Order in Contemporary Society*, Oxford: Oxford University Press.

Hagan, J. and Dinovitzer, R. (1999) 'Collateral Consequences of Imprisonment for Children, Communities and Prisoners', in M. Tonry and J. Petersilia (eds) *Prisons*, Chicago: University of Chicago Press.

Hannah-Moffat, K. (1999) 'Moral Agent or Actuarial Subject: Risk and Canadian Women's Imprisonment', *Theoretical Criminology*, 3(1), 71–95.

HM Inspectorate of Prison and Probation (2001) *Through the Prison Gate*, London: HMSO.

HM Inspectorate of Probation (1998) *Report of the HMIP on the What Works Project: Strategies for Effective Supervision*, London: HMSO.

Home Office (1998) *Prisons and Probation: Joining Forces to Protect the Public*, London: HMSO.

Home Office (1999) *Statistics on Race and the Criminal Justice System*, London: HMSO.

Home Office (2001) *Making Punishments Work: Report of a Review of the Sentencing Framework for England and Wales*, London: HMSO.

Home Office (2002) *Probation Statistics England and Wales 2000*, London: HMSO.

Hudson, B. (2001) 'Punishment, Rights and Difference: Defending Justice in the Risk Society', in K. Stenson and R. Sullivan (eds) *Crime, Risk and Justice*, Cullompton, Devon: Willan.

Jancovic, I (1977) 'Labour Market and Imprisonment', *Crime and Social Justice*, Fall/Winter, 17–31.

Jones, P. (1996) 'Risk Prediction in Criminal Justice', in A. Harland (ed.) *Choosing Correctional Options That Work*, Newbury Park, California: Sage.

Langan, P. and Farringdon, D (1998) *Crime and Justice in the United States and in England and Wales, 1981–96*, Bureau of Justice Statistics, NCJ 169284.

Lapido, D. (2001) 'The Rise of America's Prison–Industrial Complex', *New Left Review*, January, 109–23.

Lilly, R. (1992) 'The English Experience: Intermediate Treatment with Juveniles', in J. Byrne, A. Lurigio and J. Petersilia (eds) *Smart Sentencing: The Emergence of Intermediate Sanctions*, Newbury Park, California: Sage.

Lowman, J., Menzies, R. and Palys, T. (1987) *Transcarceration: Essays in the Sociology of Social Control*, Aldershot: Gower.

Luhmann, N. (1995) *Social Systems*, Stanford, California: Stanford University Press.

Maltz, M. (1984) *Recidivism*, Orlando, Florida: Academic Press.

Matthews, R. (1989) 'Alternatives to and in Prison', in P. Carlen and D. Cook (eds) *Paying For Crime*, Buckinghamshire: Open University Press.

Matthews, R. (1999) *Doing Time: An Introduction to the Sociology of Imprisonment*, London: Palgrave.

Matthews, R. and Pitts, J. (1999) 'Rehabilitation, Recidivism and Realism', *Prison Journal*, January/February.

Mauer, M. (1999) *Race to Incarcerate*, New York: New York Press.

Mauer, M. (2001) 'The Causes and Consequences of Prison Growth in the United States', *Punishment and Society*, 1(1), 9–20.

Miller, L. (2001) 'Looking for Postmodernism in all the Wrong Places', *British Journal of Criminology*, 41, 168–84.

Morris, N. and Tonry, M. (1990) *Between Prison and Probation: Intermediate Punishments in a Rational Sentencing System*, New York: Oxford University Press.

Mortimer, E., Pereira, E. and Walter, I. (1999) *Making the Tag Fit: Further Analysis from the First Two Years of the Trials of Curfew Orders*, Research Findings 105, London: Home Office.

O'Malley, P. (1999) 'Volatile and Contradictory Punishment', *Theoretical Criminology*, 23(2), 175–97.

Palmer, T. (1992) *The Re-emergence of Correctional Intervention*, Newbury Park, California: Sage.

Park, I. (2000) *Review of Comparative Costs and Performance of Privately and Publicly Operated Prisons 1998–99*, 6/000, London: Home Office.

Parenti, C. (1999) *Lockdown America: Police and Prisons in the Age of Crisis*, London: Verso.

Petersilia, J. (1999) 'Parole and Prisoner Reentry in the United States', in M. Tonry and J. Petersilia, *Prisons*, Chicago: University of Chicago Press.

Petersilia, J., Lurigio, A. and Byrne, J. (1992) 'The Emergence of Intermediate Sanctions', in J. Byrne, A. Lurigio and J. Petersilia (eds) *Smart Sentencing: The Emergence of Intermediate Sanctions*, Newbury Park, California; Sage.

Pratt, J. (1989) 'Corporatism: The Third Model of Juvenile Justice', *British Journal of Criminology*, 29(3), 236–55.

Pratt, J. (2001) 'Emotive and Ostentatious Punishment', *Punishment and Society*, 24(4), 407–39.

Rennison, C. (2001) *Violent Victimisation and Race 1993–98*, Bureau of Justice Statistics, Special Report, NCJ 176354.

Robinson, G. (2002) 'Exploring Risk Management in Probation Practice: Contemporary Developments in England and Wales', *Punishment and Society*, 4(1), 5–25.

Rose, N. (1999) *Powers of Freedom: Reframing Political Thought*, Cambridge: Cambridge University Press.

Rotman, E. (1990) *Beyond Punishment: A New View on the Rehabilitation of Criminal Offenders*, Westport, Connecticut: Greenwood Press.

Rusche, G. and Kirchheimer, O. (1968) *Punishment and Social Structure*, New York: Russell and Russell.

Sampson, R. and Lauritsen, J. (1997) 'Racial and Ethnic Disparities in Crime and Criminal Justice in the United States', in M. Tonry (ed.) *Ethnicity, Crime and Immigration*, Chicago: University of Chicago Press.

Shearing, C. (2001) 'Punishment and the Changing Face of Governance', *Punishment and Society*, 3(2), 203–20.

Silver, E. and Miller, L (2002) 'A Cautionary Note on the Use of Actuarial Risk Assessment Tools for Social Control', *Crime and Delinquency*, 48(1), 138–61.

Simon, J. (2001) 'Entitlement to Cruelty: Neo-liberalism and the Punitive Mentality in the United States', in K. Stenson and R. Sullivan (eds) *Crime, Risk and Justice*, Cullompton, Devon: Willan.

Simon, J. and Feeley, M. (1995) 'True Crime: The New Penology and Public Discourse on Crime', in T. Blomberg and S. Cohen (eds) *Punishment and Social Control*, New York: De Gruyter.

Sparks, R. (1996) 'Prisons, Punishment and Penality', in E. McLaughlin and J. Muncie (eds) *Controlling Crime*, London: Sage.

Tomasevski, K. (1994) *Foreigners in Prison*, Helsinki: European Institute for Crime Prevention and Control.

Tonry, M. and Lynch, M. (1996) 'Intermediate Sanctions', in M. Tonry (ed.) *Crime and Justice: A Review of Research*, 20, Chicago: University of Chicago Press.

Travis, J. (2000) *But They All Come Back: Rethinking Prisoner Reentry*, National Institute of Justice, Paper 7, Executive Sessions on Sentencing and Corrections: www.ncjrs.org/txtfiles/nij/181413.txt.

Wacquant, L. (2001) 'Deadly Symbiosis: When Ghetto and Prison Meet and Merge', *Punishment and Society*, 3(1), 95–133.

Wacquant, L. (2002) 'From Slavery to Mass Incarceration', *New Left Review* January/February, 41–60.

Worrall, A. (1997) *Punishment in the Community: The Future of Criminal Justice*, London: Longman.

Wray, R. (2000) 'A New Economic Reality: Penal Keynesianism', *Challenge*, 43(5), 31–59.

Young, J. (2003) 'Searching for a Criminology of Everyday Life: A Review of the Culture of Control', *British Journal of Criminology*, 43(1), 228–43.

Index